Legal
Responses
to
Indoor
Air
Pollution

Legal
Responses
to
Indoor
Air
Pollution

Frank B. Cross

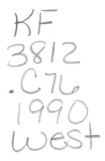

Quorum Books

New York
Westport, Connecticut
London

Library of Congress Cataloging-in-Publication Data

Cross, Frank B.
    Legal responses to indoor air pollution / Frank B. Cross.
        p. cm.
    Includes bibliographical references and index.
    ISBN 0–89930–519–9 (lib. bdg. : alk. paper)
        1. Indoor air pollution—Law and legislation—United States.
    2. Indoor air pollution.   I. Title.
    KF3812.C76   1990
    344.73′046342—dc20
    [347.30446342]   90–8963

British Library Cataloguing in Publication Data is available.

Library of Congress Catalog Card Number: 90–8963
ISBN: 0–89930–519–9

First published in 1990

Quorum Books, 88 Post Road West, Westport, CT 06881
An imprint of Greenwood Publishing Group, Inc.

Printed in the United States of America

The paper used in this book complies with the
Permanent Paper Standard issued by the National
Information Standards Organization (Z39.48–1984).

10 9 8 7 6 5 4 3 2 1

CONTENTS

EXHIBITS

PREFACE

The concept of indoor air pollution is so unknown to Americans that it appears almost to be a contradiction in terms. The public views air pollution as dirty smoke spewed from heavy industries or the oddly colored haze resultant from automobile traffic. Indoor air, by contrast, does not look dirty or polluted. Home is viewed as a refuge from air pollution. Major cities, such as Los Angeles, direct their citizenry to stay inside on particularly smoggy days.

In this context, it is understandably difficult for individuals to comprehend that indoor air is not only more hazardous than outdoor but that it is many times more hazardous. "Indoor" generally means within the home, though it also includes workplaces, restaurants, and other areas within buildings. The primary indoor air pollutants, which typically can be neither seen nor smelled, are just as hazardous as pollutants emitted into the outdoor air. These same pollutants tend to be found at much higher levels inside buildings, which capture and concentrate the emissions. In addition, people spend far more time indoors than they do outside. The combination of these features produces significant health hazards inside homes and offices.

First, some definition of indoor air pollution is required. My definition is an operational one, as there are no defined parameters for indoor air pollution. This book focuses upon the commonly understood meaning of "pollution," that is, involuntary exposures to chemicals and radiation emitted as byproducts of some economic activity. I have excluded smoking from my definition of indoor air pollution.

While sidestream smoke from cigarettes is a major polluter of indoor environments, the smoking issue differs from typical pollutants in that the greatest risks are understood and perceived, voluntarily undertaken, and directly produced by identifiable individuals, and environmental tobacco smoke calls for a different set of remedial responses. I also have excluded most occupational exposure to hazardous pollutants in the air. While many jobs require work with hazardous substances and, strictly speaking, occur inside a plant, these blue-collar exposures are already addressed by a comprehensive regulatory scheme at the Occupational Safety and Health Administration (OSHA) and are not treated as air pollution. I have included some indoor air pollution in white-collar offices, which share the attributes of residential indoor air pollution and which are largely ignored by OSHA. Thus I exclude the risks suffered by asbestos workers but consider any risk faced by students or teachers from asbestos materials used in schools.

Even after so limiting the definition of indoor air pollution and excluding major exposure problems, the remaining contamination of indoor air is responsible for tens of thousands of deaths from cancer and millions of days of illnesses, some of which are themselves doubtless fatal. Part 1 of this book summarizes the existing evidence on the enormity of the health hazard presented by indoor air pollution. While the leading killer is indoor radon, other pollutants also pose major health risks.

The remainder of this book addresses what may be done about indoor air pollution. Part 2 synopsizes the federal and state governments' action against this pollution, and Part 3 discusses the opportunities for individuals to sue responsible parties for harms suffered from contaminated indoor air. Part 4 of the book proposes future directions for government action on indoor air pollution in order to protect public health more effectively.

This book arose out of more general research into health harms caused by environmental pollution, especially cancer. Those familiar with general environmental public health regulation are aware that most government regulations are directed at relatively small sources of outdoor risk, which produce at most a handful of deaths or diseases. Given this experience, knowledge of the far greater risks of indoor air pollution is surprising, and the lack of government attention to such massive risks is shocking. For everyone truly concerned with public health protection, indoor air pollution must assume a top priority as the new frontier of government action.

ABBREVIATIONS

ACH	air changes per hour
AHERA	Asbestos Hazard Emergency Response Act
ASHRAE	American Society of Heating, Refrigeration and Air-Conditioning Engineers
BPA	Bonneville Power Administration
CERCLA	Comprehensive Environmental Response, Compensation and Liability Act of 1980 (Superfund)
CPSC	Consumer Product Safety Commission
DOE	Department of Energy
EDF	Environmental Defense Fund
EPA	Environmental Protection Agency
f/cc	fibers per cubic centimeter
FIFRA	Federal Insecticide, Fungicide, and Rodenticide Act
4-PC	4-phenylcyclohexene
GSA	General Services Administration
HUD	Department of Housing and Urban Development
HVAC	Heating, Ventilation, and Air Conditioning
MCS	multiple chemical sensitivity
mg/hr	milligrams per hour

NAHB	National Association of Homebuilders
OSHA	Occupational Health and Safety Administration
PCBs	polychlorinated biphenyls
pCi/g	picocuries per gram
pCi/L	picocuries per liter
ppb	parts per billion
ppm	parts per million
SEIU	Service Employees International Union
TEAM	Total Exposure Assessment Methodology
TSCA	Toxic Substances Control Act
UFFI	urea formaldehyde foam insulation
ug/m^3	micrograms per cubic meter
VOCs	volatile organic compounds
WL	working level
WLM	working level month

PART I

Health Risks from Indoor Air Pollution

The potential health risks from breathing indoor air get very little public attention, at least as compared with the risks of outdoor air pollution, hazardous wastes, and numerous other environmental concerns. Yet indoor air pollution almost certainly produces thousands of cases of lung cancer and millions of cases of lesser respiratory diseases every year. There is little doubt but that indoor air pollution presents a far more threatening hazard to public health than does outdoor air pollution.

The risks of indoor air pollution are surprising to many. When one considers that the average American spends 90 percent of his or her time indoors, and roughly two-thirds of his or her time in the home, however, the importance of the quality of indoor air should be obvious. Moreover, studies reveal that the known hazardous air pollutants are almost universally found at higher levels indoors than out of doors. The combination of greater time exposed to higher levels of pollutants will naturally produce greater risks.

Some indoor pollutants have received somewhat more attention from government and the press. Radon, asbestos, and formaldehyde are known to many Americans as hazardous substances that may be found in their homes or places of work and study. Individuals are also exposed to hundreds of other, lesser-known indoor air pollutants. This part of the book describes the human health consequences of exposure to these contaminants.

Chapter 1 addresses the health harms of indoor radon exposures. Radon typically enters a house from the underlying soil and is concentrated to dangerous levels. The cancer risks of this indoor pollutant dwarf those of all outdoor pollution, as radon is implicated in as many as 20,000 lung cancer deaths every year. This chapter describes the distribution of radon exposures, the extent of risk they present, and what exposure levels should be feared. The possible control measures for indoor radon are described, including their cost and effectiveness.

Asbestos, a widely known hazardous substance found in some homes, schools, and office buildings, is discussed in Chapter 2. While asbestos may be the indoor air pollutant of most concern to Americans for its ability to induce cancer, the actual risk from the indoor concentrations of the substance is rather small. In the vast majority of cases, indoor asbestos-containing materials present little or no risk. Ironically, efforts to remove these materials can produce a significant risk to building occupants far greater than if the materials were left undisturbed. This chapter addresses the sources of indoor asbestos exposure, the levels of exposure, the risks presented, and the control measures indicated for varying situations.

Chapter 3 deals with formaldehyde. Formaldehyde is used in a variety of products found in residences, particularly in pressed-wood products and some recent insulation applications. Formaldehyde is of concern because it may produce cancer in exposed individuals. While the cancer risks of formaldehyde are still disputed, the substance clearly produces disease and irritant effects at some concentrations. This chapter discusses the sources of formaldehyde exposure, the situations in which that exposure becomes significant, the attendant risk, and promising remedial measures.

The remaining significant indoor air pollutants are combined in Chapter 4. Volatile organic compounds (VOCs) are emitted by a variety of home products and have the capability of producing thousands of cancers in exposed individuals. Combustion byproducts of gas and wood-fired appliances also pollute the indoor environment and produce a significant number of diseases, especially in children, as well as some cancer risk. Biological contaminants, such as mold and allergens, are widespread in homes and offices. These pollutants may be responsible for millions of illnesses and some number of deaths from disease. Electromagnetic radiation from household appliances and wiring may cause cancer and other adverse health effects. The vaguely defined concept of "sick building syndrome" is widespread and responsible for a substantial toll of sickness. Chapter 4 summarizes the sources of all these pollutants, the extent of their hazards, and measures that can be taken to improve indoor air quality.

In total, indoor air pollution is by far the greatest involuntary environmental risk to human health. The Environmental Protection Agency (EPA) recently completed a two-year study of all environmental hazards, including hazardous wastes, industrial discharges to air and water, pesticides, and other sources. The agency found that the most severe environmental risk was indoor radon exposures and that the second greatest risk was from nonradon indoor air pollution.

1

THE HEALTH RISK FROM INDOOR RADON

Radon, scientifically known as "Rn," is an odorless and colorless radioactive gas found throughout the earth's atmosphere, as emitted from radioactive elements naturally occurring in the soil. Uranium, a common element in the earth's crust, physically breaks down or decays into radium-226, which in turn decays into radon-222. Radon-222, which has a half-life of less than four days, ultimately breaks down into its own radioactive progeny, often called radon daughters, in the form of polonium-218, lead-214, bismuth-214, and polonium-214. After some time, these elements decay into a stable form of lead. The radon daughters are especially hazardous because they are chemically active and attach to airborne particles inhaled into the lungs. The radon daughters may attach directly to the lining of the lungs and decay further. Like other forms of ionizing radiation, the radon and its daughters can cause lung cancer when inhaled, and the low level of atmospheric radon is almost certainly responsible for some number of cancers. Virtually nothing can be done about this, but fortunately the air's dilution keeps population exposures and risks low.

Rather recently, the government has discovered that radon levels in homes and other buildings may be quite high, many times the outdoor levels. Indoor radon levels are typically four times higher than comparable outdoor levels and may be ten or more times higher. The high indoor radon levels present a serious threat to public health, far surpassing the danger from much better known hazards, such as chemical wastes or nuclear power plants. Indeed, some current indoor radon levels "are the radiation equivalent of having a Three Mile Island accident . . . occur in the neighborhood every week."[1] Some persons receive more radiation exposure from their homes than uranium miners receive in their job. The Environmental Protection Agency estimates that indoor radon is responsible for up to 20,000 cancer deaths every year. The National Academy of Sciences' National Research Council's Committee on the Biological Effects of Ionizing Radiation estimates that radon may cause 13,000 lung cancer deaths annually. These rates imply that roughly 1 million Americans eventually will contract lung cancer from exposure to radon. If these estimates are accurate, radon could be second only to tobacco as a cause of cancer. Indeed, radon levels in some homes create a risk comparable to smoking a pack or more of cigarettes a day. EPA estimates that radon exposure causes nearly $500 million in direct health costs and nearly $2 billion in lost economic productivity. Obviously, radon is an enormous public health problem.

This chapter explores the sources and nature of the risk presented by indoor radon. First, I discuss how and why radon concentrates in buildings. Second, I describe what levels of indoor radon are found in various regions of the United States. Third, I address the extent of the cancer risk presented by these indoor radon levels. Fourth, I analyze the corrective measures that are available to reduce indoor radon.

Sources and Causes of Indoor Radon

The original source of indoor radon is uranium and radium found in the earth. Some amount of these elements are found in the soil of virtually every geographic area, but their relative concentration can vary considerably. Radon gas is thus emitted in varying degrees throughout the nation. The highest uranium soils have been detected in much of New England, the Reading Prong area of eastern Pennsylvania and western New Jersey, Florida, the eastern slope of the Appalachians and along the Georgia and Carolina coasts, as well as scattered areas in Wisconsin, Minnesota, and west of the Rocky Mountains. Few areas are so free of uranium in soils as to ensure the absence of a radon problem. Indoor radon concentrations are perplexingly unpredictable; "one home in a community may be heavily contaminated with radon while an adjacent home has negligible levels."[2]

Most indoor radon results when houses or other buildings are constructed upon soil that emits radon. Radon enters the house through a variety of potential routes. The gas may seep in through cracks in the foundation. Even in the absence of such cracks, most houses contain designed openings for water, sewage, or gas pipes that permit the entry of radon. Some houses contain no solid concrete foundation. Radon may slowly diffuse through even solid, uncracked concrete foundation materials. It is impossible to construct a building that prevents the entry of radon gas. Exhibit 1.1 illustrates some of the varied routes through which radon enters a dwelling.

Obviously, the level of indoor radon is at least partially dependent upon the radioactive content of the soil on which a building sits. Indoor radon exposures are often greatest in those geographic regions that have the highest radon emission rates. This is particularly evident in Colorado, where some homes have been built atop the radioactive wastes of uranium mines. The siting of a home is an important predictor of indoor radon levels. Yet location alone cannot fully explain indoor radon levels. While high natural radon areas, such as Pennsylvania, New Jersey, Florida, and other states also have high indoor contamination, radon problems are not confined to these areas. Soil gas flow and other factors also matter. For example, the Spokane River Valley has only average soil radium content, but many homes in the valley have unusually high indoor radon concentrations. High radon

Exhibit 1.1
Radon Pathways

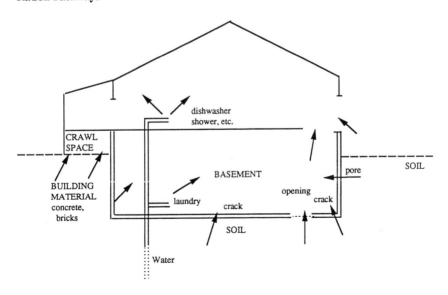

homes have been found throughout the nation, and it appears that there is enough uranium and radium in most soils to produce high indoor levels under some circumstances. EPA has found that "radon may be a problem in virtually every state."[3] Other homes have low indoor radon levels, even though they are located on highly radioactive soils. The presence of high indoor levels is sufficiently unpredictable that EPA recommends that virtually every house in the nation should be tested. Moreover, indoor radon levels are often significantly higher than would be projected based only upon location.

Building characteristics play a major role in explaining indoor radon concentrations. Houses with basements, crawl spaces, and sump holes tend to have higher concentrations. As suggested earlier, the number and size of cracks and penetrations of the foundation affect the amount of radon entering a house. One study found that "[r]adon levels in houses where [the slab] is badly cracked seem to be only about 30% higher than in houses where it is uncracked."[4] This feature of foundations seems less significant, however, than do pressure differentials.

Differences in pressure and temperature between the indoor and outdoor environments may suck high levels of radon into a house, much as a vacuum draws a gas. Differences in temperature cause pressure differentials. Heating a house creates a convection pattern that draws in air from its understructure. Wind may also depressurize the interior of a house. This effect is exacerbated by installed equipment, including exhaust fans, fireplaces, and even water heaters.[5] The pressure-differential factor apparently explains a great deal of radon entry in housing.

The rate of radon entry explains only a part of indoor radon exposure. The rate of radon exit has an equally powerful effect on indoor concentrations. Even high entry levels will not produce high concentrations, if the radon quickly exits the house. The exit of radon is largely dependent on the ventilation of a building, typically measured in air changes per hour (ACH). Buildings with high ventilation levels typically have lower levels of indoor radon and other pollutants. The dramatic effect that ventilation rates have upon indoor radon concentrations is illustrated in Exhibit 1.2.

Unfortunately, recent years have seen a dramatic reduction in the rate of ventilation for new housing. Ventilation also permits the exit of heated or air-conditioned indoor air. High ventilation rates waste energy, by requiring more fuel to maintain any given comfortable level of indoor temperature. The government's encouragement of energy

Exhibit 1.2
Effect of Ventilation on Air Quality

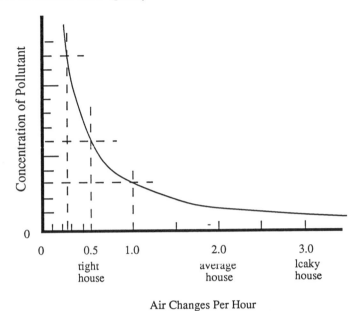

Air Changes Per Hour

conservation has therefore had the effect of reducing ventilation rates. Many older homes had ventilation rates of 1.0 or more ACH, while new homes may have rates as low as 0.2 ACH. While these lower ventilation rates conserve energy, they also reduce the exit of radon gas, thereby entrapping and concentrating radon within a building.

The extent to which energy conservation measures explain high indoor radon concentrations is disputed. Some have found that energy-efficient homes have two to five times the indoor radon concentrations.[6] EPA once estimated that the Department of Energy's weatherization program perversely would cause thousands of additional deaths from indoor radon.[7] Other recent studies have found little or no correlation between reduced ventilation rates and increased radon concentration.[8] Some energy conservation measures may reduce the rate of radon intake, thereby controlling indoor concentrations. Nevertheless, it is a physical certainty that, for any given entry rate, reduced ventilation will increase indoor radon concentrations. Radon levels will vary inversely with the ventilation rate, so that a 50 percent reduction in ventilation will double the indoor radon concentration. This reduced ventilation does not itself cause radon contamination, but it can seriously aggravate a radon problem in houses with high radon entry levels.

Another manmade source of indoor radon contamination warrants mention. Radon may be emitted from a home's building products themselves, such as concrete blocks or bricks produced from raw materials containing radioactive elements. In most cases, these materials have radium content similar to that of soil, and surveys have found radium levels around 2.0 picocuries per gram (pCi/g). Much higher concentrations have been found in concrete blocks containing phosphate slag derived from phosphate production in the southeastern United States, which has been found to contain between 20 and 60 pCi/g. Concrete incorporating phosphate slag may be found in 100,000 homes. Radon concentrations in other building materials, such as wood, tend to be far lower. Building materials do not appear to be a primary source of radon contamination, but they may account for 3 to 10 percent of all indoor radon exposure. This relatively small percentage may account for up to two thousand deaths, however, and is obviously worthy of concern.

A final potential source of indoor radon is contaminated water or natural gas that enters a house. These are not primary sources, and EPA estimates that from 2 to 5 percent of total indoor radon exposure derives from drinking water.[9] In some locations, however, water or natural gas may produce significant amounts of radon exposure. Radon gas may escape from water during showering, washing, drinking, and related activities. Radon concentrations in New England well water run into tens of thousands of picocuries per liter (pCi/L), and radon levels tend to be higher in privately supplied water. The American Medical Association estimated that privately supplied water in the New England and Appalachian regions may account for 35 percent of indoor radon air exposures in those regions.[10] Water wells in Georgia often exceed 2,000 pCi/L of radon. Texas and the Carolinas also have high average levels of radon in groundwater. In the 18 percent of homes using private wells for their water supplies, water may contribute an average of 0.5 pCi/L radon to the indoor air. In more than 1 percent of U.S. homes, well water causes indoor exposures of 1 pCi/L or greater, in addition to whatever indoor level is caused by ground emissions.[11] The typical indoor air exposure from contaminated natural gas is quite low, at around 0.1 pCi/L. Concentrations within gas may vary widely, however, and range from 100 pCi/L to less than 1 pCi/L.

In sum, indoor radon may result from a variety of sources, which makes the process of identifying and correcting hazards more complicated. It is clear, however, that housing characteristics explain the vast majority of radon concentrations. Radon is sometimes dismissed as a natural phenomenon, about which people can do little. Indoor radon, however, is primarily a result of structural factors that are well within our control.

Levels of Indoor Radon

The actual level of indoor radon concentration varies considerably throughout the United States. Most attention has been focused upon those houses found to have extraordinarily high levels. One such home had radon so high that it was the equivalent of smoking twenty-two packs of cigarettes a day. While these unusual situations obviously require prompt correction, the public health problem lies more in the unexceptional home. Even common radon concentrations are sufficiently high to produce a major risk.

Different units have been employed for measuring radon levels. One common unit of measurement is picocuries per liter (pCi/L), which expresses the radon concentration in the ambient indoor air. A second common unit is the "working level" (WL). This unit does not measure the total radon concentration directly but expresses the amount of human exposure to the actual harmful alpha radiation from radon and its progeny. Exposure to one WL for approximately 170 hours yields a cumulative exposure of one "WLM" (working level month). The different units have produced some confusion. Assuming certain equilibrium conditions, exposure to 1 WL is equivalent to a concentration of approximately 100–200 pCi/L of radon.

A large, twenty-one-state survey of indoor radon levels in private homes conducted by the Lawrence Berkeley Laboratory found average concentrations of about 1.5 pCi/L, or approximately 0.015 WL.[12] A survey by Professor Bernard Cohen of the University of Pittsburgh also found an average concentration of about 1.5 pCi/L.[13] A twenty-three-state study by Terradex Corporation found median concentrations of 1.3 pCi/L. Other smaller studies have found roughly similar average indoor radon concentrations in select locations. A survey in five Northwestern states found mean exposures of 1.2 pCi/L. A survey of energy-efficient homes in New York found average basement concentrations of 6.0 pCi/L, and first-floor concentrations averaged 2.5 pCi/L.[14] In a Minnesota study, over 35 percent of homes exceeded 4 pCi/L of radon. Homes in the Spokane Valley of Washington and Idaho averaged 13.3 pCi/L radon in winter.

These studies have also produced valuable information on the distribution of indoor radon concentrations as well. They generally agree that about 1 percent of homes average significantly higher levels of radon, of roughly 8 pCi/L (0.08 WL) or higher. One percent of U.S. homes represents a substantial number, however, representing approximately one million homes. EPA estimates that 200,000 U.S. homes have radon levels exceeding 20 pCi/L. Some smaller number of houses had much higher levels, exceeding 100 or even 1,000 pCi/L. Radon hotspots appear throughout the nation. Half the homes in Clinton, New Jersey, for example, had indoor radon concentrations exceeding 200 pCi/L during the winter. One New Jersey home had radon contamination in excess of 3,000 pCi/L.

These estimates should not be considered exact, as radon measurement is still imprecise. There is limited experience in radon measurement, and some laboratories have produced inconsistent results. Also, indoor radon levels tend to fluctuate. Radon levels tend to be higher at certain times of year, though this may simply be due to residents' tendency to leave windows and doors open at certain times of year. Radon levels will vary throughout a house, with different rooms yielding different concentrations. Upper floors, further removed from the ground, will generally have lower radon concentrations.

The indoor radon hazard has focused on single-family dwellings, which generally present the greatest risks. Some rental apartments may also have a radon problem. While apartments situated on higher floors are unlikely to have high levels of radon, concentrations may be of serious concern in ground-floor apartments.

In addition, new evidence suggests that some schools may contain high levels of radon. An EPA study of 3,000 classrooms in 130 schools in sixteen states found that 9 percent of rooms had radon levels above 4 pCi/L and 3 percent had levels exceeding 20 pCi/L. One Tennessee school had a concentration of 136 pCi/L. Eleven Nashville schools measured indoor radon concentrations exceeding 100 pCi/L and the average concentration in the city's schools was 30 pCi/L. EPA administrator William K. Reilly used this data to issue a call for universal radon testing of schools followed by action to reduce radon concentrations. The school problem is largely caused by room depressurization resulting from heating and air-conditioning units. Radon in schools has received increasing attention because children spend a great deal of time at school and because the higher metabolism of children may cause them to inhale more radon than adults. The overall school exposure is still largely unknown.

Office buildings tend to have relatively low indoor concentrations of radon. These buildings often have better ventilation and a lower percentage of total surface area in contact with the ground. A potential problem exists, however, as the National Research Council cautioned that "little is known about the distribution of radon concentrations in office buildings, especially those buildings with only one to three stories that may also have partial or full basements."[15]

While isolated measured radon levels in individual buildings may be questioned, the overall problem is clear. Scientists have conducted dozens of studies and produced an ample data base for reaching conclusions on indoor radon exposure. These data indicate that average exposures are probably below 2 pCi/L but that millions of homes have significantly higher levels. In many of these homes, radioactive exposures are higher than those in today's uranium mines.

The Risk from Indoor Radon

Radon has no known immediate adverse effects, but exposure to radon may initiate lung cancer and, possibly, stomach cancer. There is no absolutely safe level of exposure to radon. Science has found no threshold for carcinogens, which means that even the tiniest exposure to a cancer-causing substance carries some risk of cancer. This "no-threshold hypothesis" is almost universally accepted for radioactive substances. Considerable experience with radiation exposures has found no clear evidence of a safe level. As exposures decrease, of course, the relative risk also declines. At very low levels of exposure, the risk may be 1 in 1 million or less.

At very low risk levels, such as 1 in 1 million, it is difficult to demonstrate harm that is causally connected to exposures. The demonstration of cancer from lower exposures would require a huge sample exposed population of many millions and would require that other confounding factors, such as smoking, be entirely absent. The number of potential carcinogens is great, and cancer does not reveal its source. For the foreseeable future, it is impossible to directly measure the risk at low exposure levels. Given the no-threshold hypothesis, scientists assume that some small number of cancers are caused by low-level exposures. The key question is how many cancers are caused by any given exposure level. This question is answered by quantitative risk assessment, conducted by extrapolation from studies on high levels of exposure, which produce so many cancers that they may be demonstrated statistically.

There is clear evidence that lung cancer is caused by exposure to 100 WLM or more of radon daughters. This evidence derives from uranium miners during the 1940s and 1950s, when mines were poorly ventilated and exposures were high, at 500 pCi/L and more. Many excess lung cancers (roughly ten times the expected number) were attributable to these exposures. Direct evidence of lung cancer from lower radon exposure levels is inconclusive. Some studies have found no excess of lung cancer in high-radon areas of the country. On the other hand, one study compared individuals who lived at least thirty years in homes with radon concentrations exceeding 1.5 pCi/L with those who lived in homes with lower radon levels. The results of this study suggested that radon caused about 30 percent of lung cancer cases.[16] The disparate results do not mean that lower levels of radon are safe but may only mean that some experimental methods and statistical tests lack sufficient sensitivity to detect the risks or radon exposure. Established quantitative risk assessment procedures can estimate the risk at lower levels.

Quantitative estimates of the risk for lower-level exposures are produced by taking the data on high-level exposures and extrapolating downward. While some scientific dispute persists over proper extrapolation procedures, there is rough agreement in the case of radon. The Mine Safety and Health Administration has reviewed the data and concluded that exposure to 1 WLM produces a cancer risk of from one to six cases per 10,000 exposed. The International Commission on Radiological Protection estimated a risk of 1.7 in 10,000 per WLM, and the National Council on Radiation Protection and Measurements estimated a risk of 1.5 in 10,000 per WLM.[17] Animal studies have found even greater risk, of 6 to 8 in 10,000 per WLM exposure.

Some other scientists have estimated higher or lower risk levels per WLM, and any quantitative risk assessment is based on assumptions and subject to challenge. The uranium miners studied were grown males who were also exposed to other hazardous pollutants, and many smoked. The sample size of miners studied is relatively small, and exposure data are incomplete. In the case of radon and the miner studies, however, the risk assessment is unusually reliable. The EPA has stressed that "there is much less uncertainty in estimates of risk from radionuclide emissions because of the extensive data base on the effects of human exposure to radiation."[18] Unlike many toxic substances, which require extrapolation from animal studies, there is direct human evidence of cancer risk from radon. The radon risk assessments are thus far more certain than for many environmental carcinogens regulated by government. These estimates are at least as likely to underestimate the true risk as they are to overstate this risk.

The established risk assessments enable an estimate of prevailing risk from indoor exposures. The roughly 1 million homes with average exposures around 8 pCi/L produce exposures of nearly 2 WLM per year. Applying the radon quantitative risk assessment, one can estimate that one year's residence in such a home creates a cancer risk in excess of 1 in 2,500. Most people live in a home for more than a year, and the lifetime radon risk is much greater. Living an average lifetime in a home or homes with 8 pCi/L produces a total risk of roughly 1 in 50. Children may be at even greater risk of cancer, because their cells are dividing so rapidly.

For the average home, with about 1.5 pCi/L prevailing radon concentrations, the annual radon exposure is approximately 0.3 WLM. Even the exposures in this average home produce a lifetime risk of 1 in 15,000 and a total lifetime risk of approximately 1 in 300. Thus even these relatively low, average exposures yield a considerable risk of death from cancer. The risk from radon exposure itself may be even greater when combined with cigarette smoking. Smokers may be ten times more likely than nonsmokers to contract lung cancer from a given level of exposure to radon. Exhibit 1.3 portrays overall comparative risk levels from radon exposure.

The true significance of indoor radon risks can be appreciated in comparison with other environmental risks to health. EPA and other federal regulatory agencies often regulate cancer risks as low as 1 in 1 million. Few, if any, toxic air pollutants outdoors produce lifetime cancer risks in excess of 1 in 10,000. Even workplace chemical exposures seldom produce risks as high as the *average* lifetime risk from indoor radon. In short, indoor radon exposures present risks that are hundreds or thousands of times greater than those presented by environmental pollutants that most people are concerned about.

Various organizations have promulgated "action levels" for indoor radon — concentrations that warrant remedial steps to lower exposures. EPA's action level is set at 4 pCi/L. The National Council on

Exhibit 1.3
Relative Radon Risks

pCi/L	Estimated number of lung cancer deaths due to radon exposure (out of 100)	Comparable exposure levels	Comparable risk
200	44-77	1000 times average outdoor level	More than 60 times non-smoker risk
100	27-63	100 times average indoor level	4 pack-a-day smoker
40	12-38		20,000 chest x-rays per year
20	6-21	100 times average outdoor level	2 pack-a-day smoker
10	3-12	10 times average indoor level	1 pack-a-day smoker
			5 times non-smoker risk
4	1-5		200 chest x-rays per year
2	.7-3	10 times average outdoor level	Non-smoker risk of dying from lung cancer
1	.3-1		
0.2	.1-.3	Average outdoor level	20 chest x-rays per year

Radiation Protection and Measurements set its action level at 2 WLM per year, or roughly 8 pCi/L. The American Society of Heating, Refrigeration and Air-Conditioning Engineers has recommended a limit of 0.01 WL or about 1 pCi/L for new buildings. The surgeon general and the Union of Concerned Scientists both have recommended remedial action for exposures of 0.05 WL or greater.

While there is obvious variance in these recommended action levels, it is clear that a substantial number of American homes, probably exceeding one million, have radon concentrations greater than even the highest action level. Millions of homes exceed EPA's action level. EPA found that 21 percent of houses studied exceeded the 4 pCi/L action level and nearly 1 percent of houses exceeded 20 pCi/L.[19] A much higher percentage of houses exceeds the action level in some regions, such as Pennsylvania or Colorado. These exposures present a substantial risk of lung cancer. Even the lowest recommended action level would still permit an individual residual lifetime cancer risk of more than 1 in 1,000. If radon exposures were controlled as strictly as other carcinogenic environmental pollutants, the federal standard would be 0.001 pCi/L or below, and virtually every house in the entire nation would exceed the standard.

In short, radon is the greatest public health threat in the United States, save smoking. As mentioned earlier, radon may cause as many as 20,000 deaths every year, and virtually everyone agrees that the toll exceeds 1,000 deaths per year, even with the most optimistic assumptions. By contrast, most outdoor air pollutants are responsible for at most a handful of cancers. The total cancer risk from all outdoor air pollutants combined is almost certainly less than the risk from indoor radon alone.

Measures to Control Indoor Radon

While the radon hazard in the existing housing stock is considerable, remedial measures can be taken to reduce radon concentrations and the resultant risk. Different approaches are available, and their effectiveness will depend upon the specific characteristics of individual buildings. In most instances, the application of one or more techniques will significantly reduce indoor radon levels. The New Jersey Environmental Protection commissioner has flatly declared that "virtually any house or building can be cleansed of potentially dangerous indoor levels of [radon] through sophisticated ventilation and sealing techniques."[20] While this may be overly optimistic, it is indisputable that substantial improvement is possible with currently available remedial actions. EPA pilot studies have consistently demonstrated that indoor radon levels can be reduced by 90 percent or more.

The most obvious and direct response to indoor radon is to prevent its entry into a house. Because much radon seeps into houses through cracks in the floor or walls, the entry can be controlled by sealing those cracks as well as other entry points. Certain surface sealants, such as polyurethane caulks, may successfully stop the entry of radon when applied to cracks and other entry points, such as pipes and drains. Sealants have been employed in the past with some success in constraining high indoor radon concentrations. Closing soil connections with expanding urethane foam has reduced indoor radon concentrations by over 50 percent.

Unfortunately, sealants are by no means a panacea for the radon problem. It is impossible to find every crack, and some entry points are unsealable — contemporary houses require pipes and drains. Even if most entry points are effectively sealed, a house can still draw a great deal of radon from other entry points, especially if pressure differentials draw radon gas from the ground. Ironically, some sealants may themselves contain uranium. At least one study has found little benefit from sealing cracks. In addition, the sealant may last for five years or less, and new cracks may develop over time, as a house settles on its foundation. There is also concern that sealing causes high radon buildup behind this new barrier, which may cause an increase in gamma radiation from building materials. Sealing alone cannot cure the radon problem.

Sealants do offer some promise, however. Most evidence suggests that sealing entry points can reduce indoor radon concentrations by at least 30 percent. Moreover, sealing entry points is a relatively inexpensive response to the problem. Costs of professional sealing typically range from $300 to $750 per application. While the complete sealing of all internal surfaces can cost $15,000, the sealing of specific cracks or connections can be done for as little as $50.[21] In addition some skilled homeowners may be able to seal many entry points on a do-it-yourself basis.

In addition to reducing radon entry, its exit may also be encouraged, to reduce indoor concentrations. Additional ventilation provides an alternative or supplement to sealing entry points. Increased ventilation may take the form of "deweatherization" or removal of the energy-conserving processes that reduced the home's ventilation rate. Ventilation has been reduced by such simple steps as weatherstripping and caulking doors and windows. Different types of weatherization have broadly differing effects on ventilation, however. Caulking and weatherstripping reduce air exchange rates by less than 5 percent, whereas duct sealing reduces air exchange by nearly 30 percent. Increasing ventilation from 0.75 to 1.0 ACH will reduce radon concentrations by roughly one-third.

Increased ventilation also has shortcomings, however. While ventilation may be cheaply increased, simply by opening windows, this method is haphazard and may produce uncomfortable indoor conditions. Deweatherization will have its own costs, and any increase in ventilation will defeat energy conservation goals and raise the heating and cooling costs of homeowners. These added costs may well exceed $500 per year. Additional energy production required by deweatherization will have its own pollution costs to human health. In cold climates, some of these energy costs may be reduced with use of a heat exchanger that retains heat from outgoing air. These heat exchangers themselves cost hundreds of dollars, however, and they may be economically impracticable for much of the country. Moreover, outdoor weather conditions affect air exchange rates, regardless of weatherization. Despite these shortcomings, the Colorado Department of Health has found increased ventilation to provide the most cost-effective program for indoor radon control.[22]

Perhaps the most promising response to indoor radon is to eliminate or reverse pressure differentials, thereby controlling entry of radon and promoting its exit. This can be achieved by installing a powerful fan underneath the house, in the basement or crawlspace. The fan pulls contaminated air outside and at the same time corrects pressure differentials that draw radon gas into the home. An EPA study found that such fans could be very effective. The homes in this study originally had indoor radon concentrations as high as 7.4 WL, and the fans reduced the concentrations to 0.02 WL and below, a reduction of up to 97 percent. Such forced-air ventilation has also proved effective in Sweden. These fans are not universally effective, as variations in soil permeability and "large building-to-soil connections can prevent reversal of the soil-building pressure gradient over a portion of the foundation, particularly in retrofit situations."[23] In cold climates, the fan may even cause structural damage to the house. Further research is surely necessary, but this process appears to be the most effective long-run response to radon contamination. At the present time, the costs of installing such fans exceed $1,000, and the fan would cost about $140 per year in operating costs. Economies of scale and self-installation may eventually reduce the one-time cost to $500 per home. Normal exhaust fans have little benefit and may reduce indoor pressure, thereby drawing more radon into a home.

Still another remedial response, air cleaning, has occasionally been proposed. Radon decay products tend to cling to airborne particles, which are then inhaled into the lungs. Indoor air cleaners, such as electrostatic precipitators, are currently available to filter particles out of the air. Studies suggest that the newest air cleaners can remove as much as 45 to 85 percent of the radon daughters in a structure. Unfortunately, air cleaning may have the perverse effect of increasing the actual health hazard. While cleaners reduce the total concentration of particles and associated indoor radon, they leave a larger fraction of the radon unattached to particles. There is some evidence that such unattached radon causes a greater radiation dose to exposed individuals. While this risk is not entirely understood, the risk cautions against reliance on air cleaning to remediate indoor radon problems.

Radon exposures from water can readily be controlled. Activated carbon filters can remove up to 99 percent of waterborne radon, as well as other harmful contaminants, though this quality filtration will cost over $800, and the filter will eventually become radioactive itself. Water aeration also can effectively control radon levels in water supplies, at a cost of approximately $2,000. These measures are cost-effective only when very high concentrations of radon are found in water.

A variety of solutions are available for reducing indoor radon, with substructural fans appearing to be the most promising. The optimal solution will depend on the individual house, however. In some cases, no response will be effective. In other cases, drastic and expensive action is necessary. An EPA study found elaborate radon reduction measures have cost from $4,300 to $15,700 per home.[24] Anecdotal evidence suggests that correction costs may be as high as $100,000 in some instances.

It is somewhat easier to avoid high radon levels in new construction. Care should be taken to avoid locating housing atop soil with a high content of radium or uranium. Building materials can be screened for radioactive content, and less radioactive materials, such as wood, may be employed. When there is a potential radon problem, new homes can be constructed with limited ground openings and fans to avoid high indoor radon concentrations. An EPA environmental engineer suggested the following construction precautions for radon in schools:

- designing the Heating, Ventilation, and Air Conditioning (HVAC) system to operate in continuous overpressurization to repel infiltration of radon;
- placing a four-inch aggregate subslab under the four-inch concrete slab with a plastic film barrier in between;
- sealing expansion joints with plastic stripping and polyurethane caulk;
- plugging utility penetrations; and
- painting interior block walls with air-flow resistant coating and sealant.[25]

The state of Florida has proposed construction standards for residential homes, including most of these suggestions and also constructing a crawlspace, so that the floor is not in contact with soil, and preventing cracks in concrete slabs by plasticizing, prestressing, or posttensioning concrete. Such preventive measures should be effective to prevent high radon levels in new construction. Additional costs for radon prevention in new homes may be less than $500 and seldom exceed 1 percent of the total building price. Remedial action in schools and commercial buildings may be much more costly.

Notes

1. Anthony Nero, *The Indoor Radon Story*, TECHNOLOGY REV. (January 1986), p. 28.

2. Sheldon Krimsky & Alonzo Plough, ENVIRONMENTAL HAZARDS: COMMUNICATING RISKS AS A SOCIAL PROCESS (1988), p. 137.

3. INDOOR POLLUTION LAW REPORT, August 1987, p. 3.

4. B. Cohen, *A National Survey of* ^{222} *Rn in U.S. Homes and Correlating Factors*, 51 HEALTH PHYSICS 175, 179 (1986).

5. Frank Cross & Paula Murray, *Liability for Toxic Radon Gas in Residential Home Sales*, 66 N. CAROLINA L. REV. 687, 693 (1987).

6. L. Kirsch, *Behind Closed Doors: Indoor Air Pollution and Government Policy*, 6 HARVARD ENVIRONMENTAL L. REV. 339, 346 (1982).

7. Isaac Turiel, INDOOR AIR QUALITY AND HUMAN HEALTH (Stanford, Calif.: Stanford University Press, 1985) p. 40.

8. Nero, p. 37.

9. 51 Fed. Reg. 34836, 34842 (1986).

10. American Medical Association Council on Scientific Affairs, *Radon in Homes*, 258 J. AM. MED. ASSOC. 668, 669–70 (1987).

11. Anthony Nero, *Radon and Its Decay Products in Indoor Air: An Overview*, in RADON AND ITS DECAY PRODUCTS IN INDOOR AIR (W. W. Nazaroff & A. V. Nero eds. 1988), p. 23.

12. A. Nero, M. Schwehr, W. Nazaroff & K. Revzan, *Distribution of Airborne Radon-222 Concentrations in U.S. Homes*, 234 SCIENCE 992, 994 (1986).

13. B. Cohen, p. 176.

14. American Medical Association, p. 669.

15. National Research Council, *Policies & Procedures for Control of Indoor Air Pollution*, 1987, p. 17.

16. F. Steinhauser, *Epidemiological Evidence of Radon-Induced Health Risks* in RADON AND ITS DECAY PRODUCTS IN INDOOR AIR, p. 353.

17. 51 Fed. Reg. 45678, 45681 (1986).

18. 51 Fed. Reg. 34056, 34057 (1986).

19. Richard Dowd, *EPA's Radon Study Results*, 22 ENVIRONMENTAL SCIENCE & TECHNOLOGY 28 (1988).

20. Sullivan, *Radon Tests Are Urged for Homes in Parts of Jersey*, N.Y. TIMES, Sept. 13, 1987, at 62, col. 2.

21. Arthur G. Scott, *Preventing Radon Entry*, in RADON AND ITS DECAY PRODUCTS IN INDOOR AIR, p. 420.

22. The Commonwealth of Massachusetts Special Legislative Commission on Indoor Air Pollution, *Indoor Air Pollution in Massachusetts* (April 1989) p. 65.

23. Scott, p. 423.

24. *GAO Says EPA Best Suited to Lead Effort to Control "National Problem" of Radon Gas*, 17 Env't Rep. (BNA) 407 (July 11, 1986).

25. INDOOR POLLUTION NEWS, April 21, 1988, p. 5.

2

THE HEALTH RISK FROM INDOOR ASBESTOS

Asbestos, like radon, originates in the earth's crust and is widespread throughout the atmosphere. Asbestos is not a single substance but is a broad term for natural fibrous stones that describes certain minerals, known as hydrated silicates. The distinctive feature of these silicates is the occurrence of long, thin fibers that separate easily. There are many kinds of asbestos but the most common are chrysotile, crocidolite, and amosite. Some asbestos naturally erodes into the air from mineral deposits, but asbestos is also used in and emitted from a variety of manmade products. When asbestos fibers are breathed into the lungs, they damage and scar lung tissue and may cause a variety of potentially fatal diseases, including asbestosis, mesothelioma, and lung cancer.

Airborne asbestos is often found indoors. Unlike radon, emissions from the earth's crust are not the primary source of indoor asbestos exposures. While individuals are regularly exposed to asbestos outdoors, exposure levels are extremely low. Indoor exposures may be higher. Asbestos has properties that make the mineral useful to man. Asbestos is especially useful as a fire retardant, to strengthen associated materials, and as an insulator against temperature. As a result, asbestos has been sprayed on a variety of building materials to prevent fire, used to reinforce the strength of cement products, applied to resist wear and tear, and employed in insulating products, among other uses. Asbestos was used in thousands of indoor products, beginning in the 1940s and lasting through the 1970s. Many asbestos uses are inside buildings, and fibers may break off and enter the indoor air, where they are breathed by occupants. The magnitude of the resultant health risk is highly uncertain. EPA has expressed an inability to quantify the amount of health harm caused by indoor asbestos exposures. Some have suggested that indoor asbestos exposures may cause more than one thousand cancers although most estimates are much lower. Asbestos is indisputably harmful, and the remaining questions regard the extent of indoor exposure to asbestos fibers.

This chapter explores the sources and nature of the risk presented by indoor asbestos. First, I discuss the sources of indoor asbestos exposure. Second, I review the evidence on levels of asbestos found in indoor air. Third, I address the extent of the health risk presented by these indoor asbestos levels. Fourth, I analyze the responses proposed to reduce indoor asbestos.

Sources and Causes of Indoor Asbestos

Some indoor airborne asbestos derives from outdoor levels. This amount appears to be quite small, however, and the primary source of indoor asbestos is asbestos-based products found within the building. Nearly 1 million buildings contain asbestos products. A primary source of indoor asbestos is sprayed-on insulating material that contained asbestos, for purposes of fireproofing as well as insulation. In lieu of spraying, asbestos insulating material may have been trowelled on. The practice of spraying asbestos insulating material became widespread in the 1950s. Spray insulation proceeded through two distinct processes. In the wet process, a chrysotile or amosite asbestos was mixed with a binder such as cement and water, at a relatively low concentration, and then sprayed onto a ceiling or other building surface. In the dry process, a higher concentration of chrysotile or amosite asbestos was blown onto the building surface and was wetted by a water spray as it left the nozzle of the sprayer. The dry process produced a mixture that had lower density than in the wet process. As a result, fibers are more readily released from asbestos applied through the dry process. Asbestos fibers are also released during the spraying process itself. The practice of spraying on asbestos insulation was largely halted in the United States by 1980. Roughly 5 percent of buildings (about 200,000) have sprayed-on or trowelled-on materials.[1]

Another source of indoor asbestos is pipe and boiler insulation. This insulation may take the form of preformed insulating slabs, corrugated asbestos paper, or other products. These insulators usually had a relatively low asbestos content, of about 15 percent by weight. Asbestos insulation was often covered by and attached with asbestos tape or asbestos/cement compounds. This use may have been more common than sprayed-on asbestos applications. Over 15 percent of all buildings may have asbestos products in pipe and boiler insulation.[2] Asbestos has also been used in floor tile and sheet, ceiling tiles, various coatings and sealants, gaskets, and textiles. These applications are less common but are nevertheless significant uses of asbestos-containing materials.

The risk from asbestos in buildings depends on its condition. Asbestos products fall into one of three categories: "(1) those used or applied in a liquid state; (2) hard products in which fibers are embedded in some other solid material; and (3) materials that are soft and easily crushed, often referred to as 'friable.' "[3] Those asbestos products applied in a liquid state present relatively little risk. The asbestos tends to remain sealed within the product and fiber release is "unlikely, because the fibers are combined with and held down by a liquid."[4] Asbestos in hard products also presents little danger of release. The indoor asbestos problem is largely traceable to the third category of products, those referred to as "friable." Some of these friable materials are relatively well bound and present less release danger. Other friable materials are soft and crumbly and may release substantial numbers of fibers into the indoor air. Friable materials present a particular hazard when damaged, exposing more fibers to ready release. Roughly 40 percent of sprayed-on or trowelled-on asbestos may be considered damaged, and a higher percentage of pipe and boiler insulation has been damaged.[5] Fortunately, more than 85 percent of the asbestos found in buildings is amply immobilized within some binding material that largely prevents fiber release.

A wide variety of asbestos-containing products may be found within buildings. These products present widely differing health risks, depending on their nature and whether they have been damaged. While asbestos products may be found anywhere, the greatest problem does not appear to be in individual residences. A Consumer Product Safety Commission study of asbestos-containing homes in Cleveland, San Francisco, and Philadelphia found that indoor asbestos levels were no higher than those found outside. Most of the concern for indoor asbestos has focused upon schools, office buildings, rental complexes, and other large structures. EPA has studied public and commercial buildings and found that 511,000 private nonresidential buildings contain friable asbestos materials and 208,000 residential apartment buildings contain such materials.[6] Asbestos materials are found in roughly 31,000 schools, involving 15 million students. EPA estimates that 3.6 billion public and commercial buildings have some asbestos-containing materials. Others suggest that 8 million buildings may contain asbestos, including more than 50 percent of apartment complexes.

Levels of Indoor Asbestos

The number of asbestos fibers actually found in the indoor air determines the health risk. The presence of any ambient asbestos has produced considerable concern, particularly in schools, where children may be exposed. As with any carcinogen, however, it is the quantity of exposure that determines the health risk. Some levels of indoor asbestos may produce a serious cancer risk, but other lower levels may cause only a miniscule danger.

The most expansive review of asbestos harms was undertaken by the Royal Commission on Matters of Health and Safety Arising from the Use of Asbestos in Ontario. The Ontario royal commission was composed of eminent Canadian scientists, who held extensive hearings including the testimony of scores of expert witnesses, and issued a three-volume report on the health consequences of asbestos exposure. A significant section of this report dealt with indoor asbestos exposures, particularly those found in schools and office buildings. The royal commission found that the principal source of indoor airborne asbestos was damaged or disturbed friable insulating material. Even the erosion of these damaged materials produced only short-term exposure to "minimal levels of fibre concentration."[7] Most airborne indoor asbestos was caused when the eroded asbestos, having already settled onto building surfaces, was reentrained (swept back into the air) through cleaning or other building activities.

The commission sponsored its own studies to determine the indoor levels of asbestos exposure. One such study was performed by Dr. Eric Chatfield, who found that average indoor exposures to asbestos were approximately 2 nanograms per cubic meter, or 0.0006 fibers per cubic centimeter (f/cc).[8] This was roughly the concentration occurring in the ambient air outside the buildings studied. Similar levels were found in another study for the commission conducted by Dr. Donald Pinchin. In conclusion, the Royal

Commission emphasized that "the worst building exposures are considerably less than 0.01 f/cc."[9]

Several independent studies provide further data on indoor asbestos exposures. A French study by Patrick Sebastien examined buildings with sprayed-on asbestos and found median indoor exposures of 0.00015 f/cc. A U.S. study conducted for EPA by William Nicholson measured concentrations in New Jersey school buildings, distinguishing between wet-applied and dry-applied asbestos. For buildings with wet-applied asbestos, nearly all measured concentrations were less than 0.0006 f/cc, which approximated outdoor levels. A study conducted for the National Institute of Environmental Health Sciences found that "the average concentrations in the vast majority of buildings with asbestos as surfacing material do not differ significantly from background."[10] Slightly higher readings were found for dry application, where most potential exposures were 0.0015 f/cc or less. In a few schools where asbestos was visibly damaged, concentrations were as high as 0.25 f/cc.[11] Another EPA-sponsored study by Sawyer and Spooner studied office buildings in New York and Connecticut and found levels ranging from 0.000075 f/cc to 0.006 f/cc. Their study of schools with custodial activity that disturbed and entrained asbestos fibers found higher levels, of up to 0.019 f/cc.[12]

Another large study of asbestos concentrations was undertaken by EPA to measure schools in Houston, Texas. The study focused on schools with a known high asbestos content. This study found mean average exposures of 0.005 f/cc, and this mean reflected some very high measurements found in schools with highly disturbed asbestos materials.[13] This study has received some criticism for overstating actual indoor asbestos concentrations. A 1988 study of forty-five asbestos-containing homes in Cleveland, San Francisco, and Philadelphia found no measurements exceeding outdoor background levels of asbestos.

The limited data do not permit conclusive findings regarding indoor asbestos concentrations. EPA has estimated that airborne asbestos levels inside public buildings average 0.006 f/cc but that schools have a higher average of 0.03 f/cc. These figures, particularly the estimate for schools, are at the upper end of probable indoor concentrations. The Ontario royal commission and others have estimated that average exposures are well below 0.01 f/cc. All sources recognize, however, that some buildings have unusually high concentrations, far exceeding the average level of airborne indoor asbestos.

The Risk from Indoor Asbestos

In the late 1970s, governments and individuals began to notice the potential problem of indoor asbestos exposure. Evidence on the health harms of asbestos somewhat parallels that of radon. Asbestos causes lung cancer and, as a carcinogen, there is no safe level of exposure to asbestos. At very low exposure levels, the risk of cancer decreases to levels of 1 in 1 million or less. It is currently impossible to demonstrate scientifically a causal relationship with cancer at these low levels, but quantitative risk assessment can enable us to estimate the potential harm of even low exposure levels.

As with radon, evidence of the carcinogenicity of asbestos comes from high levels of occupational exposure. Some occupational exposures in the past were so high that employees literally worked in a fog of asbestos that obscured visibility. Past occupational exposures are cumulatively measured in f/cc-years, the number of years of exposure to a given concentration. Twenty-five years of exposure to an average of 10 f/cc would produce 250 f/cc-years. Disease has been clearly linked to higher levels of asbestos exposure.

One study of workers at an asbestos cement factory in Ontario separated workers into three groups: those exposed to 8–69 f/cc-years, those exposed to 70–121 f/cc-years; and those exposed to 122–420 f/cc-years. Mesothelioma mortality rates for these categories per 1,000 man-years were 1.9, 4.9, and 11.9, respectively.[14] Less clear evidence was found for lung cancer. Other epidemiological studies have produced a similar correlation for lung cancer, however, and several animal studies indicate that asbestos fiber exposure causes cancer. The legacy of past high occupational exposures to asbestos is evident in the high number of cases of mesothelioma, asbestosis, and lung cancer occurring today. Some evidence also links asbestos exposure with gastrointestinal cancers. As always, there is some uncertainty regarding past exposure levels, but the toll of cancer and other disease is so great as to leave little doubt about the potential harms of asbestos. Some have suggested that asbestos exposures have caused more than 60,000 cancer deaths in the United States every year. While this figure is probably an exaggeration, there is widespread agreement that asbestos causes several thousand cancer deaths annually.

Asbestos is even more harmful for smokers. The carcinogenic effects of tobacco and asbestos operate synergistically to increase cancer risk more than additively. Studies have shown that certain exposures to asbestos increased the lung cancer rate by five times for nonsmokers but by fifty times for smokers. The combination of asbestos exposure and smoking is a particularly deadly one.

The evidence of health harms from occupational asbestos exposures demonstrates the hazard of the substance but says relatively little about the prevailing indoor risk from asbestos. Unlike the radon situation, the asbestos exposures in schools and other buildings are far below those found to produce cancer in workers. Few individuals are exposed to as much as 1 f/cc-year from indoor asbestos concentrations. Indoor asbestos exposures are several thousand times lower than the levels that caused so much cancer in workers. Indeed, indoor exposures are far below the current occupational exposures permitted by federal regulation.

Tools of quantitative risk assessment enable us to estimate risks at even low levels. While these risk assessments typically use conservative assumptions that may tend to overstate the actual risk, the procedure provides at least a rough estimate of the maximum risk confronted. The EPA has estimated that average indoor asbestos exposures produce a risk of 1 in 100,000. The Ontario royal commission contended that even this low risk level is an exaggeration, due to EPA's selective use of data. The commission estimated that indoor exposures produced a risk of 0.07 to 2.4 in 1 million. Other scientists have reached similar results.

Even these low levels represent some risk of fatal disease, which may cause concern, especially for school exposures to children. A comparison to other risks provides context. The risk from indoor asbestos is several times lower than that presented by lightning, tornadoes, hurricanes, and any number of other natural dangers. As for schoolchildren, the drive to school is much riskier than the indoor asbestos concentrations found in most schools. A recent report concluded:

> a broad scientific consensus now holds that asbestos carries far less risk than living with a cigarette smoker, having X-rays, riding a bicycle, or breathing the air or water in some cities. By one calculation, a child is three times more likely to be killed by lightning than by attending a school insulated with asbestos.[15]

Numerous sources have now found that risk from exposure to low levels of asbestos is speculative and uncertain.

The risk estimates for asbestos may be faulted for failure to consider the varying types of asbestos. Most schools and other buildings contain chrysotile asbestos, while much of the occupational exposure was to crocidolite or amosite asbestos. Chrysotile fibers tend to be somewhat softer as compared to other forms of asbestos, which produce more rigid, needlelike fibers that "penetrate deeper into the lung."[16] Some "compelling epidemiologic data" suggest that chrysotile asbestos is less harmful than crocidolite asbestos, perhaps fifty times less harmful.[17] While the evidence on fiber type is not conclusive, it provides further assurance regarding the low risk presented by indoor exposures.

The United Kingdom Advisory Committee on Asbestos concluded that "no appreciable mortality from lung cancer can be associated" with indoor asbestos exposure.[18] Several studies of persons exposed to relatively low levels of asbestos have found no excess of lung cancer. Many public health experts believe the risk from indoor asbestos is so low as to be nonexistent. While it is difficult to isolate asbestos-caused lung cancers from the "noise" of lung cancers from other causes, mesothelioma is caused almost exclusively by asbestos. If indoor exposures to asbestos caused this disease, some cases should be observable. Yet virtually all mesothelioma is traceable to occupational exposures and no cases of mesothelioma have demonstrably been linked to indoor asbestos exposures. Doll and Peto, perhaps the world's leading epidemiologists, studied indoor asbestos exposures and found that exposures averaged only 0.0005 f/cc above background, which presented at most a negligible risk.

Although the overall risk from indoor asbestos to students and most building occupants is quite low, some groups may face much more significant risks. A study of school custodians in New York City who worked for over thirty years discovered that 40 percent of the custodians showed some evidence of asbestos-related lung disease. The lung abnormalities found were not necessarily harmful but may place the custodians at greater risk of cancer. Roughly similar results were reported from a study of Boston custodians. The type of work performed by custodians may involve activities that disturb asbestos fibers in building materials, and this group is particularly at risk from indoor asbestos exposures.

While attention over indoor asbestos has centered upon schools and commercial buildings, homeowners are increasingly concerned. Some homes may have asbestos material in insulation, ceiling surfaces, or in sheets surrounding furnaces. As many as 80 percent of homes built prior to 1979 may contain some asbestos. Residential indoor asbestos risks tend to be even lower than in commercial or public buildings. A Consumer Product Safety Commission study of "45 older homes, many containing worn asbestos" found indoor asbestos concentrations were no greater than the ambient outdoor concentrations.[19] A representative of the American Lung Association recently recommended that homeowners do nothing about asbestos-containing materials unless they were seriously damaged.

In sum, indoor asbestos exposures present little risk. Even quantitative risk assessments employing very conservative assumptions show that the risk from typical indoor asbestos concentrations is extremely low. This is not to suggest that indoor asbestos is worthy of no concern. Some buildings contain relatively high asbestos concentrations resulting from damaged friable asbestos-containing materials. These buildings require corrective action. The overall danger from indoor asbestos, however, is insignificant and no way comparable to the hazard presented by radon.

Measures to Control Indoor Asbestos

Various techniques are available to control indoor exposures to asbestos. Some of these methods involve the protection of asbestos-containing materials from the damage that may cause fiber release. Alternatively, the asbestos-containing materials may be removed from the building. None of these methods, unfortunately, is clearly effective. Moreover, some response measures may actually increase the concentrations of asbestos within a structure.

Certain custodial measures provide the simplest, and among the most effective, responses to indoor asbestos. Custodians and others can be trained to identify asbestos-containing materials in a damaged condition that may release significant numbers of fibers. Such visual inspection can evaluate the condition of material, plus evidence of water damage, amount of exposed surface area, accessibility to further damage, and presence of air streams that may distribute the fibers. Loose materials should be cleaned up and workers should be trained to use respirators. EPA has grappled unsuccessfully with an effort to establish an index for evaluating the condition of materials. Nevertheless, simple subjective visual inspection can do much to identify the sources of indoor asbestos concentrations.

When a potential problem is identified, workers must be informed to take precautions for their own exposure. Workers must also be cautioned not to sweep the floor or employ other custodial procedures that reentrain and exacerbate the asbestos problem. Specialized vacuums are available to capture the asbestos fibers that have been released. Such management and custodial control may be an effective long-term response in the case of many asbestos-containing materials, such as pipe and boiler insulation that is not directly exposed to individuals. Because management and custodial control involves the least disturbance to the asbestos-containing materials in place, this response is unlikely to increase the indoor concentrations by further damaging those materials.

Another response to indoor asbestos pollution is enclosure of the exposed asbestos-containing materials. Enclosure simply means covering up the exposed materials behind airtight barriers to prevent further damage or fiber release. For example, when the covering on pipe and boiler insulation is so damaged as to expose asbestos fibers, the insulation may be enclosed with special paint or tape. New floor tiles may be laid over old, asbestos-containing tiles. In some instances, enclosure can be an effective response, assuming that the enclosure is well constructed and remains intact. Enclosure is only a short-term response, however, as the cause of damage to the original asbestos-containing material may also damage the enclosing materials. Some areas may be difficult to enclose because they are relatively inaccessible or because they are so extensive. For example, when asbestos-containing insulation has been sprayed onto a ceiling, enclosure would require the construction of a new, lower ceiling. In addition, construction of the enclosure may itself disturb the asbestos and release fibers.

Another alternative related to enclosure is encapsulation. Encapsulation means coating asbestos materials with a bonding agent to prevent fiber release. In the case of pipe insulation, encapsulation means rewrapping the pipe. For sprayed insulation, encapsulation involves spraying a bonding agent onto the asbestos insulation. While encapsulation inhibits fiber release, many are skeptical regarding its long-term benefits. If the asbestos-containing material is already in bad condition and unable to support sealants, the application of encapsulating agents may promote further damage. The encapsulating agent seldom penetrates the entirety of the asbestos-containing materials, and a risk of fiber release remains. Consequently, reinspection and maintenance is required for encapsulated materials. Encapsulation also complicates the eventual removal of asbestos-containing materials, should that step become necessary.

The most popular control option is removal of the asbestos-containing materials from the building. This alternative is an obvious response to the problem, which eliminates the source of the indoor exposures. Ironically, removal of asbestos-containing materials may actually increase the hazard, particularly when performed in a crisis atmosphere by ill-trained workers. Removal disturbs the materials, which promotes fiber release.

When asbestos-containing materials are removed or "ripped out" of buildings, damage to the materials becomes virtually unavoidable. The damaged materials release fibers that endanger the workers removing the asbestos. In addition, these fibers settle onto building surfaces, only to become reentrained into the air by the activities of building occupants. In this way, removal may also produce a long-term risk to occupants.

Robert Sawyer of Yale, who was among the first to recognize the potential hazards of indoor asbestos, has lamented the frequent reliance on asbestos removal. He criticized recent removal efforts that "[c]onverted a situation of highly questionable risk to that of certain and well-documented hazards" and "caused contamination of school structures and grounds that have placed children, teachers and other school personnel at totally unnecessary risk of exposure."[20] Sawyer is not alone in expressing this concern. The Ontario royal commission found a "number of asbestos-control projects in schools were conducted in a manner which, according to the evidence before us, may have generated significant risk."[21] The National Institute of Building Sciences has confirmed this danger, as have many others. A Committee of the House of Representatives specifically warned that the "potential for panic and overreaction is tremendous—leading to wasted resources and possibly higher asbestos exposures if complete removal is undertaken where modest containment measures are appropriate."[22] A 1989 international symposium at Harvard reported that "asbestos removal creates higher indoor concentrations of the fibers because the containment methods are seldom efficient enough to keep the fibers from escaping."[23]

The risks from asbestos removal are frequently a consequence of improper techniques and inadequately trained removal workers. There is a lack of qualified contractors who can perform asbestos removal operations safely and effectively. As a result, some schools reportedly turned to hiring homeless people off the street to assist in "abatement" actions. In 1986 Congress estimated that 75 percent of all asbestos removal from schools had been performed improperly. This is partially due to the suddenness of public appreciation of the indoor asbestos problem and demands for prompt action. The magnitude of the risk that can be created by asbestos removal operations has been measured in several studies. Sawyer found that removal operations have produced asbestos concentrations ranging from 8 to 82 f/cc, which is far higher than the preremoval concentrations. An EPA study found even higher asbestos concentrations in the wake of removal. Canadian and French studies confirm this conclusion.

The hazards produced by removal operations can be reduced through safe practices. In a well-conducted removal, windows and doors are sealed. Plastic sheets are used to contain asbestos and airlocks may be installed to reduce fiber transmission. Showers are installed on site. During removal, vacuums filter the air and a constant mist of water is applied to cause fibers to settle. After removal, the plastic sheets, worker clothing, and other materials are carefully disposed.

Unfortunately, all these precautions fail to ensure that asbestos remains contained. The very nature of removal unavoidably disturbs asbestos-containing materials. Removal typically produces clouds of asbestos fibers, some of which escape the plastic barriers of well-conducted removal operations and migrate throughout a building. EPA found that even the best removal procedures could leave airborne asbestos concentrations of 0.5 f/cc, which is higher than the average concentration prevailing today. Other studies have shown that even well-conducted removal operations typically increase airborne fiber levels. While numerous precautions may be taken, the science of asbestos removal is still so primitive that it inevitably creates risks of its own. The physical dynamics of asbestos contamination are not well understood. One study performed for EPA discovered that asbestos levels in a school were lower immediately after removal operations but that levels rose again after classes resumed to a level above the preremoval asbestos concentration. The Consumer Product Safety Commission concluded that in-place asbestos in homes does not present a particular health hazard, and "in most cases asbestos should be left alone."[24] In addition, asbestos removal operations in structures such as office buildings and shopping centers may create risks "a thousand fold over" removal in schools, which can be fully evacuated.[25]

In addition to raising cancer risks, asbestos removal operations can be enormously costly. The more precautions are taken for safe removal, the greater these costs become. Modern removal requires " 'moon-suited' workers, warning signs, containment tents, area evacuation, and hazardous waste disposal bags, creating a scene that suggests a major environmental cleanup."[26] The costs of total asbestos removal in schools will amount to several billion dollars, based on the conservative cost estimate of $100,000 per school. EPA estimates that removal of asbestos-containing materials from all public and commercial buildings will cost $51 billion. Others believe that this figure is a gross underestimate and that total removal would cost between $750 billion and $4 trillion. These enormous costs do not include removal of asbestos from existing single-family homes.

New construction presents little asbestos risk, as the health harms of asbestos derive almost exclusively from past exposures. Dangerous applications of asbestos are seldom used anymore. In July 1989 the Environmental Protection Agency banned virtually all future uses of asbestos, with certain uses phased out over several years. By this time, there were very few indoor uses of asbestos remaining. Asbestos is not a problem with future construction — the concern involves asbestos in place from past construction practices.

Notes

1. Environmental Protection Agency, EPA STUDY OF ASBESTOS-CONTAIN-ING MATERIALS IN PUBLIC BUILDINGS (February 1988), pp. 1–3.

2. *Id.*

3. Frank Cross, *Asbestos in Schools: A Remonstrance Against Panic*, 11 COLUMBIA J. ENVIRONMENTAL LAW 73, 75 (1986).

4. Ontario Royal Commission on Asbestos, REPORT OF THE ROYAL COMMISSION ON MATTERS OF HEALTH AND SAFETY ARISING FROM THE USE OF ASBESTOS IN ONTARIO, VOLUME TWO (1984), p. 549.

5. Environmental Protection Agency, pp. 1-8 to 1-9.

6. Environmental Protection Agency, p. 8.

7. Ontario Royal Commission on Asbestos, pp. 561–62.

8. E. Chatfield, *Measurement of Asbestos Fiber Concentrations in Ambient Atmospheres* (May 1983), p. 86.

9. Ontario Royal Commission on Asbestos, p. 577.

10. Omenn *et al.*, *Contribution of Environmental Fibers to Respiratory Cancer*, 70 ENVIRONMENTAL HEALTH PERSPECTIVES 51, 55 (1986).

11. W. J. Nicholson, A. N. Roh, & I. Weisman, *Asbestos Contamination of the Air in Public Buildings* (October 1975) pp. 25–26.

12. Robert N. Sawyer and Charles M. Spooner, *Sprayed Asbestos-Containing Materials in Buildings: A Guidance Document, Part 2* (March 1979) p. I-2–9.

13. J. Constant, *Airborne Asbestos Levels in Schools* (June 1983) p. 60.

14. 51 Fed. Reg. 22612, 22617 (1986).

15. N.Y. TIMES, September 5, 1989, p. 19 (national edition).

16. Brooke T. Mossman & J. Bernard L. Gee, *Asbestos-Related Diseases*, 320 NEW ENGLAND J. OF MEDICINE 1721, 1722 (June 29, 1989).

17. *Id.* at 1728.

18. Ontario Royal Commission on Asbestos, p. 582.

19. N.Y. TIMES, September 9, 1989, p. 14 (national edition).

20. Cross, p. 90.

21. Ontario Royal Commission on Asbestos, p. 586.

22. H.R. Rep. No. 803, 98th Cong., 2d Sess. 19 (1984).

23. N.Y. TIMES, September 5, 1989, p. 19 (national edition).

24. INDOOR POLLUTION NEWS, January 28, 1988, pp. 4–5.

25. INDOOR POLLUTION NEWS, June 16, 1988, p. 6.

26. J. L. Connaughton, *Comment: Recovery for Risk Comes of Age: Asbestos in Schools and the Duty to Abate a Latent Environmental Hazard*, 83 NORTHWESTERN U. L. REV. 512, 530 (1989).

3

THE HEALTH RISK FROM
INDOOR FORMALDEHYDE

Formaldehyde is the most common and simplest member of a group of organic compounds known as aldehydes. Formaldehyde is comprised of one oxygen atom, one carbon atom, and two hydrogen atoms. The substance has been described as a "small and simple molecule" but one that can "react with and alter other chemicals in air, in liquids, and in the bodies of animals and humans."[1] Formaldehyde itself can come in various forms, including gaseous, liquid, and solid forms. At room temperature, formaldehyde is a colorless gas. While some formaldehyde occurs naturally due to the decay of biological organisms, the primary source of environmental formaldehyde is as a product of industry or through combustion.

Formaldehyde has long been recognized as having various irritant effects on humans. Breathing certain levels of formaldehyde may cause nausea, headaches, and irritation of the eyes, throat, and lungs. Liquid formaldehyde is irritating to the skin upon direct contact. Health concern over formaldehyde exposure rose dramatically following animal studies that revealed increased nasal cancer in rats exposed to high concentrations of formaldehyde. All these effects have been identified at relatively high exposures, and the irritant effects are presumed to have thresholds, below which formaldehyde exposure causes no observable symptoms. For cancer, however, there is no known safe level of exposure. While the carcinogenicity of formaldehyde is still disputed, this potential effect is cause for concern.

Outdoor formaldehyde levels remain quite low, but indoor concentrations may be many times higher. Formaldehyde can be found in a very large number of consumer products typically found in the home. Most significantly, formaldehyde is widely used in bonded-wood building materials, including wallboard and paneling. Formaldehyde emissions from these sources are high enough to cause identifiable irritant effects and potentially cause a significant risk of cancer to building occupants. The magnitude of this risk is heatedly debated, but some contend that indoor formaldehyde may be responsible for thousands of cancer deaths.

This chapter explores the sources and nature of the risk presented by indoor formaldehyde. First, I discuss how and whence formaldehyde occurs in buildings. Second, I describe what levels of indoor formaldehyde are common in different types of structures. Third, I address the health harms and risk presented by such indoor formaldehyde levels. Fourth, I analyze the corrective measures that are available to reduce unduly high indoor formaldehyde concentrations.

Sources and Causes of Indoor Formaldehyde

Commercial production of formaldehyde amounts to roughly 6 billion pounds. Manmade formaldehyde is found in thousands of products, many of which make their way into the home. While these products include toothpaste, shampoo, paper products, and cosmetics, most formaldehyde is used in adhesives and plastics. Formaldehyde-based adhesives are used in many building products, including particleboard, wallboard, ceiling panels, and other paneling. These uses may employ either urea formaldehyde or phenol formaldehyde. Urea formaldehyde is less expensive and therefore more common. Bonded-wood products such as plywood and particleboard have seen greatly increased use in recent decades, in doors, cabinets, furniture, and other commodities. Modern nonscratch cabinet finishes are a significant source of formaldehyde. Formaldehyde resins may constitute nearly 10 percent of these products.

Another leading use of formaldehyde was in urea formaldehyde foam insulation (UFFI). This product is made on-site by mixing formaldehyde with foaming agents under pressure; the insulation is typically sprayed into wall cavities, where it hardens into insulating material. This product was approved for home insulation in the United States in the early 1970s and became much more common during the

1970s' and 1980s' energy conservation movement, to cut down on residential energy losses. In the peak year of 1977, some 150,000 homes were insulated with UFFI. In all, over 400,000 homes were insulated with UFFI. Health and economic factors, however, caused a decline in the UFFI industry, which had dwindled considerably by the 1980s. Emissions from UFFI may be significant but tend to decline quickly over time. Wallboard may absorb formaldehyde from UFFI, though, and emit it more gradually. The emissions from UFFI may be increased by improper mixing and temperature at the time of installation.

Numerous other products also contain formaldehyde. Formaldehyde resins are widely used in textiles, including draperies, upholstery fabrics, and linens. Many forms of wallpaper also contain formaldehyde as an adhesive. A wide variety of kitchen and bathroom products also contain formaldehyde in some form. Fertilizers and pesticides used around the home may contain formaldehyde. Formaldehyde is also commonly employed in the manufacture of floor coverings. Formaldehyde is also a common combustion byproduct, produced by gas stoves or space heaters. Some evidence indicates that furniture (which may contain plywood, textiles, and other products with formaldehyde) is a significant source of indoor concentrations. Exhibit 3.1 is a partial listing of the manifold formaldehyde sources in a home or office.

The various formaldehyde-containing materials present differing degrees of problems. These materials differ in the rate at which they emit formaldehyde into the air. Products with urea formaldehyde resin tend to emit more formaldehyde than do comparable products with phenol formaldehyde resin. Phenol formaldehyde insulation and ceiling tile emit very little formaldehyde into the indoor air. Emissions from wood products are also influenced by the nature of the original manufacturing process, the kind of wood used, the quality of fabrication, and other features. Product characteristics also influence the emission rate. High-density, nonporous products, such as plastics, tend to release little formaldehyde. Textiles also have low emission rates, usually less than 0.1 milligram per hour (mg/hr) released. Conversely, porous formaldehyde products, such as UFFI, have high emission rates. The amount of a product's surface area also influences formaldehyde release. Mobile homes have particularly high formaldehyde levels because the formaldehyde-containing particleboard, plywood, and UFFI have a high surface area relative to the total indoor air volume of a mobile home.

Exhibit 3.1
Sources of Formaldehyde

• Acrylic	• Facial tissues and napkins	• Preservatives
• Air and furnace filters	• Fan blades	• Pressed wood furniture
• Air fresheners	• Faucets	• Radiators
• Antihistamines	• Fiberboard	• Radio and TV bases and
• Antiperspirants	• Flour preservative	housing
• Antistatic agents	• Formica	• Rayon
• Ashtrays	• Glues	• Roofing
• Binders	• Hair-setting solutions	• Sewing machine parts
• Blanket controls, bases	• Hair-waving preparations	• Shampoo
and covers	• Hardboard	• Soap dispensers
• Cigarette smoke	• Hardware	• Softwood plywood
• Coated papers used for	• Insecticides	• Sporting goods
cartons and labels	• Knobs and buttons	• Stove and refrigertor
• Coatings	• Lawn and garden equipment	hardware
• Coatings for appliances	• Maraschino cherries	• Textile waterproofing
• Cookware handles and knobs	• Mascara and other	• Toilet seats
• Counter and table tops	cosmetics	• Toothpaste
• Deodorants	• Nail hardener	• TV/radio/stereo cabinets,
• Detergents	• Nail polish	door panels, store displays
• Diaper liners	• Oil-based paints	kitchen cabinets
• Dinnerware	• Paint and wood finishes	• Utensil handles
• Disinfectants	• Particleboard	• Vacuum cleaner parts
• Door panels	• Permanent-press cotton	• Water-softening chemicals
• Drapery and upholstery	• Pesticides	• Wax and butcher wet
fabrics	• Pharmaceuticals	strength paper
• Drinking milk	• Plastic	• Wheat grains and
• Dyes	• Plumbing fixtures	agriculture seeds
• Electronic connectors	• Plywood	• Wool
• Electronic equipment	• Portable tools	

Other factors influence formaldehyde emission. Most formaldehyde is released from a product within the first five years of its existence and emission rates decline significantly with time. As a consequence, older homes seldom have high indoor levels of formaldehyde. Higher temperatures and humidity also promote formaldehyde release. The effect of temperature is pronounced—emission rates increase promptly and exponentially. Humidity has a less dramatic effect.

Formaldehyde also is produced by indoor combustion, such as in a gas stove or gas space heater. This source can emit as much as 30 mg/hr of formaldehyde. Combustion as a source of indoor air pollution is discussed in greater detail in the following chapter.

As with any indoor pollutant, ventilation influences concentrations. Higher ventilation sweeps formaldehyde from the air. Ventilation may also increase formaldehyde emissions as well, in a counteracting effect. The benefits of ventilation outweigh the harms, however, and a doubling of ventilation has been shown to reduce indoor airborne formaldehyde concentrations by 33 to 38 percent.[2]

Levels of Indoor Formaldehyde

Formaldehyde levels outdoors are quite low, averaging around 0.0004 parts per million (ppm). Levels may be higher in some polluted cities, but outdoor hourly averages seldom exceed 0.1 ppm, and overall averages are typically much lower. Indoor formaldehyde levels tend to reach substantially higher concentrations.

The earliest studies of indoor formaldehyde concentrations were performed in Europe. A study in Denmark found an average indoor formaldehyde level of approximately 0.5 ppm and a range from 0.07 to 1.9 ppm. Other European studies found indoor concentrations exceeding 2 ppm. U.S. studies have found lower levels, on average. A study of energy-efficient research homes found indoor formaldehyde levels that were nearly ten times outdoor concentrations and that averaged about 0.1 ppm or less. Concentrations found in research homes ranged widely but seldom exceeded 1 ppm, even for peak measurements. Houses with urea formaldehyde foam insulation have several times higher average indoor levels. One such house in Connecticut had an indoor formaldehyde of 10 ppm and average concentrations reached 1.8 ppm. A study of UFFI homes by the Consumer Product Safety Commission (CPSC) found average exposures of only 0.06 ppm. A very large study that collected thousands of samples found median indoor concentrations of slightly less than 0.05 ppm.

Most concern for indoor formaldehyde has focused upon mobile homes, which tend to have a higher percentage of formaldehyde-containing products in their construction and which also tend to have lower ventilation rates than conventional homes. Measurements confirm the greater indoor concentrations in mobile homes. In homes that were studied after residents complained of a potential problem, indoor formaldehyde levels have exceeded 4 ppm. A survey by the University of Washington School of Public Health found average formaldehyde levels in mobile homes ranged between 0.1 and 0.5 ppm, although 20 percent of the averages exceeded 0.5 ppm.

While mobile homes tend to show the highest formaldehyde concentrations, a potential problem exists in virtually any type of building. Although conventional homes typically have lower levels than mobile homes, the much larger number of conventional homes may produce a greater health problem overall. Apartments are equally at risk. Office buildings may also present a risk, and a recent study of several public buildings measured formaldehyde concentrations of up to 0.2

ppm. A Texas school had measured concentrations of up to 0.21 ppm and reported formaldehyde-related illnesses among its students.

Measured indoor formaldehyde levels are of uncertain reliability. Some measurement equipment has proved unreliable, and indoor levels are demonstrably affected by temporary meteorological conditions. Smoking is also a significant source of formaldehyde, and measures of indoor pollution production can be skewed by the presence of smokers. Test protocols can have a substantial effect on results.

Measured indoor concentrations of formaldehyde vary considerably. Some general conclusions may be drawn. First, older houses tend to have very low formaldehyde levels. Second, conventional homes usually have relatively low indoor formaldehyde concentrations, of about 0.05 ppm. Some newer, energy-efficient homes or those with urea formaldehyde foam insulation may have somewhat higher levels, of about 0.1 to 0.2 ppm. Third, mobile homes may have relatively high concentrations, averaging perhaps 0.5 ppm but ranging up into several ppm.

The Risk from Indoor Formaldehyde

Cancer is the most prominent adverse health effect associated with formaldehyde exposure, though the evidence of carcinogenicity is not nearly so conclusive as for radon and asbestos. In addition, formaldehyde may produce acute toxic effects, including asthma and respiratory disease, eye and lung irritation, headaches, fatigue, nausea, and other symptoms.

The ongoing debate over the carcinogenicity of formaldehyde derives from a study conducted at the behest of the Chemical Industry Institute on Toxicology. This animal bioassay in rats discovered that relatively high dose levels (14.3 ppm) of formaldehyde were plainly carcinogenic. These results were replicated by subsequent study.[3] In the experiments, formaldehyde produced nasal cancer in rats, and nasal cancer is rather rare in humans. Evidence on formaldehyde's carcinogenicity, however, raised concern that the substance might also cause more common human cancers, such as lung cancer.

The animal tests did not unequivocally establish formaldehyde's carcinogenicity, however. The overall results of the experiments were rather confusing. For example, while 50 percent of the rats developed cancer upon exposure to 14.3 ppm of formaldehyde, only 1 percent of the rats exposed to 5.6 ppm developed cancer. The latter cancer rate was not a statistically significant difference from the control group. In general, scientists believe that there is no threshold for carcinogenesis, but the stark nature of these results led some to believe that formaldehyde-induced cancer might have such a threshold level, below which exposures are noncarcinogenic.

Scientists suggested that formaldehyde itself was not carcinogenic but that the observed rat cancers resulted indirectly from the more significant irritant effects of formaldehyde. High levels of formaldehyde irritate the nasal lining and even destroy the normal mucociliary clearance process of the nose, and this might be what triggered the observed cancers. Scientists also raised other arguments why low levels of formaldehyde were safely noncarcinogenic.

The epidemiological evidence from human experience contributed little to the evaluation of formaldehyde's carcinogenicity. Indeed, studies of workers exposed to formaldehyde either found no increase in lung cancer or found a statistically significant decrease in lung cancer. Nor have occupational studies shown any increase in nasal cancer for workers exposed to formaldehyde. A recent American Medical Association study of particleboard workers found that exposure to 0.17 to 2.93 ppm caused a temporary decline in lung function but no discernible long-term lung damage. A study sponsored by the National Cancer Institute and the Formaldehyde Institute studied over 25,000 workers and found no increase in lung cancer, but other scientists reanalyzed the data from this study and concluded that workers exposed to formaldehyde had suffered an excess of lung cancer.[4] While there is some evidence that workers exposed to formaldehyde have higher levels of brain cancer and leukemia, this result is biologically rather implausible and may well be explained by other factors. The epidemiological studies permit no firm conclusions. The nature of such studies permits the detection of only substantial increases in cancer. Even strongly negative epidemiological evidence cannot disprove the carcinogenicity of a substance.

Experts continue to disagree over the danger of low-level exposures to formaldehyde. In the absence of direct evidence of carcinogenicity, the risk from low-level exposures requires extrapolative risk assessment, which relies centrally upon various unproved assumptions. Estimated risk varies widely with differing assumptions. For example, OSHA's risk assessment using very cautious assumptions for formaldehyde found that the risk from 1 ppm exposure might be as high as 264 cancers per 100,000 exposed individuals. However, using the assumptions that were deemed most likely to be true, the estimate was of 0.6 cancers per 100,000 exposed individuals.

Uncertainty about the magnitude of formaldehyde's carcinogenic effects has confounded regulatory agencies. The Environmental Protection Agency first decided that formaldehyde exposures, including indoor exposures, did not present a "significant risk" and then reversed itself and concluded that some such exposures did produce a significant risk. The Occupational Safety and Health Administration performed a similar turnabout. The Consumer Product Safety Commission sought to ban UFFI insulation, but a court reversed the rule, saying that the commission's evidence supporting the need for a ban was inadequate. This experience is discussed in more detail in Chapter 7.

The cancer burden of indoor formaldehyde exposure is not yet established. If one adopts all the most conservative assumptions in a risk assessment, the 4 million residents of mobile homes may suffer nearly 600 cancers from formaldehyde and the hundreds of millions of conventional homes with low formaldehyde levels could cause more than 11 thousand cancer cases.[5] The individual lifetime cancer risk for an individual living for ten years in a home with relatively low average formaldehyde concentrations of 0.1 ppm is a substantial 2 in 10,000.

Experience indicates that these numbers are considerably overstated, however. The most likely estimate of risk suggests that all residential indoor exposure to formaldehyde throughout the United States is responsible for about twenty-three excess cancer cases.[6] The most likely estimate of individual lifetime risk for ten years of 0.1 ppm exposure is a trivial 2 in 10 billion. The true number may lie somewhere in between the high maximum risk estimates and the low most likely estimates, and formaldehyde's carcinogenicity provides some cause for public health concern. The concern is not overwhelming, however. The British Industrial Biological Research Association declared that "[n]o reasonable person could conclude that formaldehyde constitutes a serious cancer hazard to humans."[7] A distinguished panel of physicians and epidemiologists reported in 1988 that there was "no convincing evidence" that formaldehyde caused human cancers.[8] The International Agency for Research on Cancer concluded that the evidence was insufficient to declare formaldehyde to be a human carcinogen. On the other hand, OSHA, EPA and CPSC all have regulated formaldehyde as a carcinogen. While cancer risk has received the most attention from government and the press, formaldehyde is more clearly linked to lesser health harms, such as respiratory disease and other irritant effects on building occupants.

The irritant effects of formaldehyde exposure are far more certain than the carcinogenic effects. The irritant effects appear to have a threshold; few effects have been identified at exposure concentrations below 0.05 ppm, although some evidence suggests that eye irritation may result from lower exposures. Human eyes are rather sensitive to formaldehyde and may detect concentrations as low as 0.01 ppm. Exposures of several ppm produce pronounced eye irritation. Exposures of less than 1 ppm (as low as 0.05 ppm) have been associated with tearing, stinging, and burning of the eyes, as well as an increased blink rate suggestive of some irritation.

Formaldehyde also irritates the human respiratory tract. At levels of about 1 ppm, individuals have reported a dry or sore throat and irritation of the nose. Lower airway irritation is also reported, in the form of coughing and chest tightness. Formaldehyde has been shown to aggravate bronchial asthma, and some limited evidence suggests that formaldehyde may cause the development of asthma. Between 10 and 20 percent of the U.S. population may be particularly sensitive to low levels of formaldehyde. The National Academy of Sciences reported that 30 to 50 percent of individuals reported irritant symptoms at exposures of greater than 0.5 ppm, but less than 30 percent of exposed individuals reported symptoms at lower exposures.[9] Given the varying sensitivities of individuals, the experts at the Consumer Product Safety Commission concluded that there is no threshold level for formaldehyde that is innocuous for everyone. Exhibit 3.2 reports on a broad summary of studies on the irritant effects of formaldehyde exposure.

Numerous irritant effects of formaldehyde have been identified from residential exposures. In particular, mobile home residents have complained of formaldehyde-related symptoms. The Consumer Product Safety Commission has collected numerous reports of eye and throat irritation among mobile home occupants. A survey by the Connecticut Department of Health and Consumer Protection of homes with UFFI foam found symptoms reported by over one hundred residents of seventy-four homes, where indoor concentrations ranged between 0.5 and 10 ppm. A study by the Wisconsin Division of Health found that median formaldehyde concentrations of 0.35 ppm were associated with respiratory tract irritation, headaches, nausea, vomiting, and other symptoms. Particular concern was found

Exhibit 3.2
Studies on Formaldehyde Concentration and Adverse Effects

Exposure ppm	Effect
0.0-10	Nausea, eye nose and throat irritation, headache, vomiting, stomach cramp
0.02-4.15	Diarrhea, eye and upper-respiratory tract irritation, headache, nausea, vomiting
0.09-5.6	Burning of eye and nose, sneezing, coughing, and headache; asthma or sinus problems
0.3-2.7 Av. 0.36 Median 0.4	Annoying odor, constant pricking of mucous membranes, disturbed sleep, thirst, heavy tearing
0.13-0.45	Burning and stinging of eyes, nose, and throat, headaches
0.2-0.45 Av.0.36	Irritation of eyes and upper respiratory tract, drowsiness, headaches, and menstrual irregularities
0.13,0.57,and 0.44	Headaches, concentration problems, dizziness, nausea, coughing, increases in recurring infections of the upper respiratory tract, and irritation of eyes, nose, and throat
0.08	Loss of olfactory sense, increased upper respiratory disease, subatrophic and hypertrophic alterations in nose and throat, ciliostasis of nasal mucosa, increased absorptive function of nasal mucosa
0.9-1.6	Itching eyes, dry and sore throats, disturbed sleep, unusual thirst upon awakening in the morning
0.9-2.7	Tearing of eyes, irritation of nose and throat
1.3-3.8	Menstrual disorders, pregnancy complicaitons, low birth weight of offspring

among young children, who reported vomiting, diarrhea, and respiratory problems. The Massachusetts State Commissioner of Public Health sponsored a study that concluded that indoor formaldehyde concentrations should never exceed 0.03 ppm, with a preferred level of 0.0003 ppm.

Indoor formaldehyde exposures present grounds for public health concern. The number of cancers due to such exposure is probably small, but the risk is sufficient to warrant attention. The disease and irritant effects of formaldehyde are more widespread and may pose a significant health risk to the elderly, infants, asthmatics, and others who are especially sensitive to the chemical. These sensitive individuals may suffer particularly severe irritant effects, which can become life threatening. The significant population of such sensitive individuals is shown in Exhibit 3.3. While the overall health risks of indoor formaldehyde are distinctly less than for radon, the risk may exceed that of indoor asbestos.

Measures to Control Indoor Formaldehyde

A variety of measures are available to control indoor formaldehyde, ranging from encapsulation of emitting materials to their complete removal. The effectiveness of these techniques is not yet clearly established. To date, they have produced varying results, and the long-term promise of some techniques is uncertain.

In some cases, formaldehyde emissions are attributable to improperly installed products, which may be easily corrected. Formaldehyde from pressed-wood products can be controlled by encapsulation with sealants. Certain substances bind free formaldehyde and prevent its emission into the air. These coatings have shown short-term success in reducing emissions by as much as 90 percent, but their long-term effects are uncertain. Formaldehyde may also be controlled by applying vapor-barrier paint to the walls or using vinyl wallpaper or linoleum to cover emitting sources. Evidence indicates that some paints may prevent 98 percent of emissions and wallpaper may reduce emissions by approximately 30 percent.[10] These techniques may also reduce indoor levels from urea formaldehyde foam insulation behind the walls. More effective protection from UFFI, however, requires that all cracks or gaps be sealed, that special gaskets be installed at electrical outlets and other wall penetrations, and that wall and floor junctions be sealed with substances such as acrylic latex caulking.

Removal of formaldehyde-containing products is also an option, albeit an expensive one. Removal of pressed-wood products requires

Exhibit 3.3
Sensitive Populations

Subpopulation	Size
Newborns	3.7 million
Infants	18.1 million
Elderly	29.2 million
Asthmatics	9.7 million
Smokers	70 million
Heart patients	18.5 million

a major construction job. Removal of UFFI foam dictates that interior and exterior walls be torn down and replaced. The cost of this operation can easily run into tens of thousands of dollars. In some cases, removal has not been effective in curing indoor formaldehyde problems, presumably due to improper removal techniques.

As with any indoor pollutant, increased ventilation will reduce indoor concentrations of formaldehyde. This measure has the obvious added benefit of reducing levels of other indoor pollutants as well. Ventilation is relatively less valuable for formaldehyde, however. It appears that greater ventilation levels also enhance formaldehyde emission rates, for the short term at least. Ventilation can produce pressure differences causing greater emissions, though this effect is exceeded by ventilation's benefits in sweeping pollutants out of the indoor air. Use of air conditioning and humidifiers can also reduce formaldehyde emissions, which are accelerated by heat and humidity.

Indoor formaldehyde levels can also be reduced through ammonia fumigation. Ammonia reacts with formaldehyde to produce a stable chemical. Fumigation involves leaving the house and placing large concentrations of ammonium hydroxide in the residence for roughly a day. Thorough ventilation then removes the ammonia. Studies in mobile homes suggest that ammonia fumigation may reduce formaldehyde concentrations by over 60 percent. The high ammonia levels may damage indoor fittings, furniture, and other products, however. Some recommend various types of air cleaners for indoor formaldehyde, but the effectiveness of this technique is not established. Certain common house plants, such as the spider plant, aloe vera, and pothos, apparently metabolize formaldehyde in the air and might reduce indoor concentrations by as much as 80 percent. These latter approaches obviously carry very low cost.

Controlling formaldehyde in new construction is feasible and largely accomplished. The UF foam insulation installation industry has disappeared; other forms of insulation are now employed. Industry has introduced low formaldehyde resins into compressed-wood products, which has reduced total formaldehyde content by 50 to 90 percent. Use of phenol resins reduces emission rates considerably. The amount of free formaldehyde in these products has been reduced by as much as 1 million times. Some pressed-wood products are baked at the factory to release as much formaldehyde as possible before sale. A voluntary industry standard now provides for this procedure, called off-gassing, so that the product registers no more than 0.3 ppm in a chamber test.

Notes

1. JOHN D. GRAHAM, LAURA C. GREEN & MARC J. ROBERTS, IN SEARCH OF SAFETY (Cambridge: Harvard University Press) (1988), p. 38.

2. The Commonwealth of Massachusetts Special Legislative Commission on Indoor Air Pollution, *Indoor Air Pollution in Massachusetts* (April 1989), p. 90.

3. GRAHAM et al., p. 40.

4. *International Union, United Automobile, Aerospace and Agricultural Implement Workers of America v. Pendergrass*, 878 F.2d 389, 393 (1989).

5. GRAHAM et al., p. 33.

6. *Id.*

7. E. WHELAN, TOXIC TERROR (1985), p. 166.

8. INDOOR POLLUTION NEWS, June 30, 1988, p. 4.

9. National Research Council, INDOOR POLLUTANTS (Washington, D.C.: National Academy Press) (1981), p. 331.

10. Massachusetts Special Legislative Commission, p. 97.

4

THE HEALTH RISK FROM OTHER INDOOR AIR POLLUTANTS

Government and the press have dwelt on radon, asbestos, and formaldehyde when addressing indoor air pollution. Indoor air contains hundreds of other pollutants, however, some of which probably cause greater health harm than asbestos and formaldehyde. The remaining significant indoor air pollutants are primarily volatile organic compounds (VOCs); other byproducts of combustion, microbial contaminants, pesticides, electromagnetic radiation, and the vague general category known as "sick building syndrome." In total, the Environmental Protection Agency has identified over one thousand indoor air pollutants, at least sixty of which may cause cancer. These pollutants are responsible for thousands of cancers and hundreds of thousands of diseases every year. A special commission in Massachusetts estimated that half of all illnesses in the United States may be attributed to indoor air pollution exposures. This chapter will consider the various categories of indoor air hazards. Exhibit 4.1 provides a preliminary summary of these other indoor air pollutants and the nature of the risks they present.

Volatile Organic Compounds (VOCs)

Volatile organic compounds (VOCs) represent a large class of carbon-based compounds, including formaldehyde. Hundreds of substances may be classed as VOCs. Some of the most representative and harmful VOCs are benzene, xylene, trichloroethylene, perchloro-

Exhibit 4.1
Indoor Air Pollution Sources and Effects

Pollutant	Source	Effect
Volatile Organic Compounds	paints, adhesives, solvents, cleaners building materials	cancer irritation neurotoxicity
Polycyclic Aromatic Hydrocarbons	kerosene heaters	cancer, irritation
Carbon Monoxide	combustion appliances outdoor air	asphyxiation heart disease headaches
Nitrogen Dioxide	combustion appliances	pulmonary harms
Particulates	combustion appliances	cancer, irritation
Microbiological Contaminants	water/humidity, outdoor air, carpeting	Legionnaires disease, flu, irritation
Electromagnetic Radiation	electric wires and appliances	cancer

ethylene, paradichlorobenzene, and trichloroethane. These VOCs have been the focus of a great deal of Clean Air Act regulation of outdoor pollution. The risk from outdoor pollution, however, is far less than that found indoors. First, individuals tend to spend far more time in indoor environments, as graphically illustrated in Exhibit 4.2. In addition, indoor VOC exposure levels tend to be ten or more times higher than levels out of doors. While billions of dollars have been spent to control VOCs outdoors, studies consistently reveal that indoor VOC levels are much higher and more hazardous.

Various household products emit VOCs. Organic chemicals possess many useful characteristics, including the ability to dissolve substances, and are incorporated in numerous products. A brief list of such products would include paints, varnishes, waxes, wood preservatives, aerosol sprays, cleansers, disinfectants, air fresheners, dry-cleaned fabrics, hobby supplies, and fuels. Furniture, drapes, and building materials also emit a variety of VOCs. Particleboard and insulation release many VOCs in addition to formaldehyde. An EPA study found that most VOCs were emitted from particleboard, adhesives, paints, carpets, and cleaning and pest-control operations.

The best evidence on indoor VOC exposures derives from EPA's Total Exposure Assessment Methodology (TEAM) studies. In these studies, volunteers wore a personal air sampler that directly reflected individual exposures, and additional samplers measured indoor versus outdoor sources of exposure. The TEAM study measured exposure for twenty sample VOCs. Indoor exposures were significantly and consistently higher than outdoor exposures. New Jersey subjects received an average combined VOC exposure of 200 to 338 micrograms per cubic meter (ug/m³). California exposures were lower, but Los Angeles residents were exposed to up to 240 ug/m³ of the studied VOCs. Benzene is probably the most harmful VOC and may be responsible for 50 to 100 ug/m³ of this exposure. Fortunately, VOC emissions in new buildings decline dramatically over time. The TEAM data have

Exhibit 4.2
Time Spent by Environment

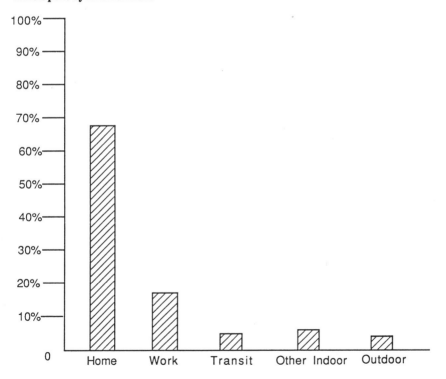

Exhibit 4.3
Indoor VOC Concentrations and Cancer Risks

Pollutant	Maximum	Mean	Cancer Risk of Maximum
Benzene	120 ug/m^3	20 ug/m^3	10 X 10^{-4}
Dichlorobenzenes	1200 ug/m^3	41 ug/m^3	–
Carbon tetrachloride	14 ug/m^3	2.5 ug/m^3	2 X 10^{-4}
Trichlorethylene	47 ug/m^3	3.6 ug/m^3	8 X 10^{-5}
Chloroform	200 ug/m^3	8 ug/m^3	5 X 10^{-3}
Ethylbenzene	320 ug/m^3	13 ug/m^3	–
Tetrachloroethylene	250 ug/m^3	10 ug/m^3	1.5 X 10^{-4}

been confirmed by other studies, which have reported indoor VOC concentrations exceeding prevailing outdoor levels by a factor of fifty or more.

EPA has evidence on the health harms of various individual VOCs, resulting from its controls on outdoor air pollution. EPA has been somewhat hesitant to estimate the health consequences of VOC exposures, but other investigators have used EPA data to demonstrate a significant risk. Using the TEAM study VOC exposure estimates for New Jersey, one study found an average lifetime cancer risk from indoor concentrations of nine selected VOCs of more than 1 in 100.[1] This study concededly employed very conservative assumptions in its risk assessment, which may lead to exaggeration of actual risk. Some individuals with especially polluted homes faced a risk several times higher. Other authors considered exposure to fifteen VOCs (including formaldehyde) and estimated a health risk of approximately 1 in 1,000.[2] The total annual cancer incidence from exposure to six specific VOCs was estimated to be between 1,000 and 5,000 cases per year.[3] The Consumer Product Safety Commission staff estimate that 1,240 annual cancer deaths are caused by indoor exposure to six VOCs — benzene, paradichlorobenzene, carbon tetrachloride, chloroform, trichloroethylene, and perchloroethylene.[4] A risk assessment for benzene alone, based on the TEAM data, suggested that indoor exposures to the chemical were responsible for 253 annual deaths (compared with 25 deaths from outdoor exposures).[5] Some VOCs are also teratogenic, causing birth defects, or fetotoxic, producing spontaneous abortion of unborn children. Exhibit 4.3 presents some VOC indoor exposure data and the attendant cancer risk levels.

VOCs also produce health effects less serious than cancer or birth defects. Many VOCs can cause respiratory irritation, eye irritation, fatigue, and headaches. Some VOCs may be neurotoxic, causing harm to the nervous system. The symptoms include central nervous system depression, visual disorders, and even unconsciousness, although these symptoms have not been observed at the levels found indoors. Other VOCs may be injurious to the liver, kidneys, and heart of exposed individuals. VOCs may also play a role in causing multiple chemical sensitivity, discussed later. Exhibit 4.4 summarizes the adverse effects associated with exposure to various organic compounds.

Indoor VOC exposures can be remediated in a variety of ways. As always, increased ventilation will dilute indoor concentrations. As with formaldehyde, however, greater ventilation may also increase the indoor emission rate of VOCs. Air cleaners may also be able to remove indoor VOCs, although their effectiveness is not well established. The most promising route to VOC control is to eliminate the offending materials. Building materials may be prebaked to cause emission of most VOCs before installation in a home. Entire buildings may be "baked out" by raising temperatures to drive VOCs out of materials before they are occupied. Sealing these materials may reduce VOC emissions by over 90 percent, but the most effective sealants may themselves emit gases that can cause adverse health effects. Home products may be selected to minimize their VOC content, although nearly all types of some products contain significant concentrations of VOCs. Proper use of these products is beneficial. Outdoor use and storage can minimize indoor levels, as can prompt disposal of leftover products. VOC levels tend to be high during and following construction work, so restricting construction to weekends or temporarily increasing ventilation may control peak exposures of building occupants. Air filtration is of very limited value in controlling indoor VOC concentrations.

VOCs represent a particularly intractable indoor air pollution problem. These compounds produce some of the most severe effects of any pollutant, yet they cannot be feasibly eliminated from indoor use. Careful monitoring of exposures and ventilation can reduce the risk, which may remain substantial.

Exhibit 4.4
Selected Organic Compounds and Their Health Effects

Compound	Health effects	Sources and uses
Formaldehyde and other aldehydes	Eye and respiratory irritation; possibly more serious long-term health effects	Outgassing from building materials (particle board, plywood, and urea-formaldehyde insulation foam); also from cooking and textiles
Benzene	Respiratory irritation; recognized carcinogen	Plastic and rubber solvents; in paints and varnishes, including putty, filler, stains and finishes
Xylene	Narcotic; irritating; in high concentrations, possibly injurious to heart, liver, kidney, and nervous system	Solvent for resins, enamels, etc.;
Toluene	Narcotic; may cause anemia	Solvents; by-product of organic compounds used in several household products
Styrene	Narcotic; can cause headache, fatigue, stupor, depression, incoordination, and possible eye injury	Plastics, synthetic rubber, paints and resins
Trichloroethane	Subject of OSHA carcinogenesis inquiry	Aerosol propellant, pesticide, cleaning solvents
Trichloroethylene	Animal carcinogen; subject of OSHA carcinogenesis inquiry	Oil and wax solvents, compounds, vapor degreasing products
Ethyl benzene	Severe irritation to eyes and respiratory system	Solvents; in styrene-related products
Chloro benzenes	Strong narcotic; possible lung, liver, and kidney damage	Paint, varnish, pesticides, and various organic solvents
Polychlorinated biphenyls (PCB's)	Suspected carcinogens	In various electrical components; in waste oil supplies and in plastic and paper products in which PCB's are used as plasticizers

Combustion Byproducts

Indoor combustion, from sources such as gas appliances and wood fires, produces numerous contaminants. This combustion may be a significant source of formaldehyde and other VOCs. Combustion also produces a host of other hazardous indoor pollutants, including carbon monoxide, nitrogen dioxide, particulates, and polycyclic aromatic hydrocarbons. While these combustion products are widely regulated in the outdoor air, indoor exposures may present a greater risk.

Perhaps the most harmful source of indoor combustion byproducts is woodstoves and fireplaces. While these sources are customarily vented, the combustion byproducts enter the indoor air due to pressurization, drafts, and cracks in the venting. This source produces benzo(a)pyrene, a well-established carcinogen, as well as carbon monoxide, nitrogen dioxide, and particulates. One study found that 84 percent of children in wood-heated homes suffer at least one episode of acute respiratory illness during a season, as opposed to less than 5 percent of children in a control group. Gas stoves (found in a majority of American homes), gas space heaters, clothes dryers, water heaters, and furnaces are often unvented and emit nitrogen dioxide, carbon monoxide, particulates, and other harmful substances. Many other of these appliances have faulty venting, which aggravates the problem. Unvented kerosene heaters, which are fairly prevalent in the southern United States, are a potentially substantial source of carbon monoxide, nitrogen dioxide, hydrocarbons, and other pollutants. Studies have shown that kerosene heaters alone can produce indoor concentrations of carbon monoxide, nitrogen dioxide, and sulfur dioxide that exceed federal outdoor standards. These kerosene heaters can also produce polycyclic aromatic hydrocarbons, which are mutagenic and carcinogenic. Adjacent garages may also produce significant carbon monoxide contamination of residences.

A study of gas space heaters found they produced exposures of 4 ppm of carbon monoxide and up to 1 ppm of nitrogen dioxide (the latter figure significantly exceeds outdoor standards). Ordinary use of gas cooking produces carbon monoxide levels of 2 to 6 ppm and average nitrogen dioxide levels of 15 parts per billion (ppb), which are below the protective outdoor air quality standard. Some homes, such as those with improperly adjusted gas stoves, may have carbon monoxide levels as high as 15 to 25 ppm. This use produces peak nitrogen dioxide exposures of 200 to 400 ppb, which is well in excess of the outdoor standard (53 ppb) for ambient average concentrations. Kerosene heaters can produce nitrogen dioxide levels over 500 ppb (as compared with less than 10 ppb in homes without combustion sources) and carbon monoxide levels up to 25 ppm. Poorer Americans often use their gas stoves and other appliances for winter heating, however, and this practice can increase indoor concentrations tenfold. The Gas Research Institute estimates that 20 percent of gas stove owners use their ovens as space heaters. Temporary exposures to these substances may also be higher—ordinary cooking behavior may produce carbon monoxide exposures of up to 50 ppm for as much as an hour.

The adverse health effects of many combustion products are relatively well defined. Very high levels of carbon monoxide (100 ppm) have caused significant decreases in lung function. Some health harms may result from prolonged exposures of 15 ppm or less. Children, the elderly, and pregnant women may be particularly sensitive to this level. Carbon monoxide also binds with blood hemoglobin and may bring on heart disease and death by impairing oxygen transport. Short-term effects of this carboxyhemoglobin include dizziness, decreased stamina, and blurred vision.

Nitrogen dioxide can produce temporary or permanent damage to lung tissue and produce such respiratory diseases as pneumonia. Some studies suggest that nitrogen dioxide has caused decreased lung function at exposures as low as 0.1 ppm. Asthmatics are particularly affected. Nitrogen dioxide exposure is also linked with headaches, impaired digestion, eye irritation, and burning pains in the chest. At concentrations of 0.05 ppm, which are common in homes with gas-fired appliances, nitrogen dioxide may produce eye irritation and affect sensory perception. Nitrogen dioxide also makes people more susceptible to infection. EPA's Clean Air Science Advisory Committee has recommended a maximum peak concentration of nitrogen dioxide no greater than 0.3 ppm, but the vast majority of homes with unvented gas space heaters exceed this concentration. The very young, the old, and the already ill are at particular risk.

Particulate exposure affects the respiratory system. Very small, fine particles deposit in the lungs and may reduce lung function and bring on respiratory disease, though the extent of harm is dependent upon the chemical identity of the particle. Indoor particulates also increase the risk of radon, which attaches to such particles and is deposited in the lung. Particulates from wood smoke are known to cause cancer and bring on respiratory disease. Benzo(a)pyrene exposures of 8 nanograms per cubic meter have been identified from woodstoves, a level several times that found outdoors. EPA studies have found that indoor particle levels can exceed outdoor air standards, and include high sulfate and acidic ion concentrations linked to pulmonary problems.

The overall burden of disease and/or death from indoor combustion byproducts is largely unknown, due to insufficient study. Studies of homes with gas cooking provide some general idea of the risk from combustion byproducts. British researchers studied children in homes with gas and electric cooking. Nitrogen dioxide measures in the gas stove homes were twice those in electric stove homes, and the boys living in gas stove homes had an 18 percent higher rate of respiratory illness.[6] A follow-up study of eight thousand children in the United States confirmed the higher nitrogen dioxide exposure levels and found that children living in gas stove homes had significantly reduced lung function as measured in controlled tests.[7] Other studies have found little association between gas stoves and respiratory illness in children. The positive evidence is strong enough, however, to suggest that indoor combustion byproducts may be responsible for respiratory disease in a large number of children and some adults. A recent Michigan study of homes with wood-burning stoves found that resident children had rates of respiratory illness of roughly twice the rates of children in homes without such stoves. Respiratory illness in general causes $15 billion in annual medical costs and nearly $60 billion in lost productivity, so the potential cost of indoor air pollution is considerable. The American Society of Heating, Refrigeration and Air-Conditioning Engineers (ASHRAE) suggests that indoor air pollution can directly reduce productivity by as much as 18 percent, particularly when ventilation is inadequate.

Indoor combustion byproducts are also responsible for some deaths. The Consumer Product Safety Commission found that there are three hundred annual deaths from indoor carbon monoxide poisoning, either through suicide or by accident. Others suggest that carbon monoxide may be responsible for thousands of deaths. Homes with woodstoves have indoor benzo(a)pyrene levels that present a substantial cancer risk. While there are no good studies on how common these concentrations are, widespread exposure to this level could be responsible for hundreds or thousands of cancer deaths.

Various steps can be taken to reduce the indoor concentration of combustion byproducts. Modifying old space heaters by adding vents helps. Gas stoves should be modified to add exhaust fans, and the burners should be kept properly adjusted to avoid yellow flames. For unvented heaters and other gas appliances, increased ventilation can reduce the indoor levels of combustion byproducts. Corrosion of gas furnaces may also cause release of carbon monoxide and other pollutants, and the Consumer Product Safety Commission has required some manufacturers to undertake repairs and even replacement of damaged furnaces. Woodstove emissions should be reduced by ensuring that doors and pipes are properly fitting. Residents should repair any cracks or other damage to furnaces, flues, and chimneys. Available air cleaners can remove particulates from the air, and gas absorption devices may reduce other indoor combustion byproducts. Confining combustion appliances to specially contained rooms produces higher concentrations in those rooms but avoids contaminating other rooms. As always, increasing building ventilation keeps indoor concentrations lower. In winter, however, increased ventilation may cause homeowners to make greater use of gas heaters and thereby increase indoor exposures. In new homes, installation of gas appliances and woodstoves can simply be avoided. Advances in manufacturing, though, have made gas appliances safer. For example, elimination of pilot lights in favor of electronic ignition can reduce emissions considerably. Building materials may remove nitrogen dioxide from indoor air through chemical reactions but vary widely in their ability to do so. For example, wallboard and cement block remove much more nitrogen dioxide than do particleboard or glass. Wool carpeting removes three times more nitrogen dioxide than does acrylic carpet. The best answer may simply be to eschew indoor combustion sources. As one author has expressed:

> Symptoms of exposure to combustion by-products are quite varied, sometimes minor, and sometimes severe. As with exposures to many pollutants, minor exposures over long periods can result in ill health in later years that has no readily discernible cause. There are so many reports of the negative health effects of combustion products, and so many people are exhibiting hypersensitivity reactions to these products that it is becoming apparent that combustion fuels should not be used in houses at all. A possible exception that might cautiously be acceptable would be to have the furnace housed totally outside the home.[8]

Biological Contamination

Various biological contaminants are found in indoor air. These contaminants include molds, bacteria, viruses, pollens, and other substances. These contaminants are capable of causing disease and even death among exposed building occupants. Distribution of these contaminants is widespread, affecting 8 to 11 million homes by one estimate and many more office buildings. The Environmental Protection Agency has suggested that biological contamination exceeds chemical contamination as a source of indoor health problems.

Viruses and bacteria often come from the exhalations of the building occupants themselves. The indoor environment, however, can contain and promote the growth of these microbes. Humidifiers, for example, effectively incubate microbial agents and have been implicated as a major source of indoor microbial contamination. Any building characteristic that enhances indoor humidity promotes the hazard from these microbes. Even a small leak or condensation can enable substantial fungal growth.

Biological contaminants also include dusts, dust mites, molds, and a variety of other human allergens. Many of these contaminants are also introduced by building occupants. In addition, indoor molds may result from wood, paint, fibers, furniture, and other products. Mattresses and furniture are associated with dust mites. Humid conditions also preserve and disseminate molds and mold spores. House dusts and plant pollens are also common in some indoor environments. Humidifiers and air conditioning also serve to disseminate these contaminants. EPA found that humidifier operation in a closed bedroom could produce particulate levels exceeding the federal outdoor standard by fifty times. Thirty percent of public buildings may have a problem of mold and mildew contamination.

Indoor products may be a source of biological contaminants, but they are not the major source. The indoor biological contamination problem is less a matter of polluting sources than of inadequate ventilation. Negative pressurization can draw in outdoor contaminants. Lack of exfiltration produces higher concentrations. Humidity and other indoor environmental conditions can have a significant effect on concentrations of biological contaminants. Humidity can result from many sources, including standing water, condensation on windows and foundations, restrooms, water-damaged carpets, and humidifiers. In homes, self-defrosting refrigerators and clothes dryers produce microbial contamination. High outdoor levels of shade can quintuple indoor levels of mold spores.[9]

The various biological contaminants cause a number of adverse health effects. Bacteria and viruses produce disease in exposed populations. The infamous Legionnaires' disease resulted from indoor exposure to a soil bacterium at an American Legion convention. One hundred eighty-two individuals contracted the disease at the convention, and twenty-five of these individuals died. Since that time there have been numerous smaller epidemics of the disease that were associated with indoor exposures. Legionella bacteria have been found in 20 to 30 percent of buildings in the Washington, D.C., area. Perhaps fifty thousand cases of Legionnaires' disease occur annually, many of which are misdiagnosed.

Another, nonfatal disease caused by indoor air, known as Pontiac fever, causes fever, headache, muscle ache, and other symptoms from indoor exposure to bacteria. More common diseases, such as influenza, measles, and chicken pox are also spread by indoor viruses. Influenza kills thousands of individuals annually in this country, although the number of these traceable to ambient indoor air pollution is unknown.

There are few studies on the indoor levels of these contaminants, but it seems clear that indoor biologicals are a material threat to health. The potential significance of indoor air pollution as a cause of influenza is illustrated by an interesting study conducted during a 1957–58 study of Asian influenza. The main building of a California Veterans' Hospital had ultraviolet air disinfection systems installed, which can destroy the influenza virus. The incidence of influenza among residents of the UV-irradiated building was 2 percent. The incidence in neighboring buildings without the systems was 19 percent.[10] This study and others demonstrated that indoor air is a major source of some diseases. A more recent study of Army training centers found that "rates of acute febrile respiratory disease were 50 percent higher in modern barracks (that had been constructed with energy-efficient designs) than in older barracks."[11]

Dusts and allergens cause a wide range of symptoms, including respiratory irritation, breathing difficulties, headaches, sneezing, skin rashes, depression, inability to concentrate, and even catatonic states. More significantly, some of these allergens may cause asthma, which affects millions of Americans. Asthma has been linked to high indoor concentrations of dust mites. Pollens and fungi spores are also a significant cause of nongenetic asthma. Mold spores are another major cause of asthma. Allergens also cause rhinitis, also known as hay fever. Allergens may cause hypersensitivity pneumonitis, which can lead to lung failure and death. In one building, four of twenty-seven workers contracted hypersensitivity pneumonitis due to dispersal of organisms through the air-conditioning system. This disease is sometimes called humidifier fever, because of its association with these devices. Children and the elderly are particularly susceptible to these sources of disease.

The health cost of biological contaminants is difficult to estimate. Some believe that these pollutants may create a larger indoor air pollution problem than any other single source, including radon. A researcher at Ball State University suggested that 50 percent of all asthma cases, amounting to 6 million individuals, are caused by dust mites. Overall, he estimated that microbes produce 6 million new cases of illness every year.[12]

Some exposure to biological contaminants is inevitable, but it can be controlled. Ventilation is very valuable, not only to exfiltrate contaminants but also to reduce indoor humidity. Installation of exhaust fans can eliminate much of the moisture that builds up from everyday activity in bathrooms and elsewhere. Ventilation of attics and basements serves the same purpose. After one building was associated with Legionnaires' disease and Pontiac fever, the air-conditioning system was dismantled and replaced with a properly designed system, after which no new cases occurred. Indoor humidity can be monitored and controlled with dehumidifiers. The Environmental Protection Agency suggests that humidity be kept within a range of 45 to 50 percent. Regular cleaning of humidifiers is essential, as they can become breeding grounds for biological contaminants. Filters for furnaces and air conditioners should also be cleaned. Cleaning wet materials and basements where water may collect, as well as the entire house, can reduce the concentration of dusts, molds, and other related contaminants. One study found that 90 percent of homes have furnishings or structural features that were wet for more than fourteen days.[13] There is some evidence that electrostatic air cleaners can significantly reduce indoor mold concentrations.[14] High-efficiency particulate filters used in hospitals are effective but are expensive for residential use. Offices can take other steps, such as eliminating reliance on water-spray systems in heating and ventilation and separating intake vents from the vicinity of cooling towers.

Moisture barriers may also be employed to cut back on the breeding grounds for microbiological contaminants. These can slow the diffusion of air and moisture through a wall. Airtight drywall is increasingly used for this purpose. Residents can use polyethylene moisture barriers on the outside and inside of external walls.

Pesticides

While most environmental concern over pesticides has focused on food residues or run-off, the greatest current risk from pesticides is probably posed by indoor exposures. The Environmental Protection Agency believes that over 80 percent of Americans' pesticide exposures result from indoor contamination. According to EPA data, 90 percent of households use pesticides in or around the home. Outdoor exposures may produce indoor problems — the computer center at the University of Kansas was virtually shut down in 1988 because insecticide fumes drifted into an outside air intake and concentrated inside the center. Many of these pesticides can be quite harmful; while the overall health burden is unknown, it may be substantial.

For a time, the pesticide chlordane was widely used beneath homes to prevent termite damage. The vapor from the pesticide penetrates openings under buildings and infiltrates indoors. The production of this pesticide has now been discontinued but exposures may persist for years. Another pesticide, pentachlorophenol, is used to preserve wood products in homes. As with formaldehyde and other chemicals used in wood, the vapor from this pesticide is slowly released into the home. Chlorpyrifos is also widely used as a pesticide by homeowners to control household insects. Propoxur, permethrin, dichlorvos, and other insecticides are also used in and around homes. The TEAM study found thirty-two different pesticides contaminating homes studied in Jacksonville, Florida. Misapplication of pesticides around public schools may produce significant exposures to children.

One study of indoor quality found frequent residential exposure to a group of pesticides, including chlorpyrifos, diasinon, chlordane, propoxur, and heptachlor.[15] Mean exposures were relatively low, however, ranging from 0.51 to 2.4 ug/m^3. Even these low levels may sometimes produce a significant cancer risk, however.

Some of the pesticides found indoors are known carcinogens. Exposures as low as a single microgram per cubic meter of air over a lifetime can produce risks as high as 1 in 1,000 for heptachlor and 3 in

10,000 for chlordane, based upon animal data. Substantial indoor application of dichlorvos (found in pest strips, sprays, and flea collars) can produce lifetime cancer risks as high as 1 in 100. These risks considerably exceed carcinogenic risks from outdoor exposures. Indeed, food exposures to pesticides are typically regulated to a level of 1 in 100,000 or less. While there are no good studies to estimate the total number of cancers attributable to indoor pesticide contamination, simple comparison of exposure levels and risk assessments suggests that indoor pesticide exposures may be responsible for hundreds or thousands of cancer cases.

Pesticides may also cause a variety of other adverse health effects, including nerve damage, fetal defects, headaches, weakness, and liver damage. An April 1990 report by a biotechnology laboratory suggested that 16 million Americans are sensitive to pesticides and that over 5 million people are highly allergic to these chemicals. The more moderate reactions included runny noses and muscle pain, but the highly allergic individuals suffer severe itching to shock and even death. These conclusions were based upon a study of the immunological responses of 8,000 subjects to exposures to the three major classes of pesticides.

Pesticide exposures can largely be contained, if not eliminated. The most severe exposures typically result when homeowners themselves apply pesticides. It is important to follow label directions carefully and to use pesticides only in well-ventilated areas. Unused quantities of pesticide should be carefully disposed of. Use of a pest control company is typically safer than self-application.

Electromagnetic Radiation

In the late 1970s office workers began to notice high levels of certain adverse health effects among those working at computer video display terminals (VDTs). In 1980 a small study found an excess of birth defects among VDT users. While most scientists discounted this finding, additional evidence arose, often finding an excess of miscarriages among those frequently exposed to VDTs. Some suggested that the harms might be explained by low-frequency magnetic radiation emitted by the terminals, radiation of a type previously believed to be entirely safe. Scandinavian studies found that pulsed magnetic fields comparable to those produced by VDTs produced biological effects in laboratory animals.

Other evidence on the potential hazard of low-frequency radiation came from epidemiological study of individuals living near high-voltage power lines. These individuals suffered an increase in childhood leukemias and other cancers, and weak magnetic fields emitted by the lines were a suspected cause. These findings also were questioned but studies soon found an excess of cancers among electrical workers frequently exposed to electromagnetic fields from power lines and transformers. Laboratory evidence lent some biological plausibility to the association. For example, animal studies found that the radiation could promote the growth of enzymes associated with cancer and alter the action of some neurotransmitters.

The most likely cause for the observed effects is electromagnetic fields, produced by electrically charged conductors. The risk appears to be associated with extremely low frequency radiation, in fields of roughly 60 hertz. Until recently, these electromagnetic fields were believed to be safe. While there is still some skepticism over the risks of this low level electromagnetic radiation, the evidence has mounted to the point of reasonable concern.

Electromagnetic radiation is of concern indoors because of the large number of electrical appliances found in the typical home or office. Small appliances that have motors, such as blenders and mixers, tend to produce substantial magnetic fields, often greater than those of larger appliances. Vacuum cleaners also project magnetic fields, largely uncontained by the appliance. Fluorescent lights, shavers, hair dryers, toasters, and other small electrical appliances also produce magnetic fields of varying concentration. Magnetic fields diminish rapidly with distance, so electric blankets and alarm clocks are of great concern, because they may be near an individual for many hours.

The magnitude of human exposure to and human risk from electromagnetic fields is not yet known. First, the quantity of exposure and the relative significance of varied sources are almost wholly unknown. Moreover, many scientists are still unconvinced by the existing studies. Even if the studies are true, the extent of risk is difficult to predict. There is a particular problem because the electromagnetic fields seem to cause harm only at certain windows of intensity. As a consequence, "[b]iological effects may be triggered at lower intensities rather than higher ones: more may not be worse."[16]

Nevertheless, there is reason to take some precautions. A study of power lines predicted a cancer risk of greater than 1 in 10,000, which warrants concern. There is direct evidence of indoor risk as well. A study of women sleeping under electric blankets and in electrically heated water beds uncovered a higher rate of miscarriages among such women, as opposed to a control group. Similar results were found in a study of Oregon homes with ceiling-cable heating, which exposes individuals to strong magnetic fields. Electromagnetic radiation may produce irritant effects as well. VDTs have been linked to allergic skin rashes, nausea, headaches, and eye problems, perhaps because static electricity fields attract particulate pollutants. A study done for the New York State Health Department suggested that exposure to common household appliances and overhead power lines may cause 10 to 15 percent of all childhood cancers.[17] Studies in Sweden have also linked childhood cancer with proximity to transformers or electrical substations.

While it is premature to take radical action against electromagnetic radiation sources, some response is appropriate. Magnetic fields cannot be easily shielded, but a study group at Carnegie-Mellon University's Department of Engineering and Public Policy proposed that new housing be wired so as to minimize electromagnetic fields and that new appliances be designed to reduce such fields. In addition, electric blankets should be avoided, particularly by women who may be pregnant. Cautious individuals also should limit their exposure to VDTs and small appliances that produce magnetic fields. Unlike other indoor air pollutants, electromagnetic fields are largely unaffected by ventilation levels.

Sick Building Syndrome

Sick building syndrome is an ill-defined condition that describes the widespread incidence of illness in certain buildings. On occasion, building occupants experience a variety of symptoms that do not fit the pattern of any identifiable disease and that are not traceable to any specific source of indoor air pollution. This pattern, generally associated with offices, has fallen under the general name of sick building syndrome. A building is generally described as "sick" if 20 percent or more of its occupants report building-related illness of one sort or another. While the specific causes of the syndrome are unknown, most suspect that the illness is caused by a "chemical soup" of various indoor air pollutants, including those described above, perhaps acting synergistically. Ironically, some of the most serious problems have been found in buildings of the Environmental Protection Agency and other federal agencies. Seventy-five percent of government office employees report that indoor air quality is a problem in their workplace.

The magnitude and complexity of the indoor air pollution problem involved in sick building syndrome is illustrated by a New York City hospital. Standing water produced a breeding ground for fungi, as did animal carcasses and excretions in air ducts. Makeshift alterations to the duct system some time in the past had produced high levels of dust. Fuel debris, lint, hair, and other substances had been sucked into ventilation, producing a powdery dark substance. Filth had accumulated to several inches of depth in fresh-air intakes, and exhausts were clogged with dirt. Outdoor-air intakes were placed in the vicinity of chemical-laden cooling towers, tar, and smokestacks. Numerous other potential problems also were identified.

The symptoms of sick building syndrome are numerous and typically include irritation of the eyes, nose, and throat; fatigue; headaches; allergic or asthmalike symptoms; nausea; dizziness; and general discomfort. In sick building syndrome, investigators are unable to find any particular substance at high enough levels to cause such symptoms. Some conditions seem clearly associated with sick building syndrome, including poor ventilation, humidification, elevated temperatures, and multiple sources of varied pollutants (usually at low levels).

The sick building syndrome may be at least partially explained by the presence of some individuals who have particular sensitivity to chemical exposures. Some evidence suggests that people today suffer more allergies and chemical sensitivities than did those living decades ago.[18] Some believe that stress from low-level exposures to pollutants such as formaldehyde or other indoor pollutants has produced this enhanced sensitivity. This condition is often called multiple chemical sensitivity (MCS), and it is seriously disputed by scientists. Some believe that the entire condition is psychological, but some individuals appear to have benefited from the elimination of indoor air pollution sources. It does appear that stress may contribute to the syndrome. One author suggests that "to the extent that sick building syndrome is an expression of our anxieties, it is a social problem, and not a medical problem at all. In short, for most of America's fifty million office workers, fear is probably the greatest occupational hazard of all."[19] EPA recognizes the synergistic effects of multiple chemical exposures and reports that such exposures "may generate acute reactions in some people, and may exacerbate the chronic effects of some pollutants such as [environmental tobacco smoke] and radon."[20] In any event, World Health Organization experts have estimated that as many as 30 percent of new or remodeled commercial buildings have unusually high rates of complaints from building occupants about their health or comfort. The total magnitude of these seemingly minor irritant effects may be quite substantial. The Consumer Federation of America has estimated that sick building syndrome may cause $100 billion a year in lost work and medical expenses.[21] Other estimates are much lower, but still typically suggest that the cost runs into billions of dollars.

The primary solution to sick building syndrome is the reduction of building "stuffiness." Over 50 percent of sick building episodes are traceable to an insufficient air exchange rate. This implies increased ventilation, lowered temperature, and reduced humidity. Modifying ventilation may also help. In some buildings, ventilation may itself circulate polluted air from outdoors, parking garages, or other pollution sources into white-collar work areas. One study found that 10 percent of the sick building syndrome cases were due to contamination from outside the building. Modifying such ventilation problems can be effective but may require expensive structural renovations. A company in Washington, D.C., charges $6,000 simply to diagnose the source of sick building syndrome, by analyzing air ventilation, filtration, distribution, humidification, and heating and cooling. They found that 64 percent of the buildings they investigated had inadequate heat exchange, 57 percent had inadequate air filters, and 35 percent had no fresh-air intake. Some suggest that 30 percent of all new buildings in California have sick building syndrome.[22] Building contents also play a role. Several instances of sick building syndrome were linked with the installation of new carpeting.

An extensive analysis by Honeywell, Inc., suggested that chemicals were the source of 75 percent of the sick building syndrome complaints, thermal problems were involved in 55 percent, microbes contributed to 45 percent, and humidity was implicated in 30 percent of the cases.[23] Honeywell's study of heating, ventilation, and air-conditioning systems in these buildings found that 75 percent had inadequate fresh outdoor air intake, 65 percent had inadequate supply of air to contained spaces, and 70 percent had inadequate exhaust of air from contained spaces. In addition, 75 percent of buildings had inadequate maintenance of the system, 60 percent had a load beyond system capacity, and 90 percent had improperly adjusted controls.[24]

The problem of sick building syndrome has focused upon commercial offices, but some residences may have a similar problem. For example, fiber glass insulation, increasingly used to replace harmful insulators, may itself cause eye irritation, skin rashes, and respiratory problems. Some limited epidemiological evidence also suggests that fiber glass fibers may cause cancer. Polyurethane foam and cellulose insulation can also cause irritant effects. Vinyl floors often contain butyl benzyl phthalate, which emits chemicals that can irritate the eyes and lungs and which appears to be carcinogenic. Wallpaper and other wall coverings require glues that emit substances intolerable to particularly sensitive individuals.

Carpeting appears to be a particularly significant source of indoor air problems. Carpets collect an enormous amount of dust and microbial growth, estimated to be as high as 10 million organisms per square foot.[25] In addition, carpet fibers produce their own synthetic dust. An even greater problem may arise from carpet backing, which can contain toxic chemicals in glues or padding. Ironically, cleaning a carpet may itself produce health problems. The carpet shampoos contain potentially toxic cleaning agents, and carpet cleaning may cause substances to become airborne that cause Kawasaki syndrome, a children's illness that produces high fevers. A Georgia company has recently introduced a new type of carpet that uses no adhesives and significantly cuts gaseous emissions.

Many carpet problems may be linked to 4-phenylcyclohexene (4-PC), used in carpet backing. The National Federation of Federal Employees reports eighty letters or phone calls complaining of irritation after the installation of carpeting with 4-PC. An EPA scientist suggests that levels as low as 17 parts per trillion of 4-PC may cause respiratory and eye irritation, and levels of 5 parts per trillion may produce symptoms in sensitive individuals and trigger multiple chemical sensitivity syndrome.

Amid all these variegated threats to health, individuals tend to seek a clear solution, such as a simple air cleaner to remove airborne contaminants. Many different forms of air cleaners are marketed. Air purifiers are available to remove particles and gases, but some of these purifiers can introduce chemicals and recirculate microbiologicals. They are at best a supplement to other measures of protecting against indoor air pollution. Particle filters may remove molds, dusts, and even asbestos but have no effect on gaseous pollutants. These filters have varying degrees of efficiency; the electrostatic precipitator, one of the most effective, produces ozone, which is itself a hazardous air pollutant. Activated carbon filters can remove gaseous pollutants, but some individuals are sensitive to the activated carbon. Activated carbon also fails to remove VOCs from indoor air. Interestingly, household plants, such as spider plants, are among the most effective filters for indoor air. Unfortunately, no filtration system is so effective that it can remove concern about sources of indoor air contamination. Air cleaning devices can contribute to healthful air, especially when integrated into a central air-circulation system, but this approach can be quite expensive.

Notes

1. M. Tancrede, R. Wilson, L. Zeise, & E.A.C. Crouch, *The Carcinogenic Risk of Some Organic Vapors: A Theoretical Survey*, 21 ATMOSPHERIC ENVIRONMENT 2187 (1987).

2. U.S. Environmental Protection Agency, REPORT TO CONGRESS ON INDOOR AIR QUALITY (1988) (Draft), pp. 4–22.

3. *Id.*, pp. 4–24.

4. INDOOR POLLUTION NEWS, June 29, 1989, p. 1.

5. Jan A. J. Stolwijk, Statement, *Hearing before the Subcomm. on Environmental Protection of the Comm. on Environment and Public Works*, 100th Cong., 1st Sess. (April 24, 1987), p. 62.

6. C. du V. Florey, R. J. W. Melia, and S. Chinn, *The Relation between Respiratory Illness in Primary School Children and the Use of Gas for Cooking. I. Results from a National Survey*, 8 INT'L J. OF EPIDEMIOLOGY 333 (1979).

7. F. E. Speizer, B. G. Ferris, Jr., Y. M. M. Bishop, and J. Spengler, *Respiratory Disease Rates and Pulmonary Function in Children Associated with NO-2 Exposure*, 121 AM. REV. OF RESPIRATORY DISEASES 3 (1980).

8. JOHN BOWER, THE HEALTHY HOUSE (1989), pp. 286–87.

9. Peter P. Kozak & Janet Gallup, *Endogenous Mold Exposure: Environmental Risk to Atopic and Nonatopic Patients*, in INDOOR AIR AND HUMAN HEALTH (R. B. Gammage & S. V. Kaye eds. 1985), p. 155.

10. National Research Council, INDOOR POLLUTANTS (Washington, D.C.: National Academy Press) (1981), p. 385.

11. U.S. Environmental Protection Agency, pp. 2–8.

12. INDOOR POLLUTION NEWS, October 20, 1988, p. 4.

13. Kozak & Gallup, p. 161.

14. M. J. Maloney, B. B. Wray, R. H. DuRant, & L. Smith, *Effect of an Electronic Air Cleaner and Negative Ionizer on the Population of Indoor Mold Spores*, 59 ANNALS OF ALLERGY (1987), p. 192.

15. U.S. Environmental Protection Agency, pp. 3–23.

16. N.Y. TIMES, July 11, 1989, p. 20 (national edition).

17. INDOOR POLLUTION LAW REPORT, July 1987, p. 8.

18. BOWER, p. 23.

19. Bardana, *Office Epidemics: Why Are Americans Suddenly Allergic to the Workplace?*, 26 SCIENCES 38, 44 (1986).

20. Environmental Protection Agency, *Report to Congress on Indoor Air Quality; Executive Summary and Recommendations* (1989), p. 16.

21. INDOOR POLLUTION NEWS, February 25, 1988, p. 5.

22. INDOOR POLLUTION NEWS, February 25, 1988, p. 3.

23. INDOOR POLLUTION NEWS, July 14, 1988, p. 5.

24. *Id.*

25. BOWER, p. 227.

PART II

Government Control of
Indoor Air Pollution

Given the magnitude of health risks from indoor air pollution that were identified and described in Part I, government regulatory action could be expected. Indoor air risks far surpass many outdoor environmental risks that have been regulated extensively, at costs ranging into the billions of dollars. Notwithstanding these risks, however, government has been slow to act against the most serious threats to indoor air quality.

Government inaction on indoor air has numerous explanations. A homeowner may tend to view his or her house as a safe refuge and may have difficulty accepting the genuine risks presented by indoor air pollution. The "villains" of indoor air pollution are less obvious and graphic than the typical oil company involved in a tanker spill or chemical dump site for hazardous wastes. The environmental and public interest lobby groups have themselves been slow to adopt the indoor air quality cause, thus depriving it of a key constituency to prod government into action.

Some government response to indoor air pollution has developed. Research activities in the area are ever-increasing. While few regulations have been forthcoming, government agencies at all levels have sought to inform the public of risks from indoor air pollution, to enable individuals better to protect themselves. The extent of these activities have varied widely by jurisdiction and by pollutant.

Chapter 5 considers the government response to indoor radon exposures. Radon remains the most significant indoor threat to health and is also one of the most prominent. Government action in this area, however, has been weak at best. The federal Environmental Protection Agency has expressed great public concern over radon threats to health, but their action has been limited to research and informational activities. Although the radon scare has prompted congressional attention, no strong legislation has even been proposed, much less passed. Some states have acted on radon, but their actions also have been limited. At the present time, voluntary private organizations have offered the most significant remedial promise.

The government response to indoor asbestos hazards is described in Chapter 6. In contrast to radon, government has been especially vigilant for indoor asbestos exposures, particularly in schools. A major nationwide cleanup program for schools has commenced, and this effort is slowly expanding to other buildings as well. Ironically, this unusually vigorous governmental response to indoor air pollution is enormously expensive and largely unnecessary. In some instances, the government's attempted remediation of indoor asbestos may exacerbate the health risks of the substance. States have taken somewhat more reasoned control operations.

Chapter 7 discusses governmental action against indoor formaldehyde exposures. Federal action on formaldehyde has been characterized by a flurry of regulatory attention and very little in the way of results. Interagency disputes and court battles have disrupted any hope of reasoned action in the area. Some regulation of formaldehyde sources has resulted, though it has been limited in scope and rather weak in degree. Individual states have taken more stringent approaches to indoor formaldehyde exposures, but these are few.

Chapter 8 analyzes the government response to the numerous other significant indoor air pollutants. The chapter addresses government actions for each major category of indoor pollutant. Unfortunately, the federal government's regulatory agencies lack any overall authority to respond to indoor air quality problems, and proposed legislation offers little further promise. The fragmented authorities of the Environmental Protection Agency, Consumer Product Safety Commission, Department of Housing and Urban Development, and other agencies yield little effective action. In the limited circumstances in which unambiguous regulatory authority exists in an agency, such as in the case of pesticides, some strong rules exist. Otherwise, government action has been restricted to research, publicity, and development of the occasional voluntary guideline. State action against most of the hazards is also absent or limited.

In sum, the present picture of government action on indoor air pollution saddens. For whatever reason, government bodies lack the motivation to address indoor air quality. The action that exists has been haphazard, uncoordinated, and often thoughtless. Particularly vigorous action responds to rather innocuous threats to health, while far greater hazards receive relatively little attention or resources. Dollars for indoor air pollution control are limited and have been too often misspent. More positively, some encouraging developments have appeared, and the area of indoor air pollution continues to receive increasing government attention, even as resources remain far below the level justified by the risks of such pollution.

5

GOVERNMENT CONTROL OF INDOOR RADON RISKS

Given the magnitude of the cancer risk from indoor radon, which apparently exceeds all outdoor pollutants combined, one might expect government control action. To date, however, government has done relatively little. There is virtually no direct regulation of the indoor radon problem, and little other government action. Most disturbingly, indoor radon appears to have a very low priority with government health and safety agencies, despite protestations to the contrary. In addition, "the legislative and regulatory framework for radon has been characterized by ambiguity and controversy about whether particular agencies have the responsibility and authority to address the problem."[1] A federal program to control exposures to indoor radon is now beginning to take shape, however, and various states have initiated their own actions in response to radon.

Federal Control of Indoor Radon

Publications reported some evidence of elevated radon levels as early as the 1960s and 1970s, but the Environmental Protection Agency did not recognize a widespread indoor radon problem until early 1985.[2] This recognition was itself rather belated. By 1980, considerable scientific evidence had mounted regarding the indoor radon hazard, as recognized in that year by the General Accounting Office, a broad-based research tool of Congress that is hardly at the forefront of environmental knowledge. The 1980 Report of the Council on Environmental Quality estimated that indoor radon could be responsible for as many as twenty thousand deaths, yet EPA did nothing for several years.

In September 1985, EPA finally initiated its "Radon Action Program." The Radon Action Program focused primarily on research into the extent of the indoor radon problem and radon mitigation approaches. While EPA's program was primarily devoted to researching the problem, the agency also incorporated measures to inform the public of the potential hazard. At his confirmation hearings, new EPA administrator William Reilly offered some promise by listing indoor air quality among his highest priorities.

EPA's research program has had some success. The agency has surveyed houses throughout the United States and thereby determined the nationwide scope of indoor radon contamination. In the course of this and other investigations, the agency has reportedly tested over 2 million homes. EPA is now preparing geological maps to identify the areas at highest risk. Unfortunately, this assessment has been delayed, and the General Accounting Office has criticized the studies as incomplete.[3] EPA also has studied the devices available for measuring indoor radon concentrations to check for accuracy and to standardize measurement methods. EPA studies of mitigation techniques enhance our knowledge of the efficacy of remedial actions. The agency also has trained government officials and private contractors in radon measurement and mitigation methods and helped create standards for certifying private organizations that test for radon contamination. This research is an important prerequisite to effective action against indoor radon contamination, but the research cannot itself correct the problem.

EPA has yet to follow up on its research with a meaningful program to reduce indoor radon concentrations in residential housing. The agency has adopted no regulations specifically directed against indoor exposures to radon. If anything, EPA has consistently run away from opportunities to regulate hazardous indoor conditions of any type, including radon.

In fairness to EPA, there is no statute that grants the agency unambiguous authority to regulate indoor air pollution. Some commentators urged EPA to use the Clean Air Act to protect indoor air quality. This act contains provisions that permit EPA to set maximum permissible concentrations for some air pollutants. The Clean Air Act refers to any pollutant that "enters the ambient air," however, and EPA has consistently interpreted this authority as limited to "outdoor" air.[4] There is no evidence that Congress was aware of indoor air pollution when it passed and amended the Clean Air Act, so there is little basis for contesting EPA's longstanding interpretation.

If the Clean Air Act is unavailable for regulation of indoor air pollution, EPA possesses broader authority under the Toxic Substances Control Act (TSCA). This law gives the agency authority to regulate against any "unreasonable risk" and authorizes many types of regulations to this end. Unfortunately, TSCA is ill suited to addressing the indoor radon problem. TSCA is directed against "chemical substances." While the term "chemical substances" could theoretically be interpreted to include virtually anything (and the statutory definition is quite broad), the context of the act is primarily directed at manufactured chemicals. At least some radioactive material is expressly included within the act's definition of "chemical substance." The ability to regulate indoor radon exposures is uncertain, however, and such radon may be outside the purview of even this broad regulatory authority.

The lack of regulatory authority over indoor air pollution could be interpreted as a complete lack of jurisdiction to address the problem through research, education and other nonmandatory approaches. EPA has not adopted this rigid view, however. The agency has employed Section 103 of the Clean Air Act to research the problem. At best, EPA has taken some rather halting steps to encourage private action to correct indoor radon hazards. EPA spends several million dollars annually in researching exposure and mitigation of indoor radon. In 1986 the agency developed and distributed pamphlets entitled *A Citizen's Guide to Radon* and *Radon Reduction Methods: A Homeowner's Guide*. EPA more recently has published other informative booklets, made available at no cost to citizens.

EPA also publishes radon guides for builders, in cooperation with the National Association of Homebuilders' Research Foundation. The agency emphasizes site evaluation prior to construction. EPA further recommends construction techniques such as installing a polyethylene vapor barrier under the slab, taking precautions to avoid cracks in the slab, sealing walls and penetrations, and home design to maintain neutral pressure differentials. The agency also offers advice for postconstruction remediation actions in homes found to have high radon contamination.

On April 20, 1989, EPA administrator William Reilly highlighted the potential problem of radon contamination of schools and called for universal testing. The agency has allocated no money for the radon-in-schools program, however, even though President Bush requested $8 million in grants. In the absence of resources, state and local governments have done very little to address the issue of student radon exposures.

EPA also has initiated several localized warning and risk communication study programs. These programs are located in regions of high radon concentrations. EPA warns individual homeowners of the risks of radon. The agency also informs them of corrective measures. The United States surgeon general issued an even more dramatic warning on September 12, 1988, in the form of a national radon health advisory urging the testing of most American homes for radon. There is little evidence, however, that these warnings have produced any real benefit or even any particular public awareness of radon hazards.

Perhaps EPA's most valuable service is the establishment of the 4 pCi/L guideline for remedial action. While the guideline was promulgated in the context of homes built in the vicinity of uranium mill tailings, the level has been widely used to evaluate naturally occurring radon problems as well. Through this guideline, the agency has created an easily understandable benchmark for radon problems. The presence of a serious radon problem is now largely defined by whether exposures exceed the 4 pCi/L guideline. This action also produced considerable criticism. Some federal agencies argued that the guideline was too low, though the level was much less stringent than other public health rules. More critics argue that the guideline is too high, leaving substantial residual risks to building occupants. Compared to other environmental regulations, the guideline is high — EPA's guideline exposures produce a significant risk of lung cancer, equal to receiving two hundred chest x-rays every year. Nevertheless, the guideline is a sensible first step. Millions of homes exceed 4 pCi/L, and this benchmark is a reasonable level to differentiate between very serious indoor radon hazards that require immediate attention and hazards that, while still serious, can await a more reflective response.

EPA has initiated one regulatory action that will contribute slightly to reducing indoor radon concentrations. In 1976 the agency adopted National Interim Primary Drinking Water Regulations that set a maximum contaminant level of 5 pCi/L of radium in drinking water. In September 1986 EPA announced its intent to reconsider this preliminary standard and reduce acceptable levels.[5] The agency suggested that prevailing radon levels in water could account for as many as 600 fatal cancers each year and that other radionuclides might cause 130 additional cancers. The agency declared that in some circumstances radon in water could produce as much as 90 percent of indoor radon but acknowledged that water accounted for only 2 to 5 percent of total indoor radon air concentrations.[6] Moreover, EPA has failed to address even this small portion of the radon hazard. The intent to reduce the maximum contaminant level for radionuclides has languished at the agency with no further formal action. EPA ignored the June 1989 deadline of the Safe Drinking Water Act for promulgation of a final regulation. Press reports suggest that the standard was stalled when EPA's Office of Air and Radiation became concerned that a tough drinking water standard would pressure the Air Office to promulgate expensive air quality standards for radon. EPA now promises a standard by September 1990, but has already expressed fears over enforcing such a standard.

Remarkably, EPA has rejected congressional offers of additional funding for indoor air projects. Internal agency analysis concedes that radon is an area of "relatively high risk but low EPA effort."[7]

EPA is not the only federal locus of concern for radon; the Department of Housing and Urban Development (HUD) also has an interest. In the mid-1970s, HUD began investigating radon contamination in a few localized western sites, such as Grand Junction, Colorado, where housing was contaminated by the tailings left over from uranium mining. HUD performed some limited testing for radon but did little else. At one point, HUD required that houses in Butte and Anaconda, Montana, be tested for radon before receiving HUD mortgage assistance, but this effort was abandoned, and HUD now simply requires that a radon disclosure notice be issued to applicants for HUD-insured mortgages at a few sites where radon contamination is known to be a particular problem. Otherwise, HUD's efforts are restricted to some limited research into problem areas and into mitigation techniques for residential housing. While HUD possesses the power to establish construction standards for its housing, the department has not developed mandatory regulations against radon contamination. Senator Frank Lautenberg of New Jersey complained that the "average homebuyer in northwest New Jersey is doing more than HUD is" in response to the radon threat.[8] HUD even argued against the EPA exposure guideline.

Other federal agencies have played a smaller role. The Department of Energy (DOE) has researched radon's health effects, geological sources of radon, and construction techniques to limit the problem. DOE has no regulatory authority over indoor air problems, however. The executive branch created two interagency coordinating committees, the Committee on Indoor Air Quality and the Committee on Interagency Radiation Research and Policy Coordination to organize the efforts of the several agencies. These programs have very small budgets, however, and their efforts are limited to researching the problem. Even coordination has been lacking; EPA and DOE have fought over radon funding. Indeed, Department of Energy conservation standards and guidelines almost certainly aggravate the indoor radon problem. DOE also fought EPA's 4 pCi/L guideline for residential exposures. By contrast, the energy conservation program of the federally run Bonneville Power Administration, discussed further in Chapter 8, contains a mitigation package to control exposure to radon, among other indoor pollutants.

Some have looked to the Consumer Product Safety Commission (CPSC) for relief, as its enabling legislation, the Consumer Product Safety Act, permits the commission to require manufacturers to repair or replace "products" that present unreasonable hazards. Courts have ruled that houses are not products under the act's definition, however.[9] The CPSC may proceed against radon-contaminated bricks and other construction materials, but these represent only a small fraction of the indoor radon problem. The commission can do little against the greater problem of indoor concentration of radon from natural sources.

Congress has acted to prod EPA and other federal agencies into responding more vigorously to indoor radon exposures. In 1986 Congress passed the Radon Gas and Indoor Air Quality Research Act, incorporated in amendments to Superfund, the federal government's statute for cleanup of hazardous waste sites. While the legislature sought to increase attention to radon, this act authorized only research. The research program was to include health research; mitigation research; and coordination of federal, state, and local radon research. This law also directed EPA to make periodic reports to Congress on the indoor radon hazard, as well as other indoor air pollution problems. Congress specifically declared that the law did not authorize EPA to "carry out any regulatory program or any activity other than research, development, and related reporting, information dissemination, and coordination activities specified in this title."[10]

In 1987 Congress passed the Radon Program Development Act. This law provides financial assistance to states to conduct their own programs against radon contamination. The law authorized up to $13 million per year to this end. The state programs are to be limited to research and information activities, however. This law also provided for a national survey of radon in schools and granted EPA the specific power to regulate private firms conducting radon testing and mitigation actions. The Reagan administration resisted even this limited action, however, contending that the bill tried to do too much too soon.

In 1988 Congress passed yet another relevant law, entitled the Indoor Radon Abatement Act of 1988. This law established a "national goal" of reducing indoor radon concentrations well below EPA's current 4 pCi/L guideline and provided some federal resources for radon reduction. The act authorized $10 million for grants to state radon development programs, $1.5 million for a study of radon in schools, $1.5 million for regulating radon testing and mitigation firms, $1 million for regional training centers at universities, and $3 million for technical assistance in radon testing and mitigation. This act also required federal agencies to study its own buildings for radon contamination and required EPA to develop model construction standards to avoid excessive levels of indoor radon. EPA also is to promote the use of these recommended construction approaches. Like its predecessors, this bill does more to recognize the problem than to solve it. The Radon Abatement Act provides no regulatory authority to protect building occupants and the amounts of money authorized for indoor radon research and control are insignificant. Congress failed to appropriate funds for many of the programs contained in the law. Congress has readdressed the radon problem periodically. The Radon Pollution Control Act of 1988 set a "goal" of reducing indoor radon below EPA's 4 pCi/L guideline down to 0.2 pCi/L. This act did little to promote accomplishment of the goal, however.

While Congress has actually done very little to encourage radon control measures, the issue remains a politically popular one. After passing three laws in the last three years, the Senate and House are considering further legislation to address indoor contamination. Like the previous laws, this new proposed legislation would actually accomplish little. Representative Tom Luken of Ohio has proposed two radon control bills, but both are limited to training and grant assistance to state and local government. EPA has resisted any effort to establish regulatory standards for housing and maintains that "indoor air research and policy programs have not sufficiently characterized [indoor air quality] problems and solutions to be able to define the appropriate long-term Federal role regarding the need for, or appropriateness of, regulatory approaches to [indoor air quality] problems."[11]

Senator George Mitchell of Maine, now majority leader of the Senate, has been the leader in legislation on indoor air quality, having proposed several bills. The most noteworthy of these is probably S. 1629, largely reintroduced in 1989 as S. 657. Representative Joseph Kennedy of Massachusetts has introduced similar legislation in the House of Representatives. In addition to the standard authorization of research and dissemination of information on indoor air, this bill also directs EPA to develop a "national indoor air quality response plan" that would attain outdoor ambient air quality standards even indoors and reduce other indoor air contaminants found to cause health harms. While Senator Mitchell's bill contains no additional regulatory authority, it may prod EPA to make greater use of its existing authority to control indoor air pollution.

In addition, Representative Pat Schroeder of Colorado and others have introduced legislation to provide a partial tax credit for the expense of installing radon mitigation equipment in residential housing. A report by senators Timothy Wirth of Colorado and John Heinz of Pennsylvania criticized such radon mitigation tax credits, however, because they "increase budget deficits, do not improve public understanding of risks, and do not induce cost-effective mitigation."[12] When first introduced, Representative Schroeder's bill had little support in Congress. Representative Bart Gordon of Tennessee recently introduced the Radon Testing for Safe Schools Act, which would require monitoring of radon levels in schools in regions that tend to have high radon concentrations.

The new legislation introduced to date reflects continuing congressional concern with indoor air quality and could doubtless contribute to reducing radon health harms associated with indoor air. At the current time, however, all significant indoor air quality legislation has been subordinated to reauthorization of the Clean Air Act to deal with outdoor pollution. Even if all these indoor air quality bills were to pass, however, they would make little direct contribution to ensuring the quality of indoor air. So long as Congress denies explicit regulatory authority to EPA and other agencies, there can be no comprehensive, effective federal program of radon control. The provision of regulatory authority appears highly unlikely, as legislators are concerned about the costs regulation might impose on the construction industry and homeowners. Indeed, even those environmental groups concerned about indoor radon have not proposed regulatory action.

State Control of Indoor Radon

Several states have seized the initiative in protecting their residents from radon contamination of housing. The state programs assume a variety of forms and take differing approaches. State radon control initiatives can be broken down into investigatory research programs, information programs, standards for radon mitigation, loan programs for mitigation, construction standards or guidelines, and regulations of real estate transactions. Some of these state actions go well beyond the federal effort to date.

States, like the federal government, have devoted resources to research investigating the extent of the radon problem. Those states known to have high geological radon levels have been in the forefront of contamination surveys. Thus Pennsylvania, New Jersey, Florida, and Colorado have all conducted surveys of the extent of radon contamination in their housing. While surveys are an important first step to mitigating high radon levels, they do little in themselves to help the situation. Moreover, some state surveys have been frustrated. Homeowners worry that state measurements may be released to the public under state open records legislation, thereby harming property values. Some states have expressed concern that misuse of the data could produce litigation against the government.[13] New Jersey has resolved these concerns by excluding radon survey data from public records. Nineteen states are conducting or have completed extensive statewide surveys of their radon problems.

States also have initiated programs to inform their citizens of the potential radon hazard of residential housing. New Jersey's program has its Department of Environmental Protection coordinate with local authorities to inform the public and establishes a toll-free telephone number for information. Pennsylvania also has such a number and publishes public notices regarding the need for testing in high-radon areas. These services cumulatively receive thousands of calls per month. Altogether, state information efforts are rather scarce and limited. Even Pennsylvania and New Jersey primarily respond to citizen questions rather than vigorously seeking out residents. In July 1989 the Pennsylvania Department of Natural Resources publicly advised all Pennsylvania residents to test their homes for indoor radon and promised free follow-up long-term tests for homeowners with high levels in the initial testing.

Some states have set standards for private firms that test for radon or that modify homes to correct radon problems. New Jersey's Department of Environmental Protection conducts a certification program for radon testing firms. The state also monitors testing companies' results to help ensure accuracy and prevent fraud. New Jersey also certifies remedial contractors. Pennsylvania hires private contractors to install remedial measures in high radon levels. The state also certifies contractors who take mitigative measures under its loans to homeowners.

Still another approach provides homeowners with loans or grants to offset the costs of mitigating high indoor radon levels. Pennsylvania is a leader in this approach, providing low-interest loans to individuals whose houses contain high levels of radon contamination. Pennsylvania offers free radon tests and loans of up to $7,000 per home for radon remediation. New Jersey also has a low-interest loan program.

Some states have also taken vigorous action to prevent future radon problems by promulgating standards for new construction. Florida's Department of Health and Rehabilitative Services adopted standards for new construction in 1986. These standards require radon testing on new homes, schools, and commercial structures in regions known to have high radon levels. Construction in these areas must adopt practices to prevent radon concentration. Postconstruction testing is carried out and, if levels of radon are high, mitigation measures are required. In 1988 Florida began imposing a one cent per square foot "radon surcharge" on building permits to fund research and new building codes. New Jersey has begun to amend its building codes in high-radon areas. A 1989 law required use of special construction standards, and proposed regulations would require a vapor barrier below the basement slab, as well as a vent pipe. Washington State recently passed an indoor air quality law that dictates changes in the state building code to ensure adequate ventilation in buildings and direct regulation of commercial buildings and schools with indoor air contamination. These steps are the only direct regulation yet adopted to protect building occupants from indoor exposures to high levels of radon.

A final state approach, which may have a significant indirect benefit in reducing radon, involves the regulation of real estate transactions. State and local associations of realtors and brokers have developed guidelines for radon contamination. Virtually all real estate transactions in New Jersey include a radon contingency clause, making the sale contingent on the house's passing a radon test or requiring corrective measures by the seller. In 1987, 80 percent of sales in northern New Jersey included a radon test of the property. The Pennsylvania Realtors' Association recommends use of radon disclosure forms in every sale. Rhode Island and Florida require that radon disclosure notices be contained in contracts for the sale of real estate. Numerous other state realty organizations have initiated similar recommendations or requirements. Radon tests in real estate transactions have been criticized, however, due to the limited accuracy of one-time, short-term testing for radon.

While some state actions are quite promising, state radon control is uneven. EPA has identified seven states, including Texas, as having virtually no programs responding to indoor radon contamination.[14] In twenty-four additional states, radon control initiatives have commenced but at a very low level. These states typically have only a single individual in charge of radon investigation and control. While these states may provide information to their citizens, they conduct no outreach and may not even perform investigatory studies to identify radon problems. Fourteen more states have performed investigatory studies but do little or nothing to assist or require mitigation of radon problems. According to EPA, only five states (Florida, Maine, New Jersey, New York, and Pennsylvania) have "operational programs" to control radon.[15] New Jersey, New York, and Pennsylvania alone account for approximately 88 percent of all state funding for radon control. While these states have particularly serious radon problems, other states also have significant indoor radon contamination but have done very little to respond to the problem. The California Department of Health Services has repeatedly downplayed the threat of indoor radon and has resisted EPA's recommendations for testing of schools. The manager of California's Indoor Air Quality Program called EPA's warning of radon's health harms "overblown" and "incomprehensible."[16] Exhibit 5.1 presents EPA's evaluation of the nature of state programs on radon exposure. State programs can provide an important complement to federal action, but states have fallen short of the full degree of protection warranted. So long as states like California resist action and other states ignore the problem, the need for a strong federal program will remain.

Exhibit 5.1
Summary of State Radon Programs

Program Type	Definition	States
Information	No active program disseminates information	Arkansas, Hawaii, Louisiana, Mississippi, Nevada, South Dakota, Texas
Formative	Preliminary surveys	Alaska, Arizona, California, Delaware, Georgia, Idaho, Iowa, Massachusetts, Minnesota, Missouri, Montana, Nebraska, New Hampshire, New Mexico North Carolina, Utah, Vermont, Washington, West Virginia
Developing	Extensive surveys	Alabama, Colorado, Connecticut, Illinois, Indiana, Kansas, Kentucky, Maryland, Michigan, Rhode Island, Tennessee, Virginia, Wisconsin, Wyoming
Operational	Comprehensive surveys demonstrating problems	Florida, Maine, New Jersey, New York, Pennsylvania

Private Control of Indoor Radon

Various private organizations have taken action to control indoor radon contamination. The most significant private organization is the American Society of Heating, Refrigeration and Air-Conditioning Engineers (ASHRAE). This organization has adopted voluntary building ventilation standards for decades. In 1973 ASHRAE adopted a new standard for indoor ventilation, Standard 62, which was adopted by most local building codes. The 1973 standard permitted very low ventilation levels, though, and the ventilation standard was amended in 1981, but the amendments were controversial and have not been adopted in many model building codes.

ASHRAE is continuously working on further revisions of its ventilation standard to protect indoor air quality. The new 1989 Standard 62 demands more ventilation in many buildings, and future standards may include differing (higher) ventilation for rooms with significant indoor air pollution sources and varying ventilation according to building occupation patterns. The threat of formal legal action has complicated ASHRAE's voluntary efforts, however. Tobacco and formaldehyde industry organizations opposed adoption of the 1981 standard and threatened to sue the society unless their concerns were represented in ASHRAE standard setting. The inclusion of these representatives has complicated effective action.

ASHRAE has taken some positive actions, in addition to establishing the now-controversial ventilation standards. ASHRAE emphasizes the need for ventilation system maintenance to reduce humidity and keep filters clear of pollutants. ASHRAE also has recommendations regarding the location of building air inlets and ventilation system design. The ASHRAE handbook emphasizes proper air cleaning (such as activated charcoal filters) for outside air and distribution of ventilation air so that it is not diverted to exhausts without first being circulated throughout the interior room. The society also has adopted exposure guidelines for indoor exposures to a small number of chemical contaminants. While ASHRAE cannot solve indoor air pollution problems, they have made an important contribution.

Other private organizations also have assumed a role in preventing indoor air pollution. The National Institute of Building Sciences has embarked upon a significant program to study measures to control indoor radon contamination. The National Association of Homebuilders (NAHB) has undertaken radon research and is helping develop model building codes. NAHB also trains builders in radon-resistant construction techniques. Unions and other employee associations are increasingly vigilant about all indoor air problems in commercial buildings. The American Federation of State, County and Municipal Employees and the Service Employees International Union have taken steps to inform their members of the risks of indoor air pollution. Dozens of businesses and universities have combined to form the American Association of Radon Scientists and Technologists to provide information about the risks of radon, to improve the accuracy of measurement of indoor radon, to improve the science of remediation, and to inform the public of this information. Some businesses, such as Honeywell, Inc., and American Telephone & Telegraph Co., have demonstrated particular concern for the quality of air in their workplaces.

It is difficult to assess the programs taken to control indoor radon exposures. Both Congress and EPA express a strong commitment to indoor air quality. States, too, have taken numerous actions on indoor radon. The clear recognition of the health risks of indoor radon should be encouraging; the government has responded much more promptly to indoor air pollution than it did to outdoor air pollution. Unfortunately, federal and state governments have repeatedly recognized the risks of radon, without taking effective action to protect building occupants from such risks. Apparently, these governments hope that individual citizens will solve the radon problem, once they are informed of its existence. This simple informational approach has not succeeded for any other major environmental health hazard, and it will not suffice for radon either. EPA administrator William Reilly declared that the "risks posed by radon gas are very real, but with a little thoughtful effort, we can solve this problem with relative ease."[17] Perhaps so, but such thoughtful effort on radon has unfortunately been lacking.

Notes

1. Sheldon Krimsky & Alonzo Plough, ENVIRONMENTAL HAZARDS: COMMUNICATING RISKS AS A SOCIAL PROCESS (1988), p. 142.

2. U.S. Environmental Protection Agency, *Report to Congress on Indoor Air Quality*, vol. 1, p. 26 (1989) (draft).

3. U.S. General Accounting Office, *Indoor Radon: Limited Federal Response to Contamination in Housing* (April 1988), p. 18.

4. 40 C.F.R. Section 35.501–1 (1981).

5. 51 Fed. Reg. 34836 (1986).

6. 51 Fed. Reg. at 34842.

7. U.S. Environmental Protection Agency, *Unfinished Business: A Comparative Assessment of Environmental Problems*, February 1987, p. xv.

8. *Radon Exposure: Human Health Threat*, Hearing before the Subcomm. on Health and the Environment of the House Comm. on Energy and Commerce. November 5, 1987, p. 21.

9. *Consumer Product Safety Commission v. Anaconda Co.*, 593 F.2d 1314 (D.C. Cir. 1979).

10. Section 404, 42 U.S.C. Section 7401 (1987).

11. INDOOR POLLUTION NEWS, August 10, 1989, p. 3.

12. INDOOR POLLUTION NEWS, December 1, 1988, p. 2.

13. Janet I. Moore, *The Radon Review: The Federal and State Governments' Responses to Indoor Radon Contamination*, 7 TEMPLE ENVIRONMENTAL LAW & TECHNOLOGY JOURNAL 39, 53 (1988).

14. U.S. Environmental Protection Agency, *Summary of State Radon Programs*, August 1987, pp. 13, 21.

15. *Id.* at 13.

16. INDOOR POLLUTION NEWS, October 20, 1988, p. 1.

17. Congressional Record, May 31, 1989, p. S5852.

6

GOVERNMENT CONTROL OF INDOOR ASBESTOS RISKS

In contrast to the slow, measured response to indoor radon contamination, the government acted very quickly in response to indoor asbestos risks in schools. Moreover, this action was not entirely informational but contained regulatory requirements as well. The federal government provided inadequate guidance to local school districts, many of which simply ignored the federal directives. Other districts overreacted, unnecessarily removing nonhazardous asbestos and concomitantly increasing the risk. While the program has evolved through several laws, the current federal controls still provide little assurance that indoor asbestos will be abated safely.

Federal Control of Indoor Asbestos

In contrast to the radon experience, the federal government has been quite active in regulating some indoor exposures to asbestos. EPA adopted rules to govern asbestos-containing materials in schools, and Congress forced the agency to go farther and strengthen its program. While the regulatory response is largely limited to the school setting, the asbestos regulations have been progressively strengthened and pressure is building to extend the controls to nonschool buildings that contain asbestos products.

Various federal agencies acted on asbestos risks to health in many contexts. In 1978 EPA's authority to control outdoor exposures was used to prohibit future use of spray-applied asbestos-containing materials for such purposes as insulation or fireproofing.[1] This ban was expanded in 1975 to prohibit all forms of asbestos application. In 1976 the agency expanded the rule further to prohibit all new uses of asbestos in buildings. The Occupational Safety and Health Administration also has an asbestos standard that applies to all private workplaces, but allowable exposures under this standard are far higher than those found in schools and other buildings.

Public concern over asbestos-containing materials in schools and other buildings began to mount during the 1970s, and in 1978 the governor of New Jersey petitioned EPA to develop rules controlling asbestos exposures in buildings. Soon thereafter, the Environmental Defense Fund (EDF) submitted a similar petition. In 1979 EPA denied both these petitions and instead initiated a program of technical assistance to state and local governments.[2] After EDF filed suit, the agency reversed its field and announced that it would initiate rulemaking to regulate sprayed asbestos products in schools. In 1979 EPA developed a Technical Assistance Program that encouraged voluntary inspection for asbestos and correction of any health hazards.

Congress became aware of student exposures to asbestos and in 1980 adopted the Asbestos School Hazard Detection and Control Act. This law authorized Department of Education research into the problem as well as grants and interest-free loans for mitigation projects. As it happened, however, the act was never funded through appropriations bills, and its authority expired in 1982. As a result, a 1984 EPA study reported that cleanup action was taken only in "wealthy" school districts.[3]

After nearly three years, EPA adopted a limited inspection rule for asbestos in school buildings under authority of the Toxic Substances Control Act. The agency required schools to "identify friable asbestos-containing building materials" in their buildings.[4] Rather than requiring response action, EPA simply directed schools to notify their employees and the school's parent-teacher association of the inspection results. While requiring inspections, EPA emphasized that "[m]any of the friable asbestos-containing materials in schools do not require abatement or removal" and can be controlled by a "reasonable effort by school officials to manage the materials."[5]

When asbestos-containing materials were discovered in a school, the agency encouraged local districts to consult with EPA regarding corrective actions. To assist this process, EPA produced a guidance document to help local governments decide on appropriate action to be taken if asbestos-containing materials are found in school buildings. EPA's guidance document became rather important and went through several iterations. The first version was known as the Orange Book, because of the color of its cover. The Orange Book was soon supplanted by the Blue Book, which in turn was replaced in 1985 by the Purple Book. These books gave increasingly detailed information on the asbestos hazard and on available response actions. The Purple Book informed administrators that typical school exposures were very low or negligible but warned of the health consequences of even low exposures to asbestos. The Purple Book recommended no action on asbestos-containing materials that had suffered no damage or deterioration. However, when these materials had suffered even minor damage or deterioration, the guide recommended removal "as soon as possible."

EPA's inspection rule and guidance had relatively minor, but erratic, effects on local actions. The rule gave schools little time to comply, and many simply failed to comply with the inspection requirement. A 1984 EPA survey found that only 34 percent of school districts studied had complied with even the major requirements of the inspection rule. Less than 10 percent of districts complied with all aspects of the rule. EPA's survey found a systematic failure to inspect for boiler room asbestos. Many schools did not perform any tests for asbestos, and of those who did such testing, 25 percent failed to inform parents of the presence of asbestos. Some school districts did comply faithfully, however, and a portion of these reacted precipitously to the discovery of asbestos-containing materials. Under pressure from parents and others, some schools undertook to remove even those materials that were in good, undamaged condition. In addition, an EPA poll found that less than one quarter of all abatement projects were conducted in accordance with EPA guidance.

Congress recognized shortcomings in EPA's inspection and response program for asbestos in schools. A House committee complained in 1984 that "technical guidance is lacking on how school officials are to evaluate risks and select appropriate corrective measures."[6] In that year, Congress passed the Asbestos School Hazard Abatement Act, with provisions similar to those of the earlier law but lodged its authority with EPA. This law provided grants and loans for abatement, and Congress appropriated $50 million for this purpose in the 1984 fiscal year. Assistance was to be based upon "the likelihood of releases of asbestos fibers into a school environment." While the act mandated a system of state inspections, EPA provided no standards or guidance, and the law accomplished little. In addition, the agency sought no additional funding for the next two fiscal years, which rendered the act "virtually useless."[7]

Two years later, the new legislation and the new Purple Book had not cured this problem, and Senator Robert Stafford of Vermont emphasized:

> EPA has issued technical guidance, but no standards for asbestos identification, hazard evaluation, and removal. As a result, schools have been uncertain about how to proceed. Too often, pressure from parents has forced school officials to remove asbestos that should have been left in place. Not only has money been spent needlessly, but in some cases, the danger has been increased by disturbing the asbestos. The problem has been exacerbated by untrained and unscrupulous contractors who have preyed on the fears of school occupants and school officials.[8]

Other representatives complained that inspection and cleanup of school asbestos had not proceeded rapidly enough. A memo from one of EPA's own regional asbestos coordinators described the EPA rule as a "dismal failure."

EPA began to spend money to remedy asbestos in schools in 1985. On June 6 the agency made its first set of asbestos abatement awards to school districts that demonstrated financial need and the need for remediation. EPA made awards to 341 schools in 198 school districts amounting in total to about $45 million, most in the form of loans rather than grants. Many school boards were denied funding, or were unaware of the availability of funding, or were unable to fulfill the extensive application requirements of the agency. The administration had little enthusiasm for the program, and Senator David Durenberger of Minnesota vividly complained:

> We have two Federal Governments addressing the asbestos-in-building problem. A Dr. Jekyll, who thinks that asbestos is a problem and that the Federal Government should have an effective program to reduce the asbestos hazard facing the Nation's school children and school personnel; and a Mr. Hyde, who has made every effort to prevent effective Federal action on the asbestos problem, so that killers like lung cancer and

mesothelioma can continue to shorten the lives of children and workers.[9]

Moreover, even Senator Durenberger's Dr. Jekyll had a dark side — the "concerned" federal government promoted radical asbestos removal actions that often elevated exposure levels. A Vermont school superintendent complained that "[b]y premature and often false press releases to the media, the EPA caused near panic among parents and teachers in many of our school systems."[10]

In this context, Congress took action to modify EPA's asbestos-in-schools program. In 1986 the legislature passed the Asbestos Hazard Emergency Response Act (AHERA). The findings and purpose of this act stated:

> The Environmental Protection Agency's rule on local education-al agency inspection for, and notification of, the presence of friable asbestos-containing material in school buildings includes neither standards for the proper identification of asbestos-containing material and appropriate response actions with respect to friable asbestos-containing material, nor a requirement that response actions with respect to friable asbestos-containing material be carried out in a safe and complete manner once actions are found to be necessary. As a result of the lack of regulatory guidance from the Environmental Protection Agency, some schools have not undertaken response action while many others have undertaken expensive projects without knowing if their action is necessary, adequate, or safe. Thus, the danger of exposure to asbestos continues to exist in schools, and some exposure actually may have increased due to the lack of Federal standards and improper response action.[11]

AHERA directed EPA to adopt regulations requiring inspection for asbestos in schools and specifying the implementation of appropriate response actions. Where asbestos-containing materials were significantly damaged, Congress ordered that some abatement action (removal, enclosure, encapsulation, or repair) be undertaken. Congress further directed EPA to study the extent of contamination from asbestos-containing materials in nonschool public buildings.

EPA began developing the rules required by AHERA in 1987. EPA first attempted to develop a negotiated rule with the participation of interested parties, but this effort failed. By October 1987, EPA promulgated a final rule on asbestos-containing materials in schools.[12] This rule required schools (actually, local education agencies) to have inspections conducted by an accredited inspector to classify any health problems. Model state accreditation plans were provided. When asbestos was found, the local education agencies were required to submit management plans to their state's governor. The regulation also contemplated that response actions, including removal, be taken in a safe and effective manner.

The AHERA regulations require local education agencies to use specially trained individuals to conduct inspections for asbestos, develop management plans for identified asbestos, and to design and conduct necessary response actions. Response actions may include operations and maintenance, repair, encapsulation, enclosure, and removal. The rule also compels periodic visual surveillance of materials containing asbestos.

One of the most significant features of the EPA rule is what it did not do. The rule scrupulously avoided any requirement of air monitoring to determine actual exposure to asbestos. Monitoring was rejected because short-term monitoring may miss peak exposures, creating a false sense of precision, and continuous monitoring was deemed too expensive. EPA elected to base any determination of asbestos hazard upon a subjective "eyeballing" of the condition of asbestos-containing materials, to be conducted by local officials. Nor did the rule provide much guidance on response actions, though it did universally authorize removal of asbestos-containing materials, in the discretion of local officials guided by accredited companies.

An organization of present and former asbestos producers, known as the Safe Buildings Alliance, challenged EPA's rule in federal court, arguing that the agency should have provided for monitoring prior to action and should have restricted removal operations. In 1988 the United States circuit court of appeals for the District of Columbia upheld the lawfulness of EPA's rule.[13] While acknowledging deficiencies in the regulation, the court emphasized the "tight timetable" imposed upon EPA action.[14] The court suggested that strict accreditation of contractors could avoid the problem of increased indoor asbestos concentrations after removal.

While EPA's regulations were upheld as legal under AHERA, these rules provide uncertain benefits, at best. The absence of any monitoring requirement means that local officials have no real evidence of the nature of the hazard from identified asbestos-containing materials. The lack of clear guidance on response actions will force local officials to rely on private asbestos contractors, who have a self-interest in removal operations, from which they profit. The federal court recognized that local officials have "harkened to the self-interested advice of newly created asbestos removal firms and ordered removal of all" asbestos-containing materials; these removals were "sometimes unnecessary, at times even detrimental, since slipshod work may increase ambient concentrations of asbestos."[15] The court emphasized EPA's new accreditation requirements, but these do not remove the inherent conflict of interest involved in having asbestos removal contractors centrally involved in decisions about proper response actions. Nor has EPA provided evidence that even well-conducted removal operations reduce indoor asbestos contamination. In the absence of any monitoring requirement, either pre- or postremoval, we can never know whether the AHERA regulations are preventing or creating a public health problem.

AHERA also has suffered problems of implementation. The law has not been fully funded and representatives have accused EPA of "foot-dragging" in implementing the law. The October 12, 1988, deadline for local inspections and management plans proved unrealistic. Schools had difficulty raising the financing necessary for compliance, while maintaining the quality of their educational programs. School districts confronted a shortage of certified inspectors of asbestos and preparers of management plans, which made it impossible to meet the act's requirements. One congressman declared that AHERA had "become a nightmare for financially strapped school districts."[16]

In view of the problems with Congress's deadline, the AHERA compliance date was extended to allow schools to request deferral of the requirements until May 9, 1989. Only 40 percent of schools met the October 12 deadline, and a third of the remaining schools completely disregarded the regulation, failing even to request a deferral of their obligations. While more than 90 percent of school systems complied by May 9, extending the deadline did not cure the fundamental problems of the law. Representative Thomas Luken of Ohio summarized the situation:

We learned that the infrastructure for carrying out the AHERA program — the accredited inspectors, management planners, and abatement contractors necessary for performing AHERA functions—is not in place. Because of this, the rush to meet the October 1988 and July 1989 AHERA deadlines may actually increase the risks from asbestos exposure to the Nation's school population.[17]

Asbestos response was hampered by other problems. The administration's 1990 budget contained only modest increases for EPA's program and proposed eliminating the grant and loan assistance to local school districts. Fortunately, EPA has begun to place more emphasis on managing asbestos in place and discouraging removal operations. Unfortunately, AHERA has yet to realize genuine benefits for public health.

New legislation introduced in 1989 is intended to improve the record of AHERA. New Jersey Representative, at the time, James Florio and New Jersey Senator Frank Lautenberg introduced a bill to extend AHERA for five years. Unfortunately, this bill does not significantly modify the approach of AHERA, but focuses on financing. The proposed legislation doubles authorizations for loans and grants, to $250 million, and sets deadlines for EPA dissemination of this money. When introducing the bill, the legislators resorted to the traditional scare tactics regarding the threat of asbestos-containing materials. In the absence of structural changes in the statute, this additional revenue is as likely to produce unnecessary, hazardous school asbestos removal as it is to cause any effective response to the limited problem of asbestos in schools.

Notwithstanding the problems in the federal government's asbestos-in-schools program, there is increasing pressure for federal action against asbestos in other categories of buildings. In November 1988 the Service Employees International Union (SEIU) formally petitioned EPA to adopt a rule extending its school asbestos control program to other public and commercial buildings. EPA rejected this petition, in part because there are not enough qualified abatement workers. The agency chose to focus on assessing and upgrading any response actions taken in nonschool buildings. The union then filed suit in federal court to compel the agency to mandate inspection and regulate abatement for all public and commercial buildings, including any residential developments with ten units or more.

The SEIU litigation produced a dialogue with EPA and building owners, and the union voluntarily suspended the adversary proceedings. The likelihood of regulation is slim, but SEIU hopes to reach a consensus with real estate, banking, and insurance industry representatives to prod EPA into action. All parties are now agreed that asbestos removal is not required in many cases and that alternative control measures should be investigated.

On a parallel track, bills to respond to nonschool asbestos-containing materials in building have been introduced in Congress. Then-representative Florio of New Jersey introduced legislation that would require asbestos inspection, management, and abatement for all government buildings. This bill also would require private building owners to follow federal standards for any voluntary asbestos abatement actions. The latter requirement is responsive to demands by both the Service Employees International Union and building owners that EPA develop standards for training and accrediting asbestos removal workers. This proposed legislation would not impose the enormous and unnecessary expense of widespread removal in private buildings.

Other federal agencies have adopted rules that respond to indoor asbestos exposure. In 1977 the Consumer Product Safety Commission banned asbestos-containing consumer patching compounds and other products containing more than 1 percent asbestos.[18] CPSC has also announced a hitherto unfulfilled intent to regulate asbestos in all consumer products. OSHA regulations apply to commercial settings, such as office employees in buildings containing asbestos products.[19] OSHA expressly indicated, however, that its relatively high exposure standard was unlikely to be exceeded in an office environment.

State Regulation

States have been vigorous in responding to indoor asbestos exposures. New York's legislation on the subject, the School Asbestos Safety Act, was adopted in 1979 and predates even the federal legislation. Recent years have seen a flurry of action on the state level. In 1987 alone, state legislatures passed thirty-three laws dealing with asbestos in some manner, many of them involving abatement actions. Forty states have passed laws intended to limit exposure to asbestos, thirty-nine states have laws that license or otherwise certify workers dealing with asbestos-containing materials, and forty-seven states have some work standards for asbestos abatement projects. While most state laws focus on school exposures, a number of states address other buildings. Twenty states conduct inspections of state-owned buildings, either under statutory requirements or as a matter of policy. Seventeen of these states provide for management plans in state-owned buildings. Four states provide for inspection and management of some limited categories of other buildings.

In general, the state accreditation programs are weaker than that established by EPA. In 1988 only Massachusetts had an accreditation program sufficient to displace federal oversight. Only New Jersey was found to have a school inspection and abatement program equal to the standards of AHERA. Some states have gone beyond federal require-ments – thirty states require inspections for state-owned buildings, and three states have some inspection requirements for private non-school buildings. These private building requirements are largely limited to child-care centers. The National Conference of State Legis-latures declared that Kansas, New Jersey, Oklahoma, and Rhode Island "have adopted their own extensive abatement standards which go far beyond federal standards."[20] Other states provide financial assistance to abatement projects in even privately owned buildings. In short, states have suddenly become quite active in responding to indoor asbestos exposures, though their responses vary widely.

Virginia has a vigorous program for control of indoor asbestos exposures. An asbestos inspection is a condition of acquiring or renew-ing a license for any hospital or child-care center in the state. Virginia also requires such an inspection before renovating or demolishing any building, with limited exceptions for individual residences and small rental units. The state also licenses abatement contractors.

Some cities have also acted against asbestos in buildings. New York City passed a law in 1985 that requires inspection for asbestos when-ever a building is to be altered, renovated, or demolished. If asbestos is found, the material must be removed or sealed insofar as necessary to prevent its disturbance. Building owners have already spent millions of dollars to remove or encapsulate asbestos and recently have sued to prevent enforcement of the law.

One area where states have gone beyond the federal government is in air monitoring. While the federal government program contains no attempt to measure asbestos exposures, at least eleven states now require some monitoring (Colorado, Florida, Louisiana, Minnesota, Montana, Nevada, New Hampshire, New Jersey, North Carolina, North Dakota, and Rhode Island). A 1988 Colorado law required establishment of numerical standards for indoor asbestos exposures, in order to avoid unnecessary removal operations. This law directs regulators to set a maximum allowable asbestos level which shall be the highest level of airborne asbestos under normal conditions which allows for protection of the general public; except that, until the commission adopts by regulation a level, the maximum allowable asbestos level for the general public shall be 0.1 fibers per cubic centimeter of air, measured during normal occupancy and calculated as an eight-hour time-weighted average. A recent North Carolina law sets a maximum airborne asbestos exposure level for public access areas at 0.01 fibers greater than 5 microns in length per cubic centimeter of air. This approach, which focuses on actual health risks from asbestos, should provide a more limited, focused, and effective response to indoor asbestos exposures.

New York was a leader in addressing indoor asbestos exposures. The New York School Asbestos Safety Act provides that the state's commissioner of health shall inform school districts of the asbestos problem, provide necessary scientific and technical information, and "cause local school districts to undertake an inspection of all public elementary and secondary school buildings." The New York law also sets up a program for "identifying and eliminating those asbestos materials which constitute imminent health hazards." The state commissioner of health is to determine the asbestos air concentrations that constitute such an imminent hazard to health. The law addresses primarily situations where exposures exceed 0.01 fibers/cc. New York also recognizes that asbestos hazards may be eliminated by containment as well as removal. The New York law, which employs air monitoring, focuses on real health hazards, and considers various remedial responses, provides a measured response to asbestos in schools.

California also has adopted sensible legislation for asbestos in schools. The California education code provides for inspections and informing local officials regarding the presence of asbestos-containing materials in schools. Before possibly unnecessary response actions, this code calls for "air monitoring to determine need for asbestos abatement." This section specifically states that for purposes of funding remedial projects, "the factors determining the need for abatement of friable asbestos or potentially friable asbestos shall include, but not be limited to, visual inspection and bulk samples and air monitoring showing an airborne concentration of asbestos in the school building in excess of the standard 0.01 fibers/cc." This emphasis on air monitoring is wise, though the law specifically declares that air monitoring is not required precedent to abating asbestos contained in pipe and block insulation. The law also directs the State Department of Health services to report "on the most effective air monitoring standard for the airborne concentration of asbestos in any public school building that is both economically and technologically feasible." California law also provides that schools in which asbestos abatement has been conducted may not be reoccupied until air monitoring demonstrates that indoor asbestos does not exceed 0.01 fibers/cc. This law provides a judicious approach to asbestos in schools that seems far preferable to the federal action. In addition, the state provides grants for asbestos abatement.

California law also addresses asbestos in some nonschool buildings. The California Health and Safety Code dictates an assessment of asbestos problems in public buildings and an "emergency" procedure for buildings in which asbestos materials produce "an imminent and severe threat to human health." This same legislation provides that the owner of any building constructed prior to 1979 must inform its employees of any asbestos-containing materials present as well as the nature of the risk that the asbestos creates. An exception to notification requirements is created for "uniquely and physically defined" areas that are not connected to a common ventilation system. For residential and commercial buildings, the California legislature recently passed a law requiring real property sellers to disclose the presence of asbestos on the property (as well as risks from radon, formaldehyde, and other environmental hazards). California has undertaken a vigorous response to indoor asbestos contamination, yet the state has avoided the panicky overreaction often associated with asbestos in schools.

Most other states have adopted some legal authority for controlling asbestos in schools, but their scope and approaches vary considerably. Arguably, such a "patchwork quilt of state statutes providing different levels of protection to schoolchildren around the country is not acceptable."[21] While an effective federal response would be optimal, EPA seems incapable of providing one. Until this effective federal response is forthcoming, state legislation can play an important role in remedying hazardous situations and restraining unnecessary removal operations. Exhibit 6.1 summarizes the state authority and policies with regard to indoor asbestos management and abatement.

Individual school districts also may respond to asbestos hazards. These districts have a poor record of compliance with federal regulations, however, and should not be relied upon to address these hazards. Typical school districts lack the expertise essential to wise remedial

Exhibit 6.1
Summary of State Asbestos Control Programs

Building Inspections

Schools	Eleven states require inspections by statute Three states conduct inspections as a matter of policy
State-Owned Buildings	Eleven states require inspections by statute Nine states conduct inspections as a matter of policy
Other Buildings	Four states require inspections of other types (e.g., municipal) of buildings

Building Management Plans

Schools	Eight states require management plans by statute or regulation
State-Owned Buildings	Nine states require management plans by statute or regulation Eight states develop and implement management plans as a matter of policy
Other Buildings	Four states require management plans in other buildings

Accreditation

39 States have some type of accreditation program

Ten states have statutes and are currently promulgating regulations

Four states license contractors with demonstrated completion of an EPA-approved asbestos training course

Abatement Standards

38 States have adopted NESHAP-type regulations and have enforcement authority from EPA

23 States have adopted OSHA-type standards relating to asbestos

Enforcement Standards

Most states can conduct on-site inspections and levy civil fines for violations

actions. Many such districts also lack the financial resources required. When school districts possess adequate resources, they too often are stampeded into unnecessary removal actions that exacerbate the indoor asbestos risk in their classrooms.[22]

Private companies also have taken action against asbestos found in commercial buildings. As early as 1979, IBM Corporation designed an asbestos control policy, providing for operations, maintenance, and abatement of asbestos-containing materials, even at a 25 percent increase in occupancy costs.[23] A survey of executives found that nearly half had inspected their buildings for asbestos-containing materials.

For those who identified asbestos, 40 percent reported their intent to remove the asbestos.[24] The presence of asbestos-containing materials tends to reduce the sales price of a building by approximately 20 percent.

The threat of potential liability, elaborated in chapters 9 and 10, has prompted many private building owners to abate asbestos in their structures. Major real estate investors, including Prudential, Aetna, and Metropolitan, "have internal policies against investing in or making loans secured by real estate assets containing asbestos." Banks are also pressuring for abatement as a condition for making loans for real estate.[25]

Notes

1. 43 Fed. Reg. 26374 (1978).

2. 44 Fed. Reg. 40900 (1979).

3. Robert D. Lang, *Danger in the Classroom: Asbestos in the Public Schools*, 10 COLUMBIA J. OF ENVIRONMENTAL LAW 111, 122–23 (1985).

4. 47 Fed. Reg. 23360 (1982).

5. *Id.*

6. H.R. Rep. No. 803, 98th Cong., 2d Sess. 19 (1984).

7. Lang, p. 125.

8. 132 Cong. Rec. S1476 (daily ed. February 20, 1986).

9. Hearing on the Asbestos School Hazard Abatement Act of 1984 – Oversight before the Sen. Comm. on Environment and Public Workers, 99th Cong., 1st Sess. 9 (July 12, 1985).

10. Hearing on Hazardous Asbestos Abatement before the Subcomm. on Toxic Substances and Environmental Oversight of the Sen. Comm. on Environment and Public Works, 99th Cong., 2d Sess. 67 (May 15, 1986).

11. 132 Cong. Rec. H8816–17 (daily ed. October 1, 1986).

12. 52 Fed. Reg. 41826 (1987).

13. *Safe Buildings Alliance v. Environmental Protection Agency*, 846 F.2d 79 (D.C. Cir. 1988).

14. 846 F.2d at 81.

15. 846 F.2d at 80.

16. CONGRESSIONAL RECORD, April 27, 1989, p. E1425.

17. CONGRESSIONAL RECORD, June 27, 1988, p. H4736.

18. 42 Fed. Reg. 63362 (1977).

19. 51 Fed. Reg. 22677 (1986).

20. INDOOR POLLUTION NEWS, April 7, 1988, p. 3.

21. Lang, p. 128.

22. Frank B. Cross, *Asbestos in Schools: A Remonstrance Against Panic*, 11 COLUMBIA J. OF ENVIRONMENTAL LAW 73, 88–92 (1986).

23. INDOOR POLLUTION NEWS, January 26, 1989, p. 6.

24. *Id.*

25. Kirkland, *What's Current in Asbestos Regulations*, 23 U. RICHMOND L. REV. 375, 385 (1989).

7

GOVERNMENT CONTROL OF
INDOOR FORMALDEHYDE RISKS

Risk from indoor exposures to formaldehyde was briefly at the forefront of government regulatory concern. This risk received considerable publicity, prompting the Consumer Product Safety Commission, the Environmental Protection Agency, and the Department of Housing and Urban Development to initiate action to control indoor formaldehyde concentrations. All these efforts went awry, however. CPSC focused exclusively on formaldehyde insulation, but the commission's planned actions were too extreme and struck down in court. EPA devoted great effort to avoiding regulation, then backed down and agreed to act, and now seems irrevocably stalled. HUD actually adopted regulations, but they were so mild that they have little effect. The formaldehyde experience reveals that regulatory authority and attention to indoor air pollution is insufficient; government must also employ effective procedures to effect the regulation. Some states have also responded to the threat of indoor formaldehyde, but state action has dwelt upon the now defunct formaldehyde insulation industry and provided little attention to the multitude of formaldehyde sources indoors.

Federal Control of Indoor Formaldehyde

The federal government's efforts to control indoor formaldehyde exposures can be described as checkered, at best. Unlike its approach to some serious indoor hazards, the government has moved directly to restrict sources of indoor formaldehyde. Unfortunately, these attempts to regulate formaldehyde were diffused among several agencies; confused by erratic, inconsistent decisions; hampered by political demands; and disabled by seemingly incompetent decisionmaking.

The Consumer Product Safety Commission first reacted to the risks of indoor formaldehyde exposure. During the 1970s the CPSC received hundreds of complaints from individuals whose homes contained urea formaldehyde foam insulation (UFFI). These individuals complained of varying irritant symptoms, presumably from formaldehyde exposure. In October 1976 the Consumer Office of the Denver District Attorney's Office requested development of a product safety standard for home insulation, including UFFI. Other consumer protection offices informally asked for action. CPSC registered these complaints and requests but took no affirmative action on UFFI.

The commission's investigation into UFFI took on greater urgency in 1979, when the Chemical Industry Institute of Toxicology reported its evidence that formaldehyde caused cancer in rats. CPSC conducted a series of field hearings in 1980, focusing primarily on the irritant effects of indoor formaldehyde exposure. The commission also began assembling data on exposure levels and harms. CPSC was unable to demonstrate a clear statistical relationship between UFFI and respiratory illness, and the commission's attention therefore turned toward the potential carcinogenic properties of formaldehyde. The commission employed a risk assessment model that extrapolated from animal data and projected that UFFI was responsible for eighty-nine cancer cases among the 2 million individuals in homes with UFFI. In 1980 the CPSC staff combined the evidence of respiratory illness and cancer and produced a proposed regulation that would ban UFFI.

The proposed prohibition on UFFI was resisted vigorously by the Formaldehyde Institute, a trade association of producing companies. The Reagan administration was also unenthusiastic about the proposed ban, but CPSC is an independent regulatory commission largely immune from presidential influence. The ban on UFFI found support from various public health organizations, such as Public Citizen, associated with Ralph Nader. The scientific community was broadly divided on the accuracy and wisdom of the commission's proposal. In April 1982 CPSC issued a final rule banning the future use of UFFI in schools and homes, on a 4-1 vote.[1]

The ban was promptly challenged by the Formaldehyde Institute in federal court. Environmental groups countersued, seeking to extend the ban to all commercial buildings. In 1983 the court overturned the CPSC rule, as unsupported by substantial evidence.[2] The court first concluded that CPSC lacked adequate data on indoor formaldehyde exposure. The exposure studies conducted were inadequate as a data base for "an exacting, precise, and extremely complicated risk assessment model." The court also suggested that the commission had overstated the carcinogenicity of formaldehyde. The court did not dispute the association of irritant effects with UFFI but observed that CPSC had not demonstrated that these irritant effects justified a complete ban on the insulation. CPSC desired to appeal this decision, but the solicitor general refused to do so. The CPSC action against formaldehyde insulation effectively terminated.

While CPSC lost in court, the commission succeeded in reality. The reports of adverse effects associated with UFFI were picked up in the media and extensively publicized. This coverage fanned public fears. By 1980 installation of UFFI had already begun to dwindle. By 1982 the UFFI industry had all but disappeared. The CPSC action, combined with preexisting public concern, effectively eliminated the use of formaldehyde insulation.

The indoor risk from formaldehyde then lay dormant at CPSC, though a variety of other products may produce exposures exceeding that of UFFI. In 1986 the Consumer Federation of America petitioned CPSC to regulate emissions from pressed-wood products, but the commission denied the petition. In 1989, however, CPSC initiated negotiations with industry representatives to control formaldehyde emissions from pressed wood. The commission found the industry's voluntary 0.3 ppm standard to be unduly high and sought a reduction to 0.1 ppm. CPSC also asked that pressed-wood products be graded for formaldehyde emissions, so that consumers might choose safer products.

The Environmental Protection Agency also considered indoor formaldehyde exposures in the early 1980s. EPA's authority to regulate formaldehyde arose under the Toxic Substances Control Act, which enables the agency to address unreasonable risks. Before initiating such regulation (under section 6 of TSCA), EPA is to determine whether a substance presents a significant risk (under section 4[f]). After formally receiving the chemical industry data on formaldehyde's potential carcinogenicity in 1980, EPA began evaluating the substance for a section 4(f) determination.

EPA's Office of Toxic Substances recommended that formaldehyde receive a section 4(f) determination on May 20, 1981, the very day that

Ann Gorsuch took office as EPA administrator under newly elected President Reagan.[3] Gorsuch directed newly appointed deputy administrator John Hernandez to review the data and make recommendations. Hernandez met with representatives of the Formaldehyde Institute and the Chemical Manufacturers Association, who downplayed the risk presented by formaldehyde. These meetings quickly became controversial, as Congress protested the lack of environmentalist representation.

In September 1981 the Natural Resources Defense Council requested an explanation for EPA's failure to list formaldehyde under section 4(f). Administrator Gorsuch expedited the agency's consideration, and in February 1982 the agency officially decided not to list formaldehyde under TSCA. This decision came in the form of a memorandum from John Todhunter, assistant administrator for pesticides and toxic substances of EPA. The Todhunter memo accepted formaldehyde's potential carcinogenicity but presented risk assessment data and concluded that the risk from formaldehyde was insignificant and below the risk levels appropriate for government regulation. Among other controversial aspects of the memo, Todhunter argued that there was a "threshold" level of exposure, below which formaldehyde might not cause cancer.

The Todhunter memo produced a firestorm of criticism that went far beyond the traditional environmentalist community. Scientists, the media, and the Congress joined in the criticism. The House of Representatives Committee on Science and Technology held extensive hearings on the formaldehyde decision, and produced a lengthy report that was sharply critical of the scientific basis for the Todhunter memo.[4] Congress and others also criticized the appearance, if not the reality, of bias in EPA's decisionmaking process. The Natural Resources Defense Council and the American Public Health Association filed suit in federal court, seeking a review of EPA's decision not to list formaldehyde under section 4(f).

At about this time, Reagan's EPA leaders suffered other difficulties, even scandals. Gorsuch was replaced by the widely respected William Ruckelshaus. Ruckelshaus negotiated with environmental organizations and agreed to reconsider the decision not to list formaldehyde. In May 1984 EPA reversed its prior position and issued a notice applying section 4(f) to formaldehyde exposure in the manufacture of apparel from fabrics containing formaldehyde and to mobile homes with manufacturing materials that contained formaldehyde.[5] The new listing decision was based upon essentially the same data that existed before, though EPA employed a somewhat more conservative approach to assessing the cancer risk.

EPA ultimately deferred to OSHA coverage of the manufacturing risks of formaldehyde in 1986, leaving only mobile home exposures to be addressed under TSCA. EPA's risk assessment did not employ worst-case assumptions but also did not assume a threshold for the carcinogenic effects of formaldehyde. The agency estimated an average indoor formaldehyde concentration of 0.25 ppm in manufactured homes and assumed ten years of exposure for occupants. EPA's most likely estimate was that these exposures would cause one cancer per year, though very conservative assumptions could yield an estimate as high as 588 cancers from formaldehyde exposures in manufactured homes. EPA concluded that these risks were sufficiently significant to justify listing under section 4(f).

Simply listing a substance under TSCA invokes no control measures. Rather, the section 4(f) decision was to trigger a future regulatory decision under section 6. Perhaps EPA's listing decision only seized a "political opportunity" to "quiet critics of the administration without taking any immediate and costly regulatory action."[6] Listing was not followed by prompt regulatory action. In 1985 EPA's expert Science Advisory Board reviewed the evidence on formaldehyde's carcinogenic risk and in 1987 the agency classified formaldehyde as a "probable human carcinogen." EPA reported an intent to issue regulations in August 1988 but failed to do so. More than five years have passed since the section 4(f) listing decision, and EPA has yet to take any regulatory action against indoor formaldehyde exposures, in mobile homes or elsewhere. At this point, federal government action on indoor formaldehyde risks has consisted of considerable sound and fury, signifying nothing.

Formaldehyde has proved a tricky regulatory problem, confounding OSHA, as well as EPA and CPSC. Interestingly, there was a point when the only federal agency regulating formaldehyde was the Department of Housing and Urban Development. HUD first announced an intent to regulate formaldehyde in 1979 and 1981, at the time of the first carcinogenicity evidence. The mobile home industry soon came to favor federal regulation, to preempt or forestall state efforts to regulate formaldehyde exposures in mobile homes. The industry also decided that HUD was their preferred locus for such regulation.

In 1984 HUD issued a regulation, based largely on input from the mobile home industry.[7] HUD chose to defer to EPA on the cancer question and based its regulation solely on the irritant effects of formaldehyde. The HUD standard for pressed-wood products in mobile homes was set at a high level of allowable emissions. HUD required that emissions not exceed 0.2 ppm from plywood or 0.3 ppm from particleboard. In most cases, these emission standards should keep ambient indoor formaldehyde concentrations at 0.4 ppm or below. At the time of HUD's action, most mobile home producers were alreading using stable resins that emit less than the HUD requirement. This regulation accomplished little, and one commentator found that the "formaldehyde example shows that environmental rulemaking can become an uneven bargaining process in which the regulated party can dictate its own standard if it has superior technical knowledge and political access."[8] The HUD standard was effectively "four times higher than the standards in effect for nuclear submarines, Air Force airplane cockpits, and NASA spacecraft, and almost twice the time-weighted average exposure level allowed for occupational workers."[9] States unsuccessfully challenged the regulations as insufficiently protective.

While HUD perhaps should be congratulated for actually promulgating a rule, the department's regulation can be criticized. Indeed, CPSC opposed the proposed standard as insufficiently protective of health. As noted, the product standards adopted were lenient. Even these rules did not apply to medium-density fiberboard, a common source of formaldehyde in mobile homes. HUD rejected an ambient standard, setting a maximum allowable exposure level in manufactured housing, which would have ensured greater protection of health. While the product standards are designed to ensure a maximum concentration of 0.4 ppm, there is no guarantee of this end. Indeed, HUD virtually conceded that homes containing medium-density fiberboard or other conditions would exceed the standard.[10] In addition, the department assumed a rather high ventilation rate that may be unrepresentative of mobile homes. HUD did require that manufacturers offer a ventilation improvement option with each home covered.

State Control of Indoor Formaldehyde

Several states have vigorously controlled indoor formaldehyde exposures. While most states have little or no program to control such exposures, major states have adopted sensible programs.

The state of Massachusetts was at the forefront of formaldehyde regulation. In November 1979, before CPSC took action against UFFI, the Massachusetts commissioner of the Department of Public Health enacted a rule banning the sale, distribution, and all uses of UFFI in the state. The Massachusetts commissioner also enacted a compulsory repurchase program in which manufacturers, dealers, and installers of UFFI were required to remove the prohibited insulation from houses where installed and refund the purchase price. The commissioner's action was based upon the irritant properties of formaldehyde, and he expressly did not rely on the evidence of carcinogenicity, although he declared that cancer risk provided an additional reason to act.

As in the CPSC regulation, companies challenged the Massachusetts action in court and initially succeeded in overturning major portions of the state rule. On appeal, however, the Supreme Judicial Court of Massachusetts reversed the lower court and upheld the most significant portions of the state's anti-UFFI rule.[11] That court concurred with the health commissioner that there was no threshold below which formaldehyde was entirely innocuous and that there was no perfectly safe method for installation of UFFI.

Following the commissioner's action, the state legislature acted further in 1985. The law provided for air testing of homes still containing UFFI, regulations of testing and remediation firms, and adopted a 0.1 ppm action level for indoor formaldehyde. The law also established a UFFI removal program for homes where levels of formaldehyde are greater than 0.1 ppm or where an occupant has experienced adverse health effects demonstrably caused by formaldehyde.

Other states have passed legislation against excessive indoor formaldehyde concentrations. California prohibited new UFFI installation after June 1, 1981, and authorized its Energy Resources Conservation and Development Commission to adopt regulations concerning UFFI as necessary to protect the public health. New York required that installers of UFFI give written notice to purchasers of the adverse effects associated with formaldehyde exposure. Texas required notification of mobile home purchasers of potential formaldehyde risks and declared that the failure of a manufactured home retailer or manufacturer to comply with its Manufactured Housing Standards Act and formaldehyde warning would provide conclusive evidence that the mobile home was not habitable.

Minnesota has adopted the most extensive and promising framework for controlling indoor formaldehyde exposure. Minnesota law requires a manufacturer of building materials or a builder whose housing contains urea formaldehyde to provide purchasers or lessees with the following written warning:

SOME OF THE BUILDING MATERIALS USED IN THIS HOME (OR THESE BUILDING MATERIALS) EMIT FORMALDEHYDE. EYE, NOSE, AND THROAT IRRITATION, HEADACHE, NAUSEA AND A VARIETY OF ASTHMA-LIKE SYMPTOMS, INCLUDING SHORTNESS OF BREATH, HAVE BEEN REPORTED AS A RESULT OF FORMAL-DEHYDE EXPOSURE. ELDERLY PERSONS AND YOUNG CHILDREN, AS WELL AS ANYONE WITH A HISTORY OF ASTHMA, ALLERGIES, OR LUNG PROBLEMS, MAY BE AT GREATER RISK. RESEARCH IS CONTINUING ON THE POSSIBLE LONG-TERM EF-FECTS OF EXPOSURE TO FORMALDEHYDE.
REDUCED VENTILATION MAY ALLOW FORMALDEHYDE AND OTHER CONTAMINANTS TO ACCUMULATE IN THE INDOOR AIR. HIGH INDOOR TEMPERATURES AND HUMIDITY RAISE FORMAL-DEHYDE LEVELS. WHEN A HOME IS TO BE LOCATED IN AREAS SUBJECT TO EXTREME SUMMER TEMPERATURES, AN AIR-CON-DITIONING SYSTEM CAN BE USED TO CONTROL INDOOR TEMPERATURE LEVELS. OTHER MEANS OF CONTROLLED MECHANICAL VENTILATION CAN BE USED TO REDUCE LEVELS OF FORMALDEHYDE AND OTHER INDOOR AIR CONTAMINANTS.
IF YOU HAVE ANY QUESTIONS REGARDING THE HEALTH EF-FECTS OF FORMALDEHYDE, CONSULT YOUR DOCTOR OR LOCAL HEALTH DEPARTMENT.

Building materials expressly include "draperies, carpeting, furniture and furnishings not normally permanently affixed to a housing unit." Sellers of such building materials are also subject to the written disclosure requirement.

Minnesota action is not limited to warnings but also contains regulatory measures. The state independently requires that all plywood and particleboard used in newly constructed housing units must comply with federal product standards and extends this coverage to medium-density fiberboard, which is not regulated by the federal government. Minnesota also requires that the seller of a newly con-structed housing unit must ensure that "the ambient indoor air of any habitable room in the unit shall not contain more than 0.4 parts of formaldehyde per million parts of air." Minnesota also enables regula-tions of building materials as necessary to ensure that indoor levels of 0.4 ppm formaldehyde are not exceeded. The state also regulates residential insulation type and installation to protect against high levels of indoor formaldehyde. Manufacturers of products that fail to meet Minnesota standards must pay the reasonable cost of repair or even relocation of consumers, in the presence of documented health problems.

Notes

1. 47 Fed. Reg. 14366 (1982).

2. *Gulf South Insulation v. U.S. Consumer Product Safety Commission*, 701 F.2d 1137 (5th Cir. 1983).

3. John D. Graham, Laura C. Green & Marc J. Roberts, IN SEARCH OF SAFETY (1988), p. 30.

4. *Review of the Scientific Basis of the Environmental Protection Agency's Carcinogenic Risk Assessment of Formaldehyde*, House Comm. on Science and Technology, 98th Cong., 1st Sess. (1983).

5. 49 Fed. Reg. 21870 (1984).

6. Graham, Green & Roberts, p. 34.

7. 49 Fed. Reg. 31996 (1984).

8. Carl Meyer, *The Environmental Fate of Toxic Wastes, the Certainty of Harm, Toxic Torts, and Toxic Regulation*, 19 ENVIRONMENTAL LAW 321, 359 (1988).

9. *Id.* at 358–59.

10. 49 Fed. Reg. at 31998.

11. *Borden, Inc. v. Commissioner of Public Health*, 448 N.E.2d 367 (Mass. 1983).

8

GOVERNMENT CONTROL OF OTHER INDOOR AIR POLLUTION RISKS

Government response to the manifold risks of indoor air pollutants other than radon, asbestos, and formaldehyde has been incomplete. Some indoor health problems have received prompt attention and effective response, while most indoor health threats are ignored by the government. Regulatory authority over indoor air pollutants is fractured, and agency actions are correspondingly erratic. Congress is now considering comprehensive indoor air quality legislation. While adoption of such legislation would represent progress, the pending bills offer little authority to protect health from indoor air contamination.

Regulatory action for the immediately foreseeable future will be constrained by existing statutes. Some laws, such as those controlling pesticide production and use, provide ample authority to protect indoor air. EPA has acted under this authority. Other indoor air pollutants, such as volatile organic compounds and combustion byproducts, have no specific enabling legislation. While EPA and CPSC potentially have authority to respond to these problems, relatively little action has been taken. For other indoor pollutants, such as microbiological contaminants, there is no basis for regulatory authority and no prospect of federal action.

States are acting to respond to indoor air contamination, but states also lack comprehensive legislation on indoor air quality. States have acted against volatile organic compounds and some combustion byproducts, though this action is primarily intended to protect outdoor air. Most indoor air pollutants have escaped state attention. Indeed, the only broad response to the complex of indoor air quality problems is being taken by voluntary private organizations, largely unhampered by limited authority, and by building owners, fearful of future litigation.

Federal Control of Other Indoor Air Pollution Risks

The federal government has no general program to monitor, prioritize, and regulate the many varied indoor air pollution problems. The Environmental Protection Agency has no statutory directive to address indoor air pollution, which diminishes the perceived urgency of the problem. Because the statutory authority for action against indoor air contaminants is sometimes ambiguous, federal agencies may be reluctant to proceed. This situation seems to be changing, however, as indoor air pollution has become an increasingly popular political issue.

EPA is showing some increased interest in indoor air quality. A recent report to Congress contained a plea for a new authority to undertake a new response:

> EPA believes that an effective national program to control indoor air pollution will require the application of generic strategies involving provisions for adequate ventilation, and provisions to avoid problems through proper building design, operation and maintenance. This approach, combined with programs targeted to specific individual high risk sources and pollutants would provide a comprehensive, but feasible and cost effective control strategy. EPA does not believe that a pollutant-by-pollutant approach encompassing target levels for individual pollutants would resolve the bulk of indoor air quality problems. Authority to develop and promote building related standards and guidelines designed to achieve adequate indoor air quality would greatly facilitate implementation of such a program.[1]

EPA has not formally proposed any specific legislative language, however, so this more promising approach is not yet on the table.

Congresspersons have introduced a number of bills on indoor air pollution. In 1987 Senator George Mitchell of Maine, who went on to become majority leader of the Senate, introduced legislation that would compel EPA to list all indoor air contaminants and publish health advisories setting safe exposure levels. The Mitchell bill, styled the Indoor Air Quality Act, also provided for grants and technical demonstrations and authorized funding of $58 million per year for five years. The proposed act also established a Council on Indoor Air Quality to coordinate the full range of federal agency activities relating to indoor air quality. This bill shortly was cut back to reduce its funding and to eliminate the requirement for safe exposure levels (for many substances, there may be no absolutely safe level of exposure). Some senators still expressed concern that the proposed legislation would "start small and explode into a new regulatory program."[2] Moreover, EPA showed little enthusiasm for new laws on indoor air pollution. In the Senate, the Mitchell bill and others on indoor air pollution have been pushed onto the back burner while that body grapples with revision and reauthorization of the Clean Air Act.

In the House of Representatives, Joseph P. Kennedy II of Massachusetts introduced legislation for indoor air quality with a dramatic statement that made the national news:

Mr. Speaker, take a deep breath.

The air that is now in your lungs passed through several hundred feet of dark, dusty, dirty ductwork before reaching this room. Twenty-seven different species of fungus have been found growing in the dank recesses of building ventilation systems. Viruses and bacteria that thrive in air ducts have been proven to cause influenza, pneumonia, tuberculosis, and dozens of other diseases, including the deadly Legionnaires' Disease. In adition to those living dangers, the air we breathe indoors can also contain high concentrations of radon, asbestos, formaldehyde, benzene, carbon monoxide, tobacco smoke, lead, chlorine, low-level ozone.[3]

The provisions of Representative Kennedy's bill closely paralleled those in the Mitchell bill. The only regulatory authority involved federal buildings. Indeed, the sponsors of the bill boast that one of its "main virtues" is "that it relies on a nonregulatory approach."[4]

The Bush administration officially opposed the Kennedy bill at hearings in September 1989. EPA argued that the bill was unnecessary because the agency already possessed ample nonregulatory authority and was increasing its commitment to indoor air quality. EPA also contended that the law was too costly and too inflexibly prescriptive. EPA opposed a "chemical-by-chemical" approach that ignored the importance of ventilation and other factors and warned that EPA advisories on indoor pollution could panic the general public. The General Services Administration also opposed the provisions involving federal buildings, which led Representative James Scheuer of New York to characterize GSA as "the most unreconstructed, unregenerate, uncaring private sector manager."[5] Lower-level EPA employees filled the hearing room with buttons expressing their support for action to protect the quality of indoor air in federal buildings where they work.

The administration in general, and EPA in particular, have been extremely hesitant to address indoor air pollution. The 1986 amendments to the Superfund statute directed EPA to prepare a report on indoor air pollution to be submitted to Congress by October 1988. The report was completed early in 1989, but the Office of Management and Budget prevented its release, apparently out of fear that it would lead to costly regulatory requirements. Concerned congresspersons then leaked the report and employed unusual parliamentary maneuvers to ensure its official release. The EPA report concluded that indoor air pollution was causing thousands of deaths and costing billions of dollars annually. Its actual recommendations were rather mild, consisting primarily of additional research and adoption of ventilation guidelines for buildings. While the report gave a boost to the proposed legislation, the White House continued to oppose the bills, and little progress has been made.

An important step was taken in November 1989, when a Senate subcommittee marked up and reported out indoor air quality legislation for the first time. The new bill requires EPA to analyze the adequacy of existing ventilation standards, to survey state and local ventilation requirements, to evaluate their adequacy and compliance costs, and to assess the potential for further standards, presumably on a federal level. This provision is the first hint of federal standards and offers some promise. Insofar as the EPA study is not to be completed for three years, however, to be followed by an indeterminate period of congressional debate, the promise of new legislation is quite limited.

The November revisions also sought to address the problem of sensitive populations, development of management training courses for indoor air pollution, and coordination of indoor air quality research. The bill also directs EPA to focus attention on the problem of multiple chemical sensitivities.

The prospect of comprehensive federal legislation for indoor air pollution is obviously assuming momentum. Such bills are not a top priority, however, and have been held hostage to other, more politically pressing issues. Barring some unexpected crisis, the likelihood of passage for indoor air quality legislation is not great. In addition, the bills under consideration lack substantial regulatory authority and would contribute relatively little to the protection of indoor air quality, even if they were passed.

EPA already possesses considerable nonregulatory authority to research and inform regarding indoor air contaminants. To date, the agency has done relatively little to exercise this authority. Not until 1986 did the agency create its Indoor Air Division, with a very small staff. Funding levels evidence the low priority given to indoor air pollution. EPA's budget for fiscal year 1990 is roughly $5 billion, of which the general indoor air quality program spends about $1 million, or 0.02 percent. While more money is spent on specific indoor air problems, such as radon, the total expenditure is far less than the $400 million budgeted for outdoor air pollution, which presents much smaller risks.

EPA has done a better job for some specific indoor air pollutants, where the agency's authority is clearer. For example, EPA has taken direct regulatory action against pesticides that contaminate indoor air. The Federal Insecticide, Fungicide, and Rodenticide Act (FIFRA) grants the agency considerable authority to protect public health from pesticide exposures. The agency entered a voluntary agreement with Velsicol, the manufacturer of chlordane, to halt production of this termiticide that contaminates indoor air. While the agreement permitted Velsicol to sell off its inventory of chlordane, this decision was challenged by the National Coalition Against the Misuse of Pesticides, and EPA prohibited all commercial use of chlordane as of April 15, 1988. EPA has also prohibited dieldrin, aldrin, and heptachlor for termiticidal use and has required protective labeling on other home-use pesticides. For example, the agency banned the use of indoor fumigating devices that used lindane in 1986. In 1984 the agency canceled all indoor applications of pentachlorophenol and creosote, used as sealants of indoor wood. Exhibit 8.1 summarizes the actions that EPA has taken to prevent indoor exposures to hazardous levels of pesticides.

EPA is preparing other FIFRA actions that may benefit indoor air quality. The agency has initiated investigation of inert ingredients in

Exhibit 8.1
EPA Regulation of Indoor Pesticide Exposures

Issue	Purpose	Status
Termiticides: --Chlordane	Protect public from exposure to termiticides containing cyclodienes	Halted sale of chlordane and heptachlor to pest control operators under MOU with Velsicol (sole manufacturer) until certain conditions are met: 1987. Manufacturers have withdrawn aldrin and dieldrin from market.
--Chlorpyrifos	Assess exposure and health issues	Need for indoor monitoring identified in 1983 report on termiticides. Testing completed.
--Public Information Materials	Answer frequently-asked questions concerning chlordane	Distribute Termiticides Consumer Information factsheet.
Non-Occupational Pesticide Exposure Survey	Measure levels of over 20 pesticides in homes	Data collection from homes in Jacksonville FL and Springfield MA to be completed.
Lindane	Protect public from unsafe exposures to lindane	Continue 1986 cancellation of use of lindane as indoor fumigant.
Wood Preservatives	Protect public from unsafe exposures to specific wood preservatives	Continue 1984 cancellation of: all indoor applications of pentachlorophenol and creosote, use of penta-

		chlorophenol in log homes, requirement for use of sealers on previously-treated wood used indoors. Continue 1986 voluntary consumer awareness program for manufacturers.
Public Information	Answer public inquiries on pesticide Issues	Maintain National Pesticide Telecommunications Network hotline (phone number: 800-858-PEST; in Texas: 806-743-3091).
Anti-Microbials	Determine exposure to anti-microbials from products used in buildings accessible to general public	Implementation of anti-microbial exposure strategy developed in 1987 ongoing. Data collection: 1987 notices of intent to suspend being sent.
Inert Ingredients in Pesticides	Identify toxic inert ingredients used in pesticides and require actions by manufacturer to reduce risks to public health, as appropriate	Implementation of 1987 policy requiring actions on both existing and new inerts ongoing. Deadline for manufacturer application to relabel or reformulate existing inerts: 1987. Program of collecting data on new inerts in progress.

pesticide formulations that may have harmful effects when concentrated in indoor air. EPA also is investigating antimicrobials used in cleaning and disinfection for potential adverse health effects.

For other categories of indoor air pollutants, EPA action is quite limited. For many VOCs, the agency is conducting exposure and risk assessments but has proposed no control action. The agency is preparing voluntary standards for combustion devices, such as kerosene heaters and gas space heaters. For biological contaminants, EPA's role is limited to basic research.

Many indoor air pollutants are produced by household products and thus the Consumer Product Safety Commission has authority to protect indoor air quality. CPSC was unpopular with the Reagan administration, which cut its staffing and budgetary authority. On one occasion, CPSC wanted to make a videotape to warn about threats from humidifiers and the commission lacked the money necessary even to rent a studio. For a time in 1988, CPSC at least professed that indoor air pollution was a top priority. By 1989, the priority status had dropped and by 1990 the commission's already small budget for indoor air quality was slashed dramatically. Research funding was all but eliminated. Cuts in research hindered ongoing research on children's respiratory health and indoor exposures to allergens and pathogens.

While CPSC resources were severely cut, the commission has taken some positive steps to research and control indoor air pollution. It has cooperated with EPA in studying the risks from and promoting voluntary standards for combustion appliances, including kerosene heaters and woodstoves. The commission is at the forefront of concern for biological contaminants, having researched sources of exposure. The commission also has helped develop methods for measuring contamination of viruses, bacteria, and fungi and is developing guidelines to minimize indoor exposure to these contaminants in residential environments. A consumer safety alert was issued in 1989, warning of the hazards presented by humidifiers and giving directions for their safe use. The commission also is working to develop a voluntary industry standard for humidifiers.

The commission has taken limited action against methylene chloride, a solvent used in paints and cleaning fluids. The Consumer Federation of America petitioned CPSC to ban methylene chloride, but the commission initially commenced a public information campaign and labeling requirement.

The Consumer Product Safety Commission also has begun to address allergic reactions to new carpet emissions. The commission is conducting research on emissions and health harms. A hot line was set up to record consumer complaints.

Federal interagency cooperation in the fight against indoor air pollution is also improving. In early 1988 EPA and CPSC signed an agreement for cooperative action against home exposures to toxic substances. The agreement provides for the agencies to share data and coordinate action without wasteful duplication. While the cooperative agreement has accomplished little, the agencies have jointly focused on indoor VOC exposures and informing the public of their hazards. For VOCs, the CPSC is participating in an interagency Integrated Chlorinated Solvents Project to assess the risks associated with certain substances and to propose regulatory options. Exhibit 8.2 reviews some major CPSC actions against indoor air pollution.

The Department of Energy (DOE) also has a considerable influence on indoor air pollution. Historically, DOE has exacerbated the problem by adopting energy conservation measures that produced greater concentrations of indoor contaminants. The Energy Conservation and Production Act directs the department to develop energy conservation performance standards that are mandatory for new federal buildings and advisory for private construction. The DOE 1979 Building Energy Performance Standards induced reduction in ventilation, which increased indoor air pollution. The most recent iteration of the mandatory standards for new federal residential buildings begins to recognize indoor air pollution, by denying building designers any energy conservation credit for savings from reduced ventilation. The standards are nevertheless likely to contribute to the indoor air pollution problem. Private groups, such as the National Wildlife Federation, complained that the standard was "likely to have a substantial impact on indoor air quality even though no credit is given for reduced infiltration levels."[6] While the department assumed a ventilation rate of 0.6 air changes per hour, the New York State Energy Office concluded that homes built in accordance with the standard would have only 0.4 to 0.5 air changes per hour, thereby "rais[ing] humidity levels and increas[ing] concentration of indoor pollutants such as carbon monoxide, radon gas, sulfur dioxide, nitrogen dioxide, and formaldehyde."[7] While the DOE downplayed these risks, even its own assumption of 0.6 air changes per hour is quite low and will reduce the exfiltration of hazardous indoor air pollutants. In addition, a recent

Exhibit 8.2
CPSC Indoor Air Quality Control Activities

Activity	Description
Mandatory Standards and Procedures	
Carbon Tetrachloride Use Ban	Ban on use of carbon tetrachloride in consumer products
Asbestos Use Ban	Ban on use of asbestos in consumer products such as patching compounds
Vinyl Chloride Ban	Ban on use of vinyl chloride in aerosol products.
Voluntary Guidelines	
Combustion Device Performance Guidelines	Recommended limits for emissions from kerosene heaters and unvented gas space heaters
Formaldehyde Emission Guidelines for Wood Products	Recommended limits on emissions from manufactured wood products
Research	
Measurement and Estimation of Exposures and Concentrations	Seven projects studying pollutant emissions, biological monitoring, and modeling
Health Effects	Three projects involving NO_2; kerosene heaters; and biologicals in humidifiers, air conditioners, and vaporizers
Risk and Hazard Assessment	Two projects involving paradichlorobenzene and solvents
Controls Assessment	Three projects investigating wood stoves and air filter evaluations
Information Dissemination	
Publications for Public Education	Indoor air "guidance", "Asbestos in Homes"
Product Label Requirements	Including warnings for asbestos and methylene chloride

change in insulation requirements for EPA's voluntary energy conservation performance standards for commercial and large residential buildings may reduce formaldehyde emissions but increase exposure to the more carcinogenic VOCs.[8]

The Bonneville Power Administration (BPA), a federally owned electric agency in the Northwest, has adopted a more responsible set of energy conservation standards for its energy-efficient homes program.[9] BPA began by estimating that in the absence of action individuals in the region would suffer significantly from indoor air pollutants. The administration quantified the risk from radon at 335 deaths per 100,000 persons, from formaldehyde at 10 deaths per 100,000 persons, and from benzo(a)pyrene of 2.6 deaths per 100,000. BPA adopted ventilation and other standards that would reduce the radon risk by roughly 10 percent, reduce the formaldehyde risk, and save additional energy.

The Bonneville Power Administration program contains a specific indoor air pollution mitigation package with the following requirements:

> exhaust fans for kitchen and bathrooms; designated outside air supplies for combustion appliances; information on indoor air quality; HUD product standards for formaldehyde emissions from structural building materials . . . and radon source control, known as the radon package.[10]

The radon package either requires construction with foundation treatments to prevent entry or the builder must assume responsibility for monitoring radon in the house. If radon measurements exceed 5 pCi/L, the builder must "retrofit the house with the appropriate mitigation measure and activate the measure."[11] BPA estimates that these measures can reduce indoor radon concentrations by 70 percent.

State Control of Other Indoor Air Pollution Risks

Several states have taken action against specific indoor air pollutants. Few states have adopted comprehensive, integrated legislation to address the full range of risks found in ambient indoor air. Individual states have gone far beyond the federal government in responding to particularized risks from given categories of indoor contaminants of concern.

States have been particularly active in addressing indoor VOC exposures, often as a byproduct of regulations for outdoor air quality. New York, for example, has established regulations that limit the VOC content of surface coating processes, such as paints. New York backed down from its plan to regulate VOC content of disinfectants, air fresheners, and insecticides, but directed manufacturers to study the feasibility of reducing this content by 25 percent. Similarly, New Jersey is developing regulations of VOCs in consumer products, including paints, deodorants, and insecticides, among other products. While these rules are aimed at correcting a serious outdoor VOC problem, they offer considerable benefit in reducing indoor exposures as well. Southern California is also developing a program to reduce VOC exposures from paints and deodorants. The Texas Air Control Board proposed to ban the sale of air fresheners containing VOCs, as well as all aerosol products in the Dallas/Fort Worth metroplex. A coalition of Northeast States for Coordinated Air Use Management also has begun developing VOC controls for products. Although these actions are encouraging, they are ironic. All these measures are designed to reduce outdoor ozone concentrations (of which VOCs are a chemical precursor). While outdoor ozone is a serious problem, it pales beside indoor VOC risks, which have received little or no independent attention as a human health threat.

Some states have taken the initiative in response to indoor air pollution. The California Air Resources Board has acknowledged the threats presented by indoor air, directing its staff to draft a plan for regulating indoor air quality. To date, the board's actions are largely limited to research. The California occupational safety agency has established ventilation system regulations for commercial buildings. Washington state recently adopted an indoor air quality law for public buildings. In addition to research, this law recommended stronger regulation of public workplaces, already authorized under the state's occupational safety and health statute. The law also directs the State Building Code Council to review its ventilation and other standards to protect indoor air quality. The state legislature rejected a law that would have placed minimum ventilation standards on all private buildings, but the bill is likely to be reintroduced for future consideration. The states of New Hampshire and Maine have set minimum ventilation standards for state office buildings. The Minnesota Department of Health is attempting to formulate a holistic indoor air pollution program, rather than focusing on individual contaminants. Several states have promulgated ventilation standards, and Exhibit 8.3 presents the leading state and local building operation rules to protect indoor air.

Regulations of specific sources of indoor air pollution are few. Massachusetts regulates sources of combustion byproducts, restricting the kinds of space heaters and portable stoves that may be used. Massachusetts also regulates certain gas appliances and prohibits, for example, constantly burning pilot lights for such appliances, requiring intermittent ignition devices in their stead. Few, if any, states have any laws addressing indoor microbiological contamination.

Exhibit 8.3
State and Local Building Operation Requirements

State or Locality	Regulations Relevant to Indoor Air Quality Control
California	The tightest of new residences must achieve at least 0.7 air changes per hour ASHRAE Standard 62 ventilation requirements adopted Workplaces must be monitored to ensure that ASHRAE Standard 62-1981 ventilation rates are met in building operation
New York (State)	Energy Conservation Construction Code adopts ASHRAE Standards 62-73 and 90-75
South Dakota	Medical Facilities Building Code specifies ventilation system design and operation requirements to supply acceptable indoor air quality
New Jersey	Public Employee Occupational Safety and Health Act requires ASHRAE Standard 62-1981 ventilation rates in State occupied buildings
Los Angeles	Adopted 1982 Edition the Uniform Building Code, incorporating minimum ventilation limits for places of assembly, garages, and residences

States are now beginning to consider regulation of electromagnetic field exposures. California is at the vanguard of this action, as the state Public Utility Commission has considered regulations on such exposures but has not yet taken official action. Instead, the commission is conducting a study to be completed at the end of 1990. While awaiting such rules some counties and other local authorities in California have begun warning of risks from electromagnetic radiation. Even this limited action is restricted to large transmission lines, however, and government has taken no significant action against indoor electromagnetic exposures from small appliances and other sources.

Private organizations also have acted to reduce risks from the many sources of indoor air pollution. The most significant of these actions was taken by the American Society of Heating, Refrigeration, and Air-Conditioning Engineers (ASHRAE). The development of ASHRAE ventilation standards was described in Chapter 5. In October 1989 ASHRAE modified its Standard 62 dealing with these problems, primarily to address the broad range of risks presented by indoor air contaminants.

The primary change in the new ASHRAE standard is to require that heating, ventilating, and air-conditioning systems be designed to provide at least 15 cubic feet per minute per person of outdoor air ventilation in mechanically ventilated buildings. This is a considerable increase from the previous requirement of only 5 cubic feet per minute per person of ventilation. Some have estimated that uniform adoption of this new standard would cure over 90 percent of indoor air pollution problems in commercial buildings. ASHRAE also requires proper maintenance of ventilation systems and procedures to insure proper interior circulation of air. ASHRAE also recommended that the public be exposed to levels of certain pollutants no greater than one-tenth the level allowed by the Occupational Health and Safety Administration for industrial settings. ASHRAE's actions represent an undeniably important advance in indoor air quality, but they are no solution. One recent article commented:

> ASHRAE's methods of determining and implementing ventilation standards fail to protect office workers for several reasons. First, ASHRAE's standards do not have the force of law. In addition, these standards are typically part of building codes, which usually apply only to new buildings. Also, agencies enforce the standards poorly. Finally, since ASHRAE's guidelines cover only thirty-four compounds, they fail to regulate hundreds of chemicals present in the workplace.[12]

While promising, this standard is only a guideline and has no independent force. While ASHRAE standards have often been adopted in enforceable building codes, previous iterations of Standard 62 have not been adopted in many codes. Preliminary reaction suggests that this new modification may also meet some resistance from code designers. Some codes still have no ventilation requirement whatsoever. The effectiveness of the ASHRAE modification is thus hostage to local authorities and those who enforce the codes. Moreover, even if the change is widely adopted, many jurisdictions may choose to apply the standard only to new construction, rather than to existing buildings.

Unforced private decisions may produce the greatest benefit in indoor air quality. Economic incentives may stimulate increased private activity for indoor air quality, in commercial buildings at least. The potential liability to tenant companies, their employees, and visitors may induce greater attention to indoor air by building owners. Some unions have adopted the indoor air pollution cause. Wise employers will recognize the significant effect that the indoor environment has upon productivity and will take steps to ensure the quality of that environment. While such private action is only incremental and evolutionary, it presently offers more promise than does government action. A representative of Healthy Buildings International, Inc., a private organization specializing in diagnosis and mitigation of indoor air pollution, projected that the 1990s would see dramatic action to improve indoor air. He predicted that "[p]roperty owners, architects, and developers will want to say, 'our building is the healthiest building. We have the healthiest environment in the city for people to work in — not only the grandest and tallest, but the healthiest.' "[13] Some such action is plausible. Unfortunately, private action will be less vigorous in residential buildings. Home purchasers are less aware of indoor air quality risks than are large institutional commercial building owners. Even attempts to inform home owners have seen relatively little success in motivating behavioral changes. It seems to be quite difficult to persuade individuals of the true measure of health risk presented by poor indoor air. Much as car purchasers often value cosmetic attributes above safety, we may expect home purchasers to continue to place more emphasis upon cost, convenience, and appearance over healthfulness when purchasing a home. While this is the homeowner's free choice, it carries societal costs and often will subject children to unreasonable risks.

Notes

1. U.S. Environmental Protection Agency, *Report to Congress on Indoor Air Quality; Executive Summary and Recommendations*, 1989, p. 2.

2. INDOOR POLLUTION NEWS, July 28, 1988, p. 1.

3. Congressional Record, March 21, 1989, p. E894.

4. Congressional Record, March 21, 1989, p. E895.

5. INDOOR POLLUTION NEWS, October 5, 1989, p. 1.

6. 51 Fed. Reg. 29754, 29760 (1986).

7. *Id.*

8. 52 Fed. Reg. 17052, 17064 (1987).

9. 54 Fed. Reg. 7822 (1989).

10. 54 Fed. Reg. at 7825.

11. *Id.*

12. Giampetro-Meyer, *Rethinking Workplace Safety: An Integration and Evaluation of Sick Building Syndrome and Fetal Protection Cases*, 8 J. ENVTL. LAW 1, 10 (1988).

13. INDOOR POLLUTION NEWS, January 11, 1990, p. 4.

PART III

Private Recovery for Indoor Air Pollution Risks

The combination of serious health hazards and little government regulation makes indoor air pollution an apparently fertile ground for private litigation. Individuals who are injured by the actions of others have various common law opportunities to recover for their damages. Many of these opportunities arise in tort law, which generally covers private injuries, but some opportunity also exists in contract law, because most indoor air pollution results from contractual relationships of some type. Those harmed by indoor air pollution may avail themselves of these opportunities to recover for ill health, property damage, or even death.

At the outset, one should recognize the twin objectives of private recovery. The first objective is compensation for those innocently injured by the unlawful behavior of others. Unlawful in this context does not mean illegal but may simply involve a lack of care for the welfare of others or a breach of terms in a contract. Justice dictates that the innocently injured have some recourse for the improper actions that produced the injury. The second objective is deterrence. Common law requires that those who unlawfully cause injury must pay the consequences, which in turn gives them an incentive to avoid causing future injuries. This objective seeks to direct behavior much as government regulation might, though it relies on financial incentives rather than the command of regulations. Thus common law recovery offers a prospect of preventing indoor air pollution.

Chapter 9 discusses the approaches to recovery for damages suffered by indoor air pollution and some of the difficulties presented by these approaches. Plaintiffs suing for damages must show that some defendant breached an accepted legal duty, such as in negligence or fraud. Homeowners may be able to recover under a contract theory known as the implied warranty of habitability, whereby a seller promises that a home is a reasonably safe place to live. In addition, the plaintiff must show that the defendant caused the harm complained of, which will be particularly difficult in the case of cancer damages. Procedural requirements, such as the timing of the lawsuit and the rules of evidence, will also complicate the plaintiff's task. Finally, the plaintiff must demonstrate the damages suffered as a consequence of the indoor air pollution. Economic damages, in the form of reduced property value or cleanup costs, may be recovered. Plaintiffs can also recover damages for health harms, though causation is more difficult to prove, and the characteristics of cancer make it extremely difficult to recover for this most severe health risk of indoor air contamination.

Chapter 11 considers the experience of indoor air pollution litigation, pollutant by pollutant. For radon, the most hazardous source of indoor air contamination, plaintiffs have brought few cases, largely due to the difficulties of proving cancer causation or recovering for a risk of future cancer. Many cases involve asbestos, though these typically seek recovery of the costs of asbestos removal, rather than any health-related damages. Asbestos litigation has produced some substantial recoveries, particularly for school districts seeking removal costs. Homeowners have sued for formaldehyde exposure, especially in mobile homes, though with mixed success. Other sources of air pollution have seen little litigation, although plaintiffs have succeeded with recovery for exposures to pesticides and some other products that contaminated indoor air.

The amount of private litigation over indoor air pollution is small but growing. Structural limitations on private litigation, however, prevent such actions ever from providing comprehensive compensation or effective deterrence of indoor air pollution. The most common and successful actions have involved relatively innocuous asbestos conditions, while radon contamination has produced little effective litigation. Indeed, problems of proof and statutes of limitation make it far easier to recover for minor irritant injuries than for cancer. The litigation system can at best produce inconsistent results and offers no solution for indoor air pollution.

9

APPROACHES TO PRIVATE RECOVERY FOR INDOOR AIR POLLUTION

The problem of indoor air pollution will remain with us for quite some time. As Part I illustrates the significance of the indoor air pollution problem, Part II reveals that government action will do little to eliminate this problem. Under these circumstances, private individuals who suffer health harms or economic losses as a consequence of indoor air pollution will seek to recover compensation for these damages. The law provides several potential avenues for such private recovery.

The injured party may choose to sue as plaintiff for recompense. To succeed, such a party plaintiff must first establish a cause of action, satisfying some standard of liability that some identifiable defendant party has violated. Second, the party plaintiff must establish causation, that the defendant's actions caused some identifiable harm. Third, the plaintiff must satisfy certain procedural requirements, such as timeliness in filing suit. Fourth, the plaintiff must prove that the defendant's actions caused a harm that is legally recoverable as damages, or some other form of relief. Throughout this process, the plaintiff has various other obstacles to overcome, such as the rules of evidence. This chapter summarizes the legal requirements of making out this case and the pitfalls complicating the prospects of the plaintiff. In most cases, litigation proceeds under state, rather than federal, law and under common law rather than statutory authority.

At the outset, it is important to distinguish between two different types of actions that may be possibly brought. In the first, a plaintiff may seek to recover for health harms allegedly caused by indoor air pollution. The second type of action will have a plaintiff seeking to recover economic damages from indoor air pollution, either in the form of abatement costs or as reduced property value caused by indoor air pollution. Somewhat different legal principles govern these two types of cases, as different principles will apply in commercial and residential real estate settings.

Establishing Liability

A plaintiff's first objective must be to find some cause of action, or legal standard of liability, that permits recovery at law. A number of potential causes of action are available to plaintiffs complaining of indoor air quality. The common feature of these theories is that the defendant breached some legal duty that was the source of plaintiff's injuries.

For injuries to health, negligence offers the longest-standing and clearest cause of action for plaintiffs. A defendant may be found negligent if it has some duty of care that it breaches by failing to take reasonable precautions to avoid harm. We all have a duty of care not to cause unnecessary, unreasonable harm through our actions. Of course, the key issue is what risk of harm is unreasonable under the circumstances. Answering this question turns to the hypothetical "reasonable person." As a very general rule, this reasonable person will prevent all harms where the benefits of such prevention exceed the costs of preventive action. In practice, courts will consider factors such as the defendant's knowledge, the defendant's resources, and general industry practices in deciding whether the defendant behaved as a reasonable person. Once negligence is shown, a plaintiff must also prove that his or her damages were proximately caused by the defendant's negligent acts or omissions.

In proving negligence, plaintiffs may be aided by the negligence per se doctrine, which holds that a defendant violating a statutory requirement is automatically negligent. When government laws exist, and when they are violated, any person harmed from the violation has a relatively easy task demonstrating negligence. For indoor air pollution, however, there are relatively few government restrictions that could invoke the negligence per se doctrine.

The circumstances of indoor air pollution provide a number of opportunities for negligence actions against different categories of potential defendants. In the residential radon context, a homeowner plaintiff may sue a builder and vendor of a home for hazardous indoor radon levels. The plaintiff first will be required to prove that the builder knew or should have known of the potential radon hazard. For houses constructed in recent years when radon risks have become well known, it is reasonable to hold builders accountable for radon contamination. Once this is shown, the plaintiff has other burdens, as described in a recent article:

If a court finds that a builder owes a duty to the purchaser of the home to protect against radon contamination, the plaintiff then must prove that the builder breached that duty by failing to exercise the care and skill of an ordinary builder under the circumstances. An alternative claim may be made against the builder for negligent siting of new construction in high radon areas. Houses built in violation of existing regulatory recommendations for radon might be considered presumptively to breach this duty of care.

Simply proving defendant's negligence is not sufficient, however; the plaintiff also must show that the failure to exercise due care in the construction of the home proximately caused the injury or damage. Builders faced with such a claim may raise a proximate cause defense, alleging that they are not responsible for the radon contamination. This defense would emphasize that, in most instances, radon gas does not enter the home as a direct result of negligent construction techniques, but rather through natural methods — radon-contaminated gas or water or the ground underlying the home. The plaintiff in turn must show that the builder's actions were the proximate cause of the excessive radon contamination and that contamination resulted in the plaintiff's injuries. In many cases, a plaintiff should be able to show that either negligent construction or negligent siting of the home exists. In addition, since radon is present at some level in all houses, the homeowner must shown that elevated exposures are caused by negligent construction, siting, or design of the home. At present, it is unclear what threshold of radon exposure will be required, but a fair guess is that the plaintiff will be required to show exposures at least in excess of applicable standards.[1]

The unique circumstances of indoor radon contamination make negligence a difficult standard, though some cases doubtless will fit the requirements of this cause of action. Negligence may also be employed against other defendants, such as real estate brokers for failure to inspect and warn[2] or architects for negligent home design. Architects have been liable for designs calling for asbestos insulation. Building contractors may be liable in negligence if poor quality construction left foundation cracks or other unnecessary pathways for radon gas to enter the home.

Negligence may be easier to prove for some other indoor air pollution problems. In the contexts of indoor asbestos or formaldehyde contamination, a defendant builder will have installed the hazardous substance, which may be found negligent. A mobile home producer and seller, for example, should be aware of potentially high formaldehyde concentrations and should test for these before sale. The same may be true in some conventional housing and for certain other indoor pollutants, such as volatile organic compounds or combustion byproducts. In commercial buildings, the parties responsible for faulty air circulation systems may also be held responsible under negligence. Building owners have sued asbestos product manufacturers for negligent failure to warn of the product's dangers. Negligence may be unavailing for many indoor air pollution problems. For example, it appears that shade trees increase the growth of microbiological contaminants and the risk of disease, but it is very difficult to imagine a court ruling that selling a house surrounded by shade trees was a negligent act.

The negligence cause of action is highly dependent on the facts of individual disputes and assessment of "reasonable" behavior on the part of judges and juries. One commentator suggests that the judges should use negligence as a sword, that the "judiciary should require procedures that will prevent injury resulting from radon exposure, even if current industry practices do not so provide."[3] At the present time, such vigorous use of negligence doctrine appears to be unlikely. It should also be noted that negligence is more promising for public health injuries than for economic damages, for reasons discussed below in the section on damages.

If applicable, a strict liability action offers benefits to plaintiffs. In strict liability, plaintiffs need not prove actual negligence on the part of defendants. All states provide for strict liability in some cases. The law in most states makes strict liability available in certain specific, limited circumstances, such as the sale of a product or the practice of ultrahazardous activities. Strict liability generally exists only for personal health injuries and is not extended to cases of economic damages.

Some indoor air contamination results from products in the home, and strict products liability should be applicable here. Some argue that certain indoor air pollutants are so extremely dangerous that they should be governed by strict liability for ultrahazardous activities, though courts are reluctant to make such a finding.

Strict liability will be generally applicable to indoor air pollution if houses can be considered products for the purpose of strict liability law. This may be particularly important in radon cases, where there is not a distinct emitting "product" in most cases. A landmark 1965 New Jersey case, *Schipper v. Levitt & Sons*,[4] applied strict products liability to a housing sale in a case involving a defective water-heating system. This case involved a mass producer of homes, however, and the precedent may be inapplicable for a small or custom builder. Mobile homes would almost certainly be considered products in many jurisdictions. Courts in other states also have extended strict products liability principles to actions brought against some home builders.

If strict liability does apply, the plaintiff still must prove certain essential elements in order to recover. Most centrally, the plaintiff must show that the product was sold in a "defective condition unreasonably dangerous to the user."[5] This "defect" may assume quite a variety of different forms. Most obviously, a defectively constructed house (e.g., one containing numerous cracks in the foundation) may be defective. Use of contaminated building products could be deemed an unreasonably dangerous defect. The siting of a home might even be considered defective. Strict liability may also be founded on the defective design of a product, such as the failure to install fans to dissipate contamination or failure otherwise to provide adequate ventilation. A housing product may even be defective because the builder and vendor failed to warn of a hazardous condition found in the house.

Defendants can respond that even houses with poor indoor air quality are not defective, using a "state-of-the-art" defense. Some courts recognize that a product is not defective if it conformed to the state of the art at the time, such as if the indoor air hazard was not reasonably known. The presence of this defense will produce problems for some radon plaintiffs, as recently discussed:

> The question now becomes whether a builder of a radon-contaminated home knew or should have known of the dangerous

condition. Certainly, the builders of homes built within the past five to ten years in radon-prone areas should be aware of the problem and the deadly dangers. As the radon problem becomes more widely publicized, even builders in other regions of the country should be expected to investigate possible radon problems in their houses. A much harder question exists for homes built fifteen or more years ago, before the danger of indoor radon was widely known. These builders may be able to take advantage of the state-of-the-art defense to absolve themselves of strict liability to injured homebuyers. Clearly, today's builders in high radon concentration areas have a duty to construct homes with radon dispersement devices and to warn potential buyers of the dangers of radon contamination.[6]

Strict liability may be even more promising for other indoor air conditions, such as excessive formaldehyde and asbestos concentrations. Some harms of these substances have been known for years, and producers should have some duty to warn of such hazards. For other indoor air pollutants the case is less clear. One might well argue that humidifier manufacturers have a duty to warn, as do manufacturers of products emitting volatile organic compounds or manufacturers of indoor combustion sources.

An action that is somewhat like strict liability is a contract case for breach of an implied warranty of habitability. When items are sold pursuant to contract, the law implies certain warranties, and many states extend an implied warranty of habitability to housing sales. This is a promise that the home sold is a suitable place to live, and a plaintiff could argue that indoor air contamination made the home so unhealthful that it should be considered uninhabitable.

The implied warranty of habitability has advantages for plaintiffs, because they need not prove that negligence or even a defect was the cause of poor indoor air quality. The basic elements of an implied warranty action are relatively easy to meet. A plaintiff must show (1) that the builder-vendor held itself out as a construction expert; (2) that the homeowner has no particular construction expertise; (3) that the builder was the provider of designs and plans; and (4) that the buyer relied on the reputation and skill of the builder. These circumstances exist for most new home sales. Contractual warranty theories present some significant barriers for plaintiffs, however.

First, most states still require that the plaintiff be in contractual privity with the defendant to maintain a warranty action. If a builder constructs a home, sells it to one person, who later sells it to a second person, the second person has no contractual relationship with the builder. While some courts have eliminated the privity requirement in implied warranty of habitability cases, most jurisdictions retain this requirement, which limits the availability of this cause of action.

Another potential shortcoming of implied warranty of habitability actions is the common presence of warranty disclaimers in housing contracts. Most builders will insist that home purchasers sign a disclaimer clause, waiving many warranties, including the implied warranty of habitability. If the disclaimer is conspicuous and clearly worded, most courts will enforce its terms and prevent plaintiffs from later complaining. Some disclaimers, such as a general inspection clause, may be ineffective against plaintiffs. For example, one commentator contends that "[a] mere general statement that the buyer 'has inspected the property' or takes the property 'as is' would not cover radon because radon is clearly a defect so latent that a reasonable prepurchase inspection would not uncover unsafe levels of gas."[7]

Still another limitation on implied warranty of habitability actions is the severity of the damages required. A house must be unfit for habitation for such an action to succeed. When indoor air creates a substantial risk of cancer or produces intolerable irritant effects, a home may be considered uninhabitable. For lesser risks and irritation, which are more common, a home may be considered to still be habitable.

Still another potential cause of action is for fraud by the seller or its agents. To prove fraud, a plaintiff must establish the following elements:

(1) a false representation of a fact by the defendant;
(2) knowledge of the defendant that the statement is false;
(3) defendant's intent to induce the plaintiff to rely on the false representation;
(4) plaintiff's justifiable reliance upon the false representation; and
(5) damage to the plaintiff as a result of such reliance.

The standards for proving, or even alleging, fraud are stricter than for negligence, strict liability, or implied warranty of habitability actions.

Nevertheless, in some circumstances, fraud actions will be most appropriate in indoor air litigation.

In the housing context, the false representation of fact need not necessarily be a false statement. Silence in the face of known hazards can be a fraudulent omission by a seller of housing. The seller's awareness of indoor air contamination (or reckless disregard of such problem) is required under fraud. One can readily imagine a mobile home producer aware of a formaldehyde problem or a regular home builder aware of a severe radon problem who fails to disclose such a problem to a purchaser. A fraud case could well succeed on these facts. Many banks and brokers now require radon disclosure forms by sellers, and any misrepresentation on these forms would be clear fraud. Misleading testing for radon could also be actionable fraud. Many parties have alleged that asbestos products manufacturers have fraudulently concealed the risks of asbestos from purchasers of their products.

Even if a seller were actually unaware of indoor air contamination, a homeowner or commercial tenant might still recover under the doctrine of negligent misrepresentation. Even an honestly intended statement, if false, may produce liability. This is particularly true if the circumstances suggest that the party should have become aware of the untruth of the statement. Real estate brokers are particularly susceptible to claims for fraud. Fraud claims are promising for both health and property damages, but contractual disclaimers may be so broad as to waive fraud actions, as well as the implied warranty of habitability.

Plaintiffs' lawyers have also tried several other theories of liability, depending upon the facts of the particular action. Some have argued that asbestos companies engaged in a conspiracy to mislead the public regarding the potential harms of their products. Others have argued that situations, such as buildings with asbestos-containing products, constitute a legal "nuisance" that defendants have a duty to abate. Many states have laws regulating unfair or deceptive trade practices that provide good causes of action for plaintiffs, especially when the source of indoor air contamination is a product.

Congress supplemented the above common law causes of action when it enacted the Comprehensive Environmental Response, Compensation and Liability Act of 1980 (CERCLA), also known as Superfund. While this act focused upon abandoned hazardous waste dumps, it may have some applicability to indoor air pollution problems as well.

CERCLA provides that a party may clean up a release of hazardous substances and then sue certain responsible parties for the cleanup costs. Some parties have "cleaned up" an indoor air pollution problem, such as by the removal of asbestos-containing products, and then sought recovery of these costs under CERCLA. The available damages under CERCLA are limited to these abatement expenses and do not include health harms or diminished property value, but the act does have important procedural benefits to plaintiffs, particularly in asbestos-removal litigation. Courts and commentators remain divided on whether CERCLA is properly applied to the indoor air context.

Causation

In addition to demonstrating that a defendant has violated some legal duty, a plaintiff must demonstrate some damages caused by the defendant's violation. In the case of plaintiffs suing for health harms, they must link their symptoms to the defendant's actions. The same is true for claims of property damage. If suing for the expenses of abating indoor air problems, the plaintiff must show that the remediation was necessary.

Causation is most difficult in the case of health harms. Most health harms are not clearly and exclusively linked with any cause. The problem is particularly intractable in the case of cancer. Proof of causation of cancer is extraordinarily difficult in litigation. The problem arises first because cancer has a very long latency period—the disease usually does not strike until decades from the time of the exposure that triggered the disease. Second, most air pollutants cause lung cancer, which has a plethora of other potential causes. When lung cancer develops, it is impossible to be certain that it was caused by indoor air pollution as opposed to cigarette smoke, outdoor pollution, or other sources. Third, we have relatively little knowledge of how and why cancer develops. As a result, it seems to be a disease of probabilistic risk. Virtually any exposure to a carcinogen *may* cause cancer, and no commonly present exposures produce anything approximating a certainty of cancer. Thus, while thousands of Americans probably contract cancer from radon, volatile organic compounds, and other indoor air pollutants, each individual faces a risk of, for example, 1 in 1,000 of cancer. Thus very few individuals actually have a probability of cancer from indoor air pollution, and after a cancer is suffered, it is difficult to prove that indoor air pollution was the cause of this specific cancer. For other contexts, such as electromagnetic fields, the task will be even more difficult.

Traditional common law principles require that a plaintiff prove a greater-than-50-percent probability of causation. Thus, if a million individuals are exposed to a 1 in 1,000 risk, a thousand people will contract cancer, but none of them may recover from their disease. This causation paradox is difficult for plaintiffs to escape.

In addition, the "abstract theoretical difficulties of demonstrating causation [of cancer] are probably dwarfed by practical difficulties of proof."[8] Few homeowners have monitored the indoor concentrations of pollutants in their homes, and they will thus have difficulty proving exposure. Even those plaintiffs who prove exposure must still prove the risk associated with that exposure. Scientists differ on cancer risk assessments, and both sides of the litigation will be able to present witnesses debating relative risks. The cost of this proof will also be daunting to many plaintiffs. An expert report to Congress stated that "it is clear that proof of the causal connection between exposure and injury is an almost overwhelming barrier to recovery, particularly in smaller cases (regardless of their merit) because the cost of mounting the massive probative effort and the arrays of technical and scientific evidence will be prohibitive."[9] Some plaintiffs have sought to ease these problems by suing for the risk of future cancer, but this theory is not universally accepted.

The plaintiff's task will be somewhat easier for other types of health harms. The irritant effects of indoor air pollution may themselves be quite severe, making life miserable for homeowners or renters. These irritant effects usually appear almost immediately upon exposure to the harmful substance. The causation for many irritant effects is itself disputed, however. There is ongoing scientific debate, for example, on whether formaldehyde causes certain adverse health effects and at what level of exposure. Some scientists believe that reported irritant effects are largely psychosomatic responses. Many individuals claim to suffer from multiple chemical sensitivity, yet the existence of this condition is not universally recognized. In addition, the medical conditions presented by many irritant responses may be caused by many different sources. For example, someone suffering respiratory illnesses may have been harmed by indoor combustion byproducts, but there are many other possible sources of these illnesses. In addition, individuals who suffer from indoor air pollution are typically particularly sensitive to pollution (because of asthma, age, or other conditions), and courts have not established the extent to which defendants should be responsible to protect unusually sensitive individuals from commonplace conditions. Microbiological contaminants have so many sources that it will often be impossible to link disease to indoor contamination. In some circumstances, however, a sudden endemic of an unusual illness, such as Legionnaires' disease, at a specific site will strongly suggest causation. Even in these special circumstances, the plaintiff will be required to trace the source of the contaminant.

Proof of causation for lost property value actions will be somewhat simpler. Here, a plaintiff will claim that the presence of indoor contaminants or potentially harmful products used in a building have reduced the resale value of the building. Of course, building value is affected by numerous factors beside indoor air quality. Financial experts can be employed to testify as to the effect of indoor pollution, however, and this is the sort of judgment commonly made by courts.

Abatement actions will also have an easier time proving causation. In these, a plaintiff spends his or her money correcting an indoor air pollution problem and then sues the party responsible for the contamination in order to recover abatement costs. The only literal causation issue here is whether the expenses were actually incurred and for the purpose of correcting indoor air contamination. While causation is simple, these cases face financial barriers. The typical recovery in an abatement action for most pollutants is relatively small, and litigation costs may make such actions impractical. For large commercial buildings, however, abatement actions may be feasible. Asbestos removal, for example, can be quite an expensive operation.

One final causation problem is common to all these types of indoor air pollution litigation. For a plaintiff to recover, he or she must be able to identify a defendant who is responsible for causing the indoor air pollution. Sometimes the responsible defendant will be obvious; a purchaser of a mobile home, for example, will promptly know whom to sue. In other cases, however, identifying defendants is more difficult. If a home has been sold several times, it may be difficult for a plaintiff to trace the parties responsible for products causing indoor air contamination. If a building contains products with asbestos, the manufacturer of those products may be difficult to trace. The problem of identifying defendants is greater when problems arise some time after construction or sale. Moreover, even when defendants can be identified, they may have gone out of business or declared bankruptcy and their assets may be unreachable.

Statutes of Limitations and Repose

All states have statutes of limitations that place time limits on when lawsuits may be brought. A plaintiff must bring an action within a certain amount of time after a breach of contract or commission of a tort or lose his or her legal claim. These laws protect potential defendants from an eternity of potential liability and help ensure that cases are brought when evidence is available. All states have their own statutes of limitations, which typically differ for contract or tort actions. Contract statutes of limitations may extend up to fifteen years but are typically much shorter, at about four years. Tort statutes of limitations vary more widely but typically extend from one to six years from the date of injury.

In some indoor air litigation contexts, such as irritant responses to new products, plaintiffs should have no difficulty meeting the limitations statutes. These statutes of limitations may present significant problems for other indoor air pollution plaintiffs. In the case of cancer harms, these typically occur long after the statute of limitations has passed. In other instances, hazardous asbestos-containing materials may only be discovered years after their construction or installation, and the statute of limitations will have passed. Traditional legal principles exempt the government from statutes of limitations, so school plaintiffs may avoid being time-barred.

Courts have recognized the rigidity of limitations statutes and softened their application in some circumstances. For example, the statute of limitations does not run during the time that a defendant is fraudulently concealing the presence of a tort or breach of warranty. In addition, many courts are adopting a discovery rule for applying statutes of limitations. Under this rule, the statute of limitations does not begin running until the plaintiff actually discovered or should have discovered the presence of a cause of action. The discovery rule can considerably ameliorate the statute of limitations but it has varied applicability in different jurisdictions.

Benefits of the discovery rule are also undercut by the enactment of statutes of repose. Many states have adopted these statutes of repose, which set an absolute limit on the time of liability. Some of these statutes are limited to specific defendants, usually including architects and contractors. Statutes of repose begin running from the time of manufacture or sale, not from the time of the injury suffered or the time of its discovery. The statutes of repose typically allow a longer time period to sue than do statutes of limitations, such as twelve years. For cancer and some other cases, however, the statutes of repose will complicate potential litigation. CERCLA offers particular benefits to some plaintiffs, because it is a federal action not subject to state statutes, and because the CERCLA cause of action does not commence until the time of cleanup.

Remedies

The objective of any litigation is to obtain some remedy to compensate plaintiffs for their injuries. The ability to establish a defendant's liability means little if remedies are seriously incomplete. While relatively little attention has centered on remedies, this area has considerable importance in indoor air quality litigation.

One remedy appropriate to many cases will be damages for health harms incurred. Thus, if an individual suffers cancer as a consequence of air contamination, he or she might receive in excess of $1 million in damages to compensate for medical expenses, loss of earnings, pain and suffering, or other harms. Plaintiffs suffering irritant effects from indoor air may also receive a substantial recovery of tens or hundreds of thousands of dollars. Juries can appreciate how unrelieved misery from allergic or other irritation is worthy of compensation. To recover these damages, of course, a plaintiff must show that defendant's actions caused their harms.

In the case of cancer, it is particularly difficult to sue for cancer incurred. The disease's latency period means that "by the time cancer occurs, defendants may be insolvent, critical evidence may be destroyed, proof of causation will be complicated, and the action may be time-barred by applicable statutes of limitations."[10]

Because of the difficulties attendant to suing for cancer incurred, a number of plaintiffs are seeking to recover for suffering a risk of future cancer. Upon discovering that they have been exposed to high radon levels, for example, a family might sue a builder for exposing them to such a risk of cancer. Under traditional principles of tort law, a risk is not considered a real harm, and courts would not allow someone to sue for such a "mere risk." Courts and commentators have increasingly recognized the great difficulty of *post facto* cancer damages recovery, however, and there is growing sentiment to allow some recovery for a risk of future cancer. There is still limited precedent for such actions, however, and even sympathetic jurisdictions would require a plaintiff to show a greater-than-50-percent risk of future cancer before permitting recovery. Even the indoor environment seldom produces cancer risks this great, so few plaintiffs will have an opportunity to recover for a future risk of cancer standing alone.

Courts are more willing to grant some damages for a risk of incurring cancer in the future if this risk is coupled with some already existing harm. This is known as the "extent of the injury" rule and permits plaintiffs to sue for future risks that arise out of a present manifest injury. The rule permits plaintiffs to recover for all demonstrable adverse future consequences of a present injury. This rule inevitably follows from the procedural rule against "claim-splitting," which bars bringing more than one lawsuit from a given tort. Because a later action for cancer would be barred by an initial action for irritant effects, courts will permit some recovery for a risk of future cancer when accompanied by a present harm.

In the case of some indoor air pollutants, this extent of the injury rule should permit recovery for risk of future cancer. For formaldehyde exposure, present irritant effects may be accompanied by future cancer risk, which should be litigable in the same trial. For other pollutants, such as radon, no obvious present harm is caused by the substance. Creative plaintiffs' attorneys have propounded a theory that exposure to a carcinogen immediately produces some identifiable chromosomal damage to a person's cells. While a diagnosable cancer would not result for years, these attorneys argue that the chromosomal damage provides sufficient present injury to justify bringing the risk of future cancer to trial. While this issue is not settled, some courts seem amenable to the theory that chromosomal damage (which has no immediately noticeable adverse effect on victims) can constitute a present harm under the extent of the injury rule.

If a plaintiff can reach court on a risk of future cancer under the extent of the injury rule, it remains uncertain what risks are compensable. Some courts have still required a greater-than-50-percent probability as a condition upon recovery. This position is indefensible, because the preclusion of claim-splitting would leave many victims without later recourse. Consequently, a number of courts have authorized recovery for much smaller risks, such as 3 percent. While these precedents benefit plaintiffs, few substances cause even a 3-percent risk of cancer and the ability to obtain damages for such smaller risks is undefined. The amount of recovery for such small risks may also be too low to justify litigation.

A somewhat more promising theory for many plaintiffs is recovery for fear of future cancer. Someone exposed to a significant risk of future cancer may suffer emotional distress as a consequence. There is now a medically recognized condition, called cancerphobia, to describe such a fear of future cancer. Courts historically have been somewhat reluctant to recognize the compensability of this type of psychological harm, for fear of false claims. As a result, some courts would only recognize emotional distress damages that arose out of a present physical injury. Courts are increasingly willing to permit recovery for psychological distress, and chromosomal injury may satisfy the present injury requirement even in more restrictive jurisdictions.

Of course, to recover for cancerphobia from indoor air or any other source, the plaintiff's fear of cancer must be a reasonable one. The public misperceives many cancer risks, such as asbestos. Enclosed nonhazardous asbestos products have produced significant fear in individuals who rather blithely accept much greater risks from other sources. Courts have not adopted a uniform standard for reasonability, but some demonstrable percentage risk should be required before permitting recovery. The availability of mental distress damages may also depend on the plaintiff's theory of liability. While emotional distress damages may be recovered for intentional or negligent torts, there may be no recovery for actions in strict liability or breach of warranty.

Another possible recovery for those exposed to a risk of future cancer is damages for future medical surveillance. When a plaintiff was exposed to a carcinogen, he or she might seek regular medical surveillance to detect the development of any cancer. Such early detection greatly enhances the prospects for effective treatment of cancer. Courts are divided on the availability of potential recovery for medical surveillance. Some have granted damages, while others have placed obstacles in the path of recovery or denied it altogether. Like fear of cancer recovery, future medical surveillance damages should be limited to instances when the damages are reasonably related to the risk. Mere exposure to a carcinogen should not suffice; plaintiffs should demonstrate that a defendant created a material risk. On the other hand, some courts have required a greater-than-50-percent probability of future cancer for medical surveillance damages, which is far too strict. Lesser cancer risks warrant monitoring for development of the disease. Proof of existing injury may not be required to recover costs of medical surveillance.

In addition to the above health-related damages, plaintiffs may seek to recover economic losses associated with indoor air pollution. In the case of substances such as radon, volatile organic compounds, or other carcinogens, the health-related damages may be small, because cancer will not have developed. The primary objective may be to prevent the risk or to escape the risk. Economic damages may cover the costs of remediation or permit sale of the property by covering the reduced property value caused by indoor contamination.

Current precedent forecloses some options for a party suing for only economic losses. The "economic loss" doctrine has ruled out recovery under theories such as negligence or strict liability for some economic damages. The doctrine holds that "economic losses that arise out of commercial transactions, except those involving personal injury or damage to other property, are not recoverable under tort theories of negligence or strict products liability."[11] These losses must be recovered under some contract theory, such as breach of warranty. This doctrine particularly precludes tort actions for diminished property value. The theory of the economic loss doctrine is that a contract captures a complete bargain struck between two parties, who set forth in that contract the remedies for any problems that may arise. The doctrine contains significant exceptions, however. If a product damages other property or causes health harms, for example, tort theories may be used. Some argue that tort should be available if a product creates a risk of health damages as well. This doctrine primarily arises in asbestos abatement actions, which defendants argue are purely economic and not properly subject to tort actions and remedies. Denial of tort remedies can significantly impair a plaintiff's prospects of success.

When plaintiffs can bring actions for economic losses to real estate, either in contract or through an exception to the economic loss doctrine, the standard measure of damages is reduction in property value. It is now demonstrable that high levels of radon or the presence of asbestos-containing materials can significantly reduce the value of buildings. While the effect of other pollutants is less clear, it seems likely that a mobile home with very high formaldehyde levels will have a reduced value. Plaintiffs can recover this reduction in property value as damages, unless repair or other correction of the contamination problem would be more efficient than granting reduced property value. In many instances, repair may be the preferred alternative for plaintiffs, regardless of its cost.

Many plaintiffs may not wish to move their home, or, as in the case of schools, the plaintiff may be unable to move. In these cases, the plaintiff may seek repair of the problem regardless of the cost. As a general rule, repair costs are only recoverable when they are less than the reduction in property value. This rule is not rigid, however, and when a plaintiff has a particular "personal reason" for repair, rather than reduced market value, courts have shown some willingness to grant restoration costs as damages. This is particularly true when the uncorrected building presents a serious public health hazard. Fortunately, costs of correcting many indoor air pollution problems, including radon, are relatively inexpensive and should often be recoverable if sought by a plaintiff.

Some individuals victimized by indoor air contamination may not wish to correct the problem but simply desire to escape the offending structure. These individuals can seek to escape their contract for the building under the remedy of rescission. If a plaintiff can demonstrate fraud or a breach of the implied warranty of habitability, courts generally will permit him or her to rescind the contract. While rescission is less likely to be available under tort theories of action, a plaintiff might also receive rescission under the contractual doctrine of mutual mistake. As recently explained:

> When the parties to a transaction are mistaken regarding a basic assumption of the contract, either may rescind upon discovery of the mistake. In the present controversy, when indoor radon levels are unknown [by the parties prior to sale], the parties were mistaken regarding the fundamental safety of the residence. Courts have granted rescission of real estate contracts for mistakes of lesser magnitude.[12]

Rescission will not be universally available. If a purchaser has assumed the risk of mistake, such as through a valid contractual disclaimer, rescission will be denied. Nor will rescission be available when a mistaken condition can be corrected easily and inexpensively. Another drawback to rescission is that some jurisdictions require plaintiffs to elect among their remedies, and an equitable action for rescission may preclude recovery of other contract damages.

For many indoor air plaintiffs, the most lucrative recovery may take the form of punitive damages. The law provides for punitive damages in order to punish particularly objectionable conduct and to deter future conduct of that nature. Punitive damages are generally limited to cases in which a defendant's behavior has been especially egregious or reckless. Punitive damages are seldom available in contract actions but may be received for negligence or, especially, for fraud. Punitive damages today are far more common and far larger in amount than they were even a decade ago. Courts and commentators are increasingly critical of the trend to granting punitive damages, and various devices are being adopted to restrain such awards. For example, some courts require a comparability between actual damages and punitive damages and reject verdicts where punitive damages far exceed compensatory actual damages. Notwithstanding these efforts, punitive damages are granted fairly often in cases in which a defendant has endangered a plaintiff's health, and these damages can materially increase such a plaintiff's recovery in indoor air litigation.

Notes

1. F. Cross & P. Murray, *Liability for Toxic Radon Gas in Residential Home Sales*, 66 N. CAR. L. REV. 687, 720–21 (1988) (citations omitted).

2. Note, *Clearing the Air on Radon Testing: The Duty of Real Estate Brokers to Protect Prospective Homebuyers*, 15 FORDHAM URBAN L.J. 767 (1987).

3. S. F. Conaway, *Grappling with Silent Invaders of the Home: Legal Remedies for Radon Gas Contamination*, 5 TEMPLE ENVT'L LAW & TECH. J. 36, 43 (1986).

4. 207 A.2d 314 (N.J. 1965).

5. RESTATEMENT (SECOND) OF TORTS, section 402A (1965).

6. Cross & Murray, p. 714.

7. Note, *Radon Gas: Ramifications for Real Estate Transactions in Pennsylvania*, DICKINSON L. REV. 1113, 1147–48 (1987).

8. Frank Cross, ENVIRONMENTALLY INDUCED CANCER AND THE LAW (1989), p. 168.

9. *Injuries and Damages from Hazardous Wastes — Analysis and Improvement of Legal Remedies*, Report to Congress by the Superfund Section 301(e) Study Group (September 1982), p. 71.

10. Cross & Murray, pp. 724–25.

11. *Superwood Corp. v. Siempelkamp Corp.*, 311 N.W.2d 159, 162 (Minn. 1981).

12. Cross & Murray, pp. 737–38.

10

EXPERIENCE IN RECOVERY
FOR INDOOR AIR POLLUTION

The litigation process offers some hope for remedy or compensation for indoor air pollution. To date, success in litigation has been mixed. The theories described in the preceding chapter have produced some major recoveries, particularly for property damages. Litigation has been of little promise, however, for some of the greatest indoor air problems.

Radon Litigation

Some have projected an enormous number of lawsuits being filed to recover for residential radon contamination. Some cases have been filed, and litigation appears to be on the upswing.[1] The anticipated explosion of cases has not occurred, however, and very few decisions are reported.

Plaintiffs were wholly unsuccessful in the first reported residential radon decision, *Wayne v. Tennessee Valley Authority.*[2] In this case, Mark and Phoebe Wayne began construction of a home for themselves on their Tennessee ranch. They purchased concrete blocks for their basement in 1968. The concrete blocks were produced from radon-contaminated phosphate slag from Tennessee Valley Authority fertilizer production. The Waynes moved into their new home in 1969 and lived there until 1979, when they were alerted to the potential radon problem. Monitoring revealed high indoor radon levels, and the Waynes moved out of their house, on the advice of EPA and the Tennessee

Public Health Department. The Waynes then sued the producers of the concrete blocks and the Tennessee Valley Authority, seeking $14 million in damage for health harms and the loss of the use of their home. Their action alleged breaches of implied warranties, negligence, and strict liability. The district court dismissed their claim as barred by the statute of limitations. The Waynes then sought to avoid the statute by arguing that defendants had fraudulently concealed the radon hazard.

The appellate court rejected the Wayne's claim, primarily because the blocks were purchased in 1968. The court found that knowledge of potential radon hazards was not available until "the latter half of the 1970s."[3] The Waynes were unable to demonstrate that the Tennessee Valley Authority was aware of and fraudulently concealed the radon risks during the relevant time period. While the Waynes lost their case, the decision suggests some promise for future success in cases where radon contamination is traceable to more recent sources.

Some success was achieved in the next reported radon action, *Brafford v. Susquehanna Corp.*[4] The Braffords were a South Dakota family who lived in their home three years before discovering high indoor radon measurements. Their property was contaminated by uranium mill tailings produced by the Susquehanna Corporation, which was the presumptive source of the indoor radon. The Braffords sued Susquehanna, seeking compensation for their increased risk of cancer, mental grief, and the loss of their home, as well as special recovery under a South Dakota statute. Defendants moved to dismiss portions of the claim, but the court held that established chromosome damage justified the Braffords' claim for increased future risk of cancer and that the Braffords also could sue for punitive damages. Shortly after this ruling, defendants settled with the Braffords for an undisclosed sum.

Some success was also achieved in *T & E Industries v. Safety Light Corp.*,[5] where a business facility was contaminated by ore tailings left on the property. The New Jersey Department of Environmental Protection ordered the current owner to take immediate remedial action. T & E Industries, the owner, sealed floor cracks and drains and increased ventilation in the building. The owner then sued the dumper of the tailings under CERCLA for costs incurred. The court ruled that the defendant was liable for response costs, but that the defendant was not liable for relocation expenses, pending remediation.

Numerous other cases have been brought. One of the best known cases involves Dr. Joel Nobel, a Pennsylvania homeowner, who discovered radon levels exceeding 50 pCi/L in his house. Nobel is suing a contractor who installed an allegedly cracked ventilation system and seeks $100,000 damages for costs of remedial work needed to eliminate the radon problem, as well as emotional distress and risk of future cancer. Nobel uses the implied warranty of habitability, among other theories.

At this time, there have been few radon cases, and the decisions reflect rather uncommon circumstances. The promise of lawsuits for indoor radon contamination remains uncertain. Commentators have projected success for radon litigation, which could lead to extensive litigation.[6] This projection has not yet come to pass, but there is considerable potential for radon litigation, particularly for problems found in new housing. The National Home Builders Association, the Home Owners Warranty Corp., and other trade associations have predicted an increase in liability actions in the 1990s.

A recent Oklahoma decision offers special future promise to radon plaintiffs. In a case involving a uranium shipping cylinder, the Oklahoma court ruled that strict liability applied in cases of exposure to radiation. Even a high degree of care could not protect a defendant from liability. This case involved a user of radioactive materials and may not encompass natural sources of radiation, as often found in housing. The decision does open up the possibility of a new, powerful argument for radon plaintiffs, however.

Asbestos Litigation

In contrast to the radon experience, there has been considerable litigation over indoor asbestos exposures. This may be due to the federal government's more active role in asbestos monitoring and the fact that asbestos contamination is particularly a problem in institutional public buildings. Few asbestos cases have involved personal injury or risk to health, however, as the litigation has focused on recovery of removal costs.

Workers exposed to high levels of asbestos on the job produced the first wave of asbestos litigation, which has so far yielded billions of dollars in judgments and bankrupted companies. A second wave of litigation began in the early 1980s, with school districts filing property damage claims for the costs of asbestos removal. The school districts were soon followed by local governments and by some private building owners. The extent and success of the second wave of litigation is still unsettled.

The earliest cases seeking to recover asbestos abatement costs produced mixed results. One early New Jersey action permitted a strict liability claim to proceed to trial and granted a school district the benefits of the discovery rule, to avoid the statute of limitations.[7] An early Tennessee case dismissed a cause of action under warranty but permitted plaintiffs to bring their negligence, strict liability, and fraud claims.[8] The earliest jury trial, in South Carolina, resulted in a verdict for the defendant asbestos producers, though this result was partially overturned and remanded for a new trial.

One leading plaintiff success was in *City of Greenville v. W. R. Grace & Company.*[9] Greenville, South Carolina, built a new city hall in the early 1970s, using asbestos fireproofing products, though Grace was aware at the time of the hazards of asbestos. Moreover, the particular product used had "poor bonding characteristics" and was particularly likely to crumble. After a decade, the asbestos material began crumbling and contaminated carpets and other indoor areas. Greenville did not present any fiber measurements, and Grace's independent measurements found only low levels of contamination. Greenville sued in negligence and breach of warranty for the costs of removing asbestos, and a jury returned a verdict for the city granting $6.4 million in maintenance and removal cost damages and $2 million in punitive damages.

Grace asked the trial judge to overturn the jury verdict, on several theories. Grace used the economic loss doctrine (discussed in Chapter 9) to argue that Greenville could not maintain its negligence action. Because the case involved a threat to public safety, however, the court affirmed the negligence finding. Grace next argued that it had breached no warranty because it conformed to the state of the art at the time of construction. The court did not recognize any such defense in South Carolina warranty actions. The court also affirmed the jury's assessment of actual and punitive damages. The most interesting aspect of this case is the judge's cavalier attitude toward the need for removal. Greenville had no measurements of actual asbestos exposure. Grace conducted its own, concededly limited, study of asbestos contamination and found it to be low. The court ignored this evidence, stressing the limitations of air testing, and observing that even "[i]f no person ever gets sick from the asbestos in the City Hall, that would not change the fact that Greenville's building is contaminated and it must deal with that contamination." Grace sought to present evidence that the risk from asbestos in the building was small, less than comparative risks from drinking soft drinks or eating peanut butter. The court, however, excluded the evidence of comparative risk. Apparently, the judge ultimately was persuaded by evidence of the no threshold hypothesis, that there is no perfectly safe level of asbestos exposure. Grace appealed the decision, but the Fourth Circuit Court of Appeals unanimously upheld the judgment.

The Greenville case is perhaps the most prominent case of recovery for indoor asbestos risks, but certain factors make it unique. In this case, the asbestos-containing materials had no utility, being used as filler, for which paper could have substituted. The plaintiffs were able to demonstrate that Grace had actual knowledge of the hazard and used a form of asbestos particularly susceptible to crumbling and consequent human exposure. Greenville had no difficulty identifying a solvent defendant in W. R. Grace, and its government status enabled the city to escape the statute of limitations. Nevertheless, the decision established precedents favorable to plaintiffs.

Colorado was the site of a major success for a private asbestos plaintiff. Western Office Partners purchased a large downtown office building in Denver in 1984. Western Office Partners later discovered that the seller of the building had been precluded from performing a 1982 renovation because of the presence of asbestos-containing materials throughout the building. Western Office Partners sued under a fraud theory and obtained a verdict of $6.75 million in actual damages and $2.43 million in punitive damages. Other cases also have succeeded, and the state of the law can be summarized.

On the key issue of theories of liability, building owners have used quite a number of arguments. These include express or implied warranties, strict liability, negligence, fraud, trespass, restitution, and civil conspiracy. Because the parties typically are in a contractual relationship, warranty is the most obvious claim. Warranty cases have confronted particular problems, however, from the statute of limitations. Contract claims generally have shorter statutes of limitations for suing, and the discovery rule exception to statutes of limitations is largely limited to tort. In addition, warranty law requires that the plaintiffs give notice to the defendant of the alleged breach, to enable its correction, before a suit may be successfully filed.

Tort theories, such as negligence and strict liability, offer benefits to plaintiffs. Plaintiffs have generally been able to demonstrate a breach of duty under negligence, such as the duty to warn of the hazards of asbestos installation. Strict products liability also offers advantages even over negligence, but some jurisdictions, such as Michigan, do not recognize strict liability in these cases. Many jurisdictions limit strict liability to personal injuries and do not recognize the doctrine for purely economic losses. A November 1989 New York decision, however, applied strict liability to a claim by an office building owner against a former producer of asbestos products. The court held that the producer was more aware of potential asbestos hazards than even a "sophisticated commercial buyer" of real estate.

A key obstacle to any tort theory has been the economic loss doctrine, holding that plaintiffs in a contractual relationship may only sue in warranty when they suffer only economic loss. While commentators continue to dispute the proper application of the economic loss doctrine to indoor asbestos cases,[10] most plaintiffs have been permitted to proceed in tort. Some jurisdictions do not recognize the economic loss doctrine. Other courts have ruled that the harm from asbestos is not classic economic loss but rather is property damage (to other indoor products), which is an exception to the doctrine. Still other courts have emphasized that this dispute is not a classic one over whether the buyer received the benefit of the bargain but involves risks to personal safety. In general, "the courts seem willing to find a way to define the injury as a type of property damage rather than economic loss."[11] Consequently, most negligence actions have been able to proceed.

Other plaintiffs have alleged fraudulent or negligent misrepresentations by sellers of asbestos-containing materials. These actions have a higher burden of proof but offer an opportunity to escape statutes of limitations by alleging fraudulent concealment. One decision has ruled that such a fraud claim in an indoor asbestos suit had merit.[12] Another potentially successful theory is equitable restitution, in which a plaintiff performs a defendant's abatement duty. To succeed here, a plaintiff must demonstrate that it abated an asbestos hazard and that such action was immediately necessary to satisfy the requirements of public health or safety. In these circumstances, the plaintiff assumed the defendant's duty to protect public health and deserves the restitution of its costs.

Other building owners have sought to recover their indoor asbestos abatement expenses as cleanup costs under CERCLA. This cause of action has several benefits for asbestos plaintiffs, especially an ability to avoid state statutes of limitations, which are based on the date of the installation of asbestos, not on the date of the cleanup. To date, no asbestos case has accepted CERCLA liability for indoor abatement expenses, but there are limited precedents for other indoor air pollutants. In 1989 the United States Supreme Court accepted a case on the application of this statute to indoor asbestos cleanup by a private building owner. The promise of this cause of action depends on the Court's ultimate ruling, and if the Court upholds the case, CERCLA may become the primary source of recovery for asbestos abatement costs.

In sum, indoor asbestos plaintiffs have generally been able to meet the requirements of various theories of liability necessary to recover their abatement costs. Given the relatively widespread and long-standing appreciation of asbestos hazards on the part of manufacturers, negligence, fraud, and restitution claims have been relatively successful. While this success is paramount for plaintiffs, other obstacles may yet prevent recovery.

One problem common to all toxic tort litigation is the identification of responsible parties. This task is somewhat easier in the indoor asbestos cases, because the building owners often possess a contract or other documents identifying the parties who produced the materials in question. Analysis of the product may also reveal the producer. In some instances, however, plaintiffs have been unable to identify the specific company that produced the asbestos-containing materials, and several claims have been dismissed for this reason. Some plaintiffs have identified and sued all producers of asbestos-containing materials and argued that they should share the abatement costs, in proportion to their market share. While there is some precedent for this market-share liability, it has failed in the indoor asbestos cases. Identifying responsible parties remains a barrier to some asbestos abatement actions, and one case was dismissed when product analysis proved that the asbestos-containing material was *not* produced by a named defendant. School districts have lost other cases when they simply were unable to prove that any given manufacturer was responsible for friable asbestos found in their buildings.

The greatest difficulty for indoor asbestos plaintiffs may be the statute of limitations. Most asbestos-containing materials were installed in the mid-1970s or earlier. Contract statutes of limitations are typically four years or less, and tort statute limitations seldom exceed six years. While the discovery rule offers some amelioration of these time rules, many states have adopted statutes of repose that place a maximum period for initiating litigation, regardless of the date of discovery. Several cases have been dismissed under the statutes of limitations or repose.

Plaintiffs in other cases have had some success evading the time limits for bringing suit. One court found a statute of repose unconstitutional under a state constitution and another held that a statute of repose was not intended to benefit parties such as manufacturers and sellers of asbestos-containing materials. School plaintiffs have successfully taken advantage of a traditional common law rule that statutes of limitations do not apply to government plaintiffs, though more than one court has rejected this claim. Obviously, this theory is of no avail to private building owners. A church that sued asbestos producers for costs of removal of asbestos-containing acoustical tiles was barred by a statute of repose, regardless of a fraudulent concealment claim.[13] A university had its case dismissed under the statute of limitations, which held the discovery rule inapplicable to real property damages.

Procedural issues may also be important in asbestos abatement cost recovery litigation. A number of school districts have sought to combine in a large class action against manufacturer defendants. The class action procedure offers economies of scale to plaintiffs, easing litigation costs and avoiding repetitious actions. Courts have certified several class actions in these asbestos cases, though others have been denied. A class action may also facilitate settlement and provide the plaintiffs with enhanced bargaining leverage. Several large class actions have been settled, the most dramatic being a case brought by eighty-three school districts in which W. R. Grace & Co. and United States Gypsum Co. agreed to pay in excess of $55 million in a settlement.

While the asbestos property damage cases have produced extensive analysis of various legal issues, they have given remarkably little attention to the actual need for and reasonableness of the abatement action in question. Most cases did not involve air sampling or other evidence of actual risk to building occupants. While defendants have sought to raise these issues, they have received little scrutiny, and juries and judges seem fearful of the well-known carcinogenic potential of asbestos. In addition, total removal has been accepted as the presumptive response to indoor asbestos, with relatively little consideration for less costly and possibly more effective actions. One recent decision, however, dismissed a school district claim, emphasizing:

the risk of future injury from the defendant's product is remote and highly conjectural. Eagle-Picher's asbestos cement, as well as a number of other asbestos products, have been present in the plaintiff's schools for over twenty-five years. However, Catasqua presents no evidence that these products have caused a single asbestos related interest. .... There has also been no showing that the past presence of these products in the plaintiff's schools create a substantial likelihood that someone will suffer an illness in the future.

Because the plaintiff had not shown a "significant health risk," its case was dismissed under the economic loss doctrine.[14] While the court's discussion of health risk is rather abbreviated, the decision represents an important step forward in at least considering the actual hazard presented by asbestos-containing materials, before awarding compensation for removal activities.

Some juries also have resisted asbestos abatement claims where no real risk is present. In November 1989 a Los Angeles jury rejected a cost recovery action by a private building owner. The jury apparently accepted the defendant's argument that the asbestos-containing materials in the building had caused no actual indoor contamination requiring removal. In October 1989 a Pennsylvania jury rejected a cost recovery action by a school district. The defendant, W. R. Grace & Co., emphasized that "the presence of small amounts of asbestos contained in fireproofing materials used in buildings does not constitute a health hazard" and contended that "the jury verdict reflects a growing consensus of opinion that the inordinate expenses for the removal of asbestos-containing building materials is unwarranted." These recent decisions may reflect an increased skepticism, or at least an increased scrutiny, of the need for asbestos removal.

In addition to the abatement cost recovery actions, there are a few cases alleging personal injury from nonoccupational indoor exposures to asbestos. One researcher who worked in the Library of Congress while it was being renovated with asbestos products sued a manufacturer after he incurred asbestosis. The court permitted this case to proceed to trial, as the plaintiff had the benefit of the discovery rule to evade the statute of limitations in his personal injury action. An Illinois school janitor, however, failed in his claim for damages from cancer, because he was unable to provide evidence as to the manufacturer of the asbestos-containing products to which he was exposed.

A New York woman recently has brought suit against the Yonkers Board of Education, alleging that her son's death from mesothelioma was caused by exposures at his junior high school between 1967 and 1970. She claimed that friable asbestos had visibly deteriorated, dropping chunks of asbestos-containing materials, releasing fibers. The court rejected the school board's motion for summary judgment, holding that the plaintiff had presented sufficient evidence to go before a jury. The court granted summary judgment for the architect who designed the school in 1959, however, ruling that the use of asbestos in school building construction was consistent with generally accepted practices at that time.

The indoor asbestos cases demonstrate the potential for successful litigation over indoor air pollution problems. Unfortunately, these cases illustrate the limitations of the common law liability system. Some possibly deserving plaintiffs have lost their cases on what might be called technicalities. Private plaintiffs have found it particularly difficult to succeed. Other possibly undeserving plaintiffs have won, even in the absence of a real need for abatement action. Patently inconsistent results have been reached in different jurisdictions.

While asbestos in homes probably poses the least health threat of any type of building, homeowner actions are on the rise. Three California homeowners sought to bring a class action on behalf of all those whose homes contained asbestos materials, estimated at more than 1 million homes. The court rejected this class action, ruling that asbestos products have "rainbow-like diversity and a bewildering array of potential uses," and were therefore not amenable to the class action format.[15] Homeowners have begun to succeed in individual actions, particularly against insurance companies. The Bourn family in California sued a carpet company, whose employees sanded asbestos-containing vinyl tiles from a concrete floor, thereby releasing substantial numbers of asbestos fibers into the indoor air. The Bourns' house was contaminated at levels many times the federal standards for asbestos exposure, and they requested that their insurance company pay the $40,000 cost of cleanup. The Bourns sued the insurance company, and the jury found that the company acted so improperly that it awarded $1 million in punitive damages. The judge overturned this award but let stand $215,000 in economic and emotional distress damages.

In February 1990, a North Carolina couple won a $50,000 award after their home was contaminated by improper removal of an asbestos-backed vinyl floor. The jury found that a carpet installer had removed the flooring negligently and in breach of contract, because the job was not done in a workmanlike manner. Removal had produced visible dust and required replacement of furniture and other personal property. A South Carolina couple recently received $45,000 in compensatory damages and $25,000 in punitive damages for asbestos contamination resulting from improper removal of flooring.

Potential insurance liability has also arisen in an Indiana case. A homeowner plaintiff there alleged that water damage released asbestos fibers that made her home uninhabitable. Her insurance company denied coverage under the economic loss doctrine, but the court found sufficient property damage to enable her case to go forward. While relatively few residential asbestos abatement claims have been brought to date, the potential number of such actions is enormous.

Formaldehyde Litigation

While not as prominent as the asbestos abatement litigation, numerous cases have been decided involving indoor exposures to formaldehyde. The formaldehyde cases also are somewhat more representative of indoor air pollution litigation in general, because they involve health harms in a residential setting.

The formaldehyde cases also predate the explosion of asbestos litigation, as the first reported formaldehyde decision began in the early 1970s.[16] In this case, William and Arline Heritage bought a mobile home, which was apparently contaminated with high levels of formaldehyde. They alleged that Arline Heritage had suffered "painful, disabling, and incapacitating personal injuries" from exposure within the home. The Heritages sued under a theory of strict products liability. The jury found that the mobile home was not defective, so judgment was entered on behalf of defendants. The jury may have been persuaded by evidence that the risks of formaldehyde were "scientifically unknowable" to defendants at the time. Defendants' expert witness testified that formaldehyde was not known to cause such harms as suffered by Arline Heritage. The appellate court affirmed the use of this variation of the state-of-the-art defense in Alaska strict products liability actions. The Alaska Supreme Court remanded the case for a new trial, however, because the jury instructions implied that plaintiffs were required to prove negligence on the part of the seller.

The Alaska Supreme Court opened further doors to plaintiffs in a second formaldehyde action. Joseph and Lucille Shooshanian were building a retail store and installed urea formaldehyde foam insulation on the advice of their general contractor. The formaldehyde reportedly gave off "noxious and malodorous fumes" that drove away the Shooshanians' customers. The plaintiffs sought recovery under warranty, strict products liability, negligence, and a state law prohibiting certain unfair trade practices. The trial court dismissed the entire case, and the Shooshanians appealed. The Alaska Supreme Court first reversed the dismissal of plaintiffs' breach of warranty claim, taking a liberal view of the notice required in such actions. The court next reversed the dismissal of the strict products liability claim, rejecting the economic loss doctrine, because the Shooshanians alleged health effects, even though they claimed no personal injury damages. The court also reversed the dismissal of the negligence and unfair trade practice claims.

While the Alaska trial courts were resistant to the early formaldehyde claims, other plaintiffs succeeded before juries. In 1982 a South Carolina woman was awarded $600,000 after she suffered pulmonary insufficience and asthma from formaldehyde exposure in her mobile home. Later that year, a Denver jury awarded $50,000 in actual damages and over $500,000 in punitive damages for formaldehyde exposures in a mobile home. Thousands of additional formaldehyde actions were filed.

Most plaintiffs seeking recovery for formaldehyde exposure have successfully met a theory of liability. Plaintiffs have succeeded under the implied warranty of habitability, even when the plaintiff was not the original owner of the mobile home. Strict products liability cases also have succeeded. While some defendants have disputed whether a mobile home is a product, courts have tended to apply strict liability to homes against a builder-vendor. In addition, formaldehyde emissions usually result from specific wood or insulation products in a home, thus justifying the use of strict products liability. Other plaintiffs have succeeded under specific statutes governing warranties and other consumer protection guarantees. Others have successfully recovered in negligence.

The economic loss doctrine has arisen in a limited number of cases. Most formaldehyde litigation involves health damages, which automatically sound in tort. Even when a plaintiff seeks only property damages, courts have been hesitant to invoke the economic loss doctrine and limit the plaintiffs to contract claims. One action seeking costs for retrofitting and diminished home value succeeded in tort, because the court observed that formaldehyde may cause cancer and because plaintiffs were not seeking "to protect their expectation interests nor secure the benefit of the bargain."[17]

In one interesting case, the defendant maintained that the plaintiff was primarily at fault herself for her health harms.[18] Defendant maintained that the homeowner was at fault because she was hypersensitive to formaldehyde and failed to return the home to the dealer or to attempt to sell the home elsewhere. They also alleged that she took hypertension medication that may have heightened her reaction to formaldehyde, that she failed to use a humidifier supplied by the defendant, and that she brought a deodorizer and other formaldehyde sources into the home. The jury ultimately found that the plaintiff was 75 percent responsible for her health harms. Because of this finding, the plaintiff could not recover her health harms, but she still received $15,000 for loss of home value under breach of implied warranty of habitability.

Nor has the statute of limitations been a significant problem in the formaldehyde litigation. Allergenic health reactions to formaldehyde are immediately perceptible, and homeowners are easily able to sue within the statutorily required period. Indeed, formaldehyde emissions are particularly heavy immediately after purchase and decline considerably after a year or more. The statute of limitations may be a barrier to cancer damage claims from indoor formaldehyde, but these are uncommon, as formaldehyde does not appear to be a major source of cancer.

In the formaldehyde cases, the extent of actual health harms and the reasonableness of damages have been among the most litigated issues. Some of these cases have turned on the health evidence. In a Colorado case, air monitoring revealed formaldehyde levels between .49 ppm and .97 ppm in a mobile home. In addition to minor irritant effects and nausea, the residents alleged that the formaldehyde exposure caused more serious health problems, including hepatitis, that in turn led to financial setbacks for the family. Medical experts conflicted over the basis for the liver disease, and the jury awarded $50,000 in compensatory damages. The jury also awarded punitive damages totaling $510,000. The judge found the punitive damages to be too disproportionate to the actual damages and reduced the punitive award to $150,000.[19] Upon appeal, the court reversed even the lowered punitive damages award, holding that the defendants had not demonstrated "wanton and reckless disregard" for health and were unaware that formaldehyde caused such serious health problems as suffered by plaintiffs.[20]

An even more extensive judicial discussion of the health dangers of indoor formaldehyde is found in a California case.[21] In this action an eighty-two-year old widow purchased a mobile home. She immediately noticed an unpleasant odor, and subsequent testing revealed formaldehyde concentrations of about 0.5 ppm. After living in the mobile home, she developed headaches and nausea, as well as irritation of her eyes, nose, and throat. She complained, the mobile home seller eventually installed some vents, and the problem did not abate. The homeowner then sued and received an award of $90,000 compensatory damages, $55,000 punitive damages, and $90,000 as a civil penalty provided for under California statutory law. The defendant maintained that there was no connection between formaldehyde and the plaintiff's symptoms, but the court dismissed this claim as "frivolous." The court took notice of the State Department of Health Services' finding that formaldehyde could cause health effects at levels as low as 0.05 ppm. In addition, a certified industrial hygienist testified that 0.1 ppm was an excessive exposure to formaldehyde. The defendant also disputed the punitive damages award, and the court agreed, finding that the statutory civil penalty took the place of punitive damages.

A Washington case addressed a critical issue in formaldehyde litigation – the extent to which actions may be brought by individuals who are particularly sensitive to formaldehyde exposures.[22] In this case, Maureen Tiderman bought a new mobile home, in tandem with a friend. Both buyers experienced eye and throat irritation and Tiderman began suffering from asthma. Eventually, she was diagnosed as having a supra cord obstruction, which is a collapse of the airway in her throat. Prior to moving into the mobile home, Tiderman was described as "a person in excellent health who regularly engaged in strenuous physical activity and made her living as a physical education teacher."[23]

Tiderman sued the mobile home manufacturer under negligence, breach of warranty, strict liability, and state consumer protection law. The defendant argued, among other things, that Tiderman was peculiarly sensitive to formaldehyde and that the mobile home was of reasonable quality. The trial court found for plaintiff, the court of appeals reversed on a jury instruction involving special sensitivity, and the Washington Supreme Court reversed the appellate court, reinstating the trial judgment. While defendant contended that "only an insignificant percentage of the population has such a severe and long-lasting reaction to formaldehyde," the Washington Supreme Court found this irrelevant, because the manufacturer should have been aware that "formaldehyde was *harmful to some extent* to a reasonably foreseeable and appreciable percentage of users."[24] Because an appreciable number of persons will suffer somewhat from formaldehyde, the court held that the manufacturer had a duty to make its product safe for that smaller number of persons who will suffer unusually serious responses to formaldehyde. This holding has considerable importance because formaldehyde and some other indoor air pollutants appear to have particularly harmful effects on a more sensitive subgroup of the population.

The most significant jury verdict in formaldehyde litigation occurred in March 1990, when a Missouri jury awarded the Pinkerton family $16.2 million in damages for exposure to formaldehyde in flooring materials. Plaintiffs began suffering illnesses shortly after moving into their home. A state test at the house indicated that the homeowners had a daily formaldehyde intake of 3 to 10 ppm, which is hundreds of times higher than even the occupational standard for formaldehyde. The formaldehyde emissions were traced to particleboard flooring in the house.

The Pinkertons sued the manufacturers and distributors of the particleboard, seeking recovery in strict products liability and breach of implied warranty of fitness. They complained that the manufacturer should have stored the formaldehyde for six months of de-gassing before selling it. Alternatively, plaintiffs contended that defendants could have used an alternative resin that did not contain formaldehyde, when constructing the particleboard. The manufacturer responded that the alternative resin would increase costs 37 percent and that they had been unable to find a market for the more expensive nonformaldehyde particleboard.

Plaintiffs contended that their exposure to high levels of formaldehyde had caused permanent impairment of their immune systems, heightened chemical sensitivity, an increased risk of cancer, and reproductive system disorders. An expert toxicologist estimated that the exposure doubled the Pinkertons' risk of developing cancer in the future. The jury returned a verdict finding defendant manufacturers liable for nearly $200,000 in compensatory damages, after the distributors settled out of the case. The jury also assessed punitive damages of $16 million against the manufacturers.

Other Indoor Air Pollutant Litigation

There are relatively few reported decisions involving other indoor air pollutants. An increasing number of such cases are being brought to trial, however, and some cases are succeeding. The litigation over the myriad sources of indoor air pollution often suffers even greater difficulties than for radon, asbestos, and formaldehyde. The most severe indoor air pollution threats involve cancer or other diseases that are difficult to trace to any specific source of indoor contamination.

One of the first indoor air pollution cases to go to trial involved a carpet installed in a business office in 1980. The Beebes, the business owners, began suffering dizziness, nausea, inability to concentrate, burning eyes, and other symptoms. They hired a chemist to analyze the office surroundings, and the chemist suggested that the source of the health problems was 4-phenylcyclohexene, a byproduct found in the resin for the adhesives used to bind carpet fibers to their backing. After the carpet was removed, the symptoms improved. The symptoms returned when they used a heater, however, perhaps because the heating coils had been covered with dust from the carpet installation. A physician subsequently diagnosed Glen Beebe as suffering from multiple chemical sensitivity. The Beebes sued the carpet manufacturer in 1981, arguing that they had suffered over $1 million of lost earnings.

The Beebes argued that their exposure to 4-phenylcyclohexene from the carpet brought on the multiple chemical sensitivity. A study of EPA offices had shown that the substance could produce sickness, but the judge at the trial excluded this evidence, because the carpet at EPA offices was produced by a different manufacturer than that purchased by the Beebes. Trial preparation stretched out over eight years, and a jury ultimately returned a verdict for the defendant carpet manufacturer.

The Beebes apparently lost their case because evidence on the harms of 4-phenylcyclohexene was not conclusive and because medical experts cannot even agree on whether there is such a condition as multiple chemical sensitivity, much less the causes of any such condition. Several other lawsuits have been brought alleging health harms from carpet fumes, cases that may have a better prospect for success. A California resident settled for over $600,000, after he brought a lawsuit alleging that carpet glue and inadequate ventilation caused him to become dizzy and fall and hit his head. After this accident, he was comatose for several months.

Other plaintiffs have succeeded in their cases alleging symptoms from indoor air pollution sources. Students and teachers at a California school sued when roofing materials entered a classroom via air intakes. The plaintiffs suffered dizziness, fatigue, and respiratory problems, allegedly caused by solvents and plasticizers in the roofing materials. This reportedly led to heightened sensitivity to other substances, including household cleaners. The plaintiffs alleged that the company applying the new roofing materials oversprayed and failed to take precautions to prevent fumes from entering the school. After a trial, one teacher was awarded $250,000 in damages, and another received $13,000. The defendant company then settled the remaining cases for an unspecified amount.

The plaintiffs' victory in the California school case was made easier because the source of offending chemicals was clear. Cases complaining of disease from sick building syndrome or VOCs are usually complicated by the many potential sources and causes of common symptoms. There is a widespread expectation among attorneys and building owners, however, that sick building syndrome cases will proliferate during the 1990s.

A somewhat different approach to indoor air pollution problems is illustrated by a case involving state employees in Kentucky. In early 1988 workers complained of pulmonary problems and other sensitivities. The exact source of the problems could not be identified, but the building has a relatively low ventilation rate. While plaintiffs have sued for damages, the first decision involved the employees' refusal to return to work in the building. A court refused an injunction permitting the employees to stay away from the building, thereby enabling the government to force them to return to work. This decision was based largely upon exposure monitoring that failed to discover any particularly significant contamination of the indoor air.

Most VOC cases have involved allergy-type symptoms, though the greatest health threat of VOCs is cancer. At least one plaintiff has sued for leukemia allegedly contracted from indoor exposures resulting from benzene emissions from a motor oil test kit. The plaintiff, Otis Mason, was an engineering instructor who used the kit in his classroom. Mason claimed that Texaco, the kit's manufacturer, breached a duty to warn and train the sales representatives of a distribution company marketing the kit. Mason also sued the companies who distributed and sold the kit to the school. A jury awarded Mason's heirs over $9 million, of which $3.15 million was assessed against Texaco.

An appellate court reversed and remanded this decision against Texaco due to a faulty jury instruction. The appellate court ruled that the distributors of the kit were knowledgeable, and that Texaco had no duty to monitor their behavior. Mason may still recover from the other defendants, though their assets may prove insufficient to satisfy the award.

It is difficult to succeed in litigation for indoor exposures to combustion byproducts. The primary symptoms caused by the combustion byproducts are respiratory illnesses, which have so many other sources that proof of causation will be extremely difficult. There may be recovery, however, for extreme episodes, such as carbon monoxide poisoning. For example, a Virginia apartment resident died from carbon monoxide poisoning, and his heirs have brought suit alleging that the landlord was responsible because "the furnace and hot water heater were operating with inadequate, unsafe and improper ventilation which was dangerous to human life."[25] In a Florida case, a restaurant's grand opening was spoiled when an outside generator vented carbon monoxide fumes into the restaurant. A woman who was overcome by the fumes received a total of $200,000 compensation from settlements and a trial verdict. In March 1990, a woman received a $2.8 million settlement after her husband died from carbon monoxide fumes that had seeped into his motel room.

Plaintiffs also face difficulty succeeding in an action alleging biological contamination of indoor air. One unusual case has been brought in San Francisco. The genesis of this action was a fire that triggered the commercial building's sprinkler system. The building owner allegedly delayed the cleanup of the interior and ultimately provided an inadequate cleanup. An advertising company tenant in the building subsequently sued the owner, complaining that the water caused microbial contamination, which caused its employees to suffer lung disease, headaches, and other illness and left the workers hypersensitive to fungal exposure. The advertising company then moved to another building and sued their original landlord for millions of dollars in lost business.

White-collar workers exposed to microbial contamination may recover for disease under workers' compensation statutes in force in all states. These laws typically provide for automatic, no-fault compensation for health harms arising out of an accident on the job. A New York appellate court recently dealt a blow to this theory, however. An attorney sought benefits based on his allergic reaction to dust circulated during the firm's remodeling, and the Workers' Compensation Board awarded compensation, attributing an accident to a malfunctioning air-conditioning system. The appellate court overturned this finding, ruling that the inhalation of dust could not be an accident warranting workers' compensation recovery. Other states have taken a somewhat broader view of the accident requirement and may provide a workers' compensation recovery opportunity. Other circumstances also may enable recovery. An employee of Raytheon alleged that he was exposed to toxic substances, which caused him to become dizzy, lose his motor control, fall and strike his head, and subsequently lapse into a coma. He brought a workers' compensation claim against his employer as well as tort claims against those involved in constructing and furnishing the building. This case ultimately settled for an undisclosed sum. In addition, a Florida librarian recovered under workers' compensation when she alleged that indoor air pollution caused her to suffer coughing, eye irritation, sore throats, and inability to speak in the building.

Attempts at recovery for health harms from miscellaneous air pollutants have generally been unsuccessful, with the exception of indoor exposures to pesticides. The most prominent pesticides case involved a Virginia couple who died the week after their home was fumigated by Orkin Exterminating Co. This case led to criminal indictments of Orkin under the Federal Insecticide, Fungicide, and Rodenticide Act for allowing the site to be reoccupied before aeration was complete, for failure to remove pillows and mattresses before fumigation, and for failure to warn adequately. The company also failed to monitor for indoor exposure levels. Orkin was convicted and fined $500,000. The presence of criminal actions obviously eases the private plaintiff's burdens and Orkin settled with the family's estate for $2.5 million. In another pesticide case, decided in December 1989, America, Inc., treated a home with chlordane to exterminate termites. Plaintiffs alleged that this treatment caused them identifiable medical problems, produced anxiety that hastened the death of a ninety-year-old relative, and harmed their property value. Evidence demonstrated that the defendant had unsafely and illegally applied the pesticide in this case and in sixty other homes over four years. A jury awarded plaintiffs $260,000 in compensatory damages and $500,000 in punitive damages. Velsicol, the manufacturer of the chlordane, had previously settled with plaintiffs for an undisclosed amount.

Numerous other pesticide cases have been tried, with relative success for plaintiffs. A 1989 Georgia decision awarded $400,000, including $130,000 punitive damages, to a family whose house was sprayed for termites. The applicator failed to follow the label, and the family then suffered headaches, vision problems, and allergic reactions. A federal appellate court ruled that Orkin's sales pitch violated the Illinois consumer protection statute and upheld a $625,000 recovery by a family who suffered immune system injuries. An Ohio court ruled that a homeowner could proceed against an exterminator but not against the manufacturer of the pesticide. In South Carolina a strange decision resulted from Orkin's application of chlordane. A homeowner alleged that he and his daughter suffered health harms from termite extermination, and the defendant disputed the causation of the harms. A jury awarded $1 in actual damages and $24,999 in punitive damages.

More than one hundred cases have been filed throughout the country alleging health problems from pesticide applications that contaminated indoor air. The National Coalition Against the Misuse of Pesticides has now formed a clearinghouse to assist plaintiffs' attorneys by pooling their knowledge. This can provide invaluable assistance to the typical plaintiff, who has few resources and little expertise.

Notes

1. M. Galen, *Lawyers Grapple with Radon Issue*, NAT'L L.J., July 21, 1986, at 8.

2. 730 F.2d 392 (5th Cir. 1984), *cert. denied*, 469 U.S. 1159 (1985).

3. 730 F.2d at 395.

4. 586 F. Supp. 14 (D. Colo. 1984).

5. 680 F. Supp. 696 (D.N.J. 1988).

6. Frank Cross & Paula Murray, *Liability for Toxic Radon Gas in Residential Home Sales*, 66 N.C. L. REV. 687, 739 (1988).

7. *Cinnaminson Township Board of Education v. U.S. Gypsum Co.*, 552 F. Supp. 855 (D.N.J. 1982)

8. *County of Johnson v. United States Gypsum Company*, 580 F. Supp. 284 (E.D. Tenn. 1984)

9. 640 F. Supp. 559 (D.S.C. 1986), *aff'd*, 827 F.2d 975 (4th Cir. 1987).

10. Note, *Asbestos in Schools and the Economic Loss Doctrine*, 54 U. CHI. L. REV. 277 (1987).

11. Note, *Asbestos Abatement: The Second Wave of the Asbestos Litigation Industry*, 27 WASHBURN L.J. 4454, 491 (1988).

12. *City of Manchester v. National Gypsum Co.*, 637 F. Supp. 646, 655 (D.R.I. 1986).

13. *First United Methodist Church of Hyattsville v. United States Gypsum Company*, 882 F.2d 862 (4th Cir. 1989).

14. *Catasauqua Area School District v. Eagle-Picher Industries, Inc.*, Civil Action No. 85-3743 (E.D. Pa. 1988).

15. INDOOR POLLUTION NEWS, April 21, 1988, p. 6.

16. *Heritage v. Pioneer Brokerage & Sales, Inc.*, 604 P.2d 1059 (Alas. 1979).

17. *Pearl v. Allied Corp.*, 566 F. Supp. 400, 403 (E.D. Pa. 1983).

18. *Peterson v. Bendix Home Systems, Inc.*, 318 N.W.2d 50 (Minn. 1982).

19. *Alley v. Gubser Development Co.*, 569 F. Supp. 36 (D. Colo. 1983).

20. *Alley v. Gubser Development Co.*, 785 F.2d 849 (10th Cir. 1986).

21. *Troensegaard v. Silvercrest Industries, Inc.*, 220 Cal. Rptr. 712 (Cal. App. 1 Dist. 1985).

22. *Tiderman v. Fleetwood Homes of Washington*, 684 P.2d 1302 (Wash. 1984).

23. 684 P.2d at 1303.

24. 684 P.2d at 1305.

25. INDOOR POLLUTION NEWS, April 21, 1988, p. 3.

PART IV

The Future of Indoor Air Pollution Control

The first three parts of this book, taken together, present a discouraging picture of the legal system's reaction to indoor air pollution. Part I demonstrated the enormity of the health costs of current levels of indoor air pollution. Yet Part II revealed the incomplete and erratic nature of the government's efforts to remedy the problem. Private efforts to recover for indoor air pollution are also ineffective, as described in Part III.

There is real opportunity, however, to correct some deficiencies of the status quo and create an effective response to indoor air contamination. Influential political actors, both in Congress and in the executive branch, are now awakening to the risks presented by indoor air. Some indoor air quality issues have even assumed prominence with the public at large. This attention has not yet reached the critical mass necessary to drive effective action against indoor air pollution. The potential responsiveness of these parties creates at least an opportunity for the modifications in existing structures necessary to control the morbidity and mortality associated with contaminated indoor air.

Chapter 11 sets forth several general principles for reforming the law's response to indoor air pollution. Foremost among these reforms is the simple need for recognition of the magnitude of the indoor air quality problem confronting Americans. Measured by any reasonable yardstick, indoor air pollution should be at or near the top of the government's priorities for public health protection. Yet indoor air issues dwell near the bottom of current priorities, when considered in terms of resources spent. Little can be done until these priorities are reversed. Various psychological and structural features conspire to keep indoor air quality low on the government's agenda for environmental action. These obstacles can be overcome, however, and anyone with a principled concern for public health will demand that indoor air quality receive additional resources and attention.

The mere provision of additional resources will contribute significantly to the government's response to indoor air contamination, but additional measures are necessary to ensure that such response is effective and efficient. Express statutory authority is required for government action on indoor air pollution. Action is presently stalled in part due to the ambiguity of authority for action by the Environmental Protection Agency and other administrative bodies. Legislation creating express authority over indoor air would stimulate executive action, direct that action along constructive lines, and overcome inconsistency and disagreement among federal agencies with some jurisdiction over indoor air issues.

Such statutory authority should contain a third reform in the federal government's approach to indoor air quality protection — the authority to impose enforceable standards and other regulatory requirements to protect indoor air. The government presently focuses upon an informational approach that relies on research and education of the public in hopes of prompting private responses to contaminated indoor air. While this approach has political appeal, it has proved ineffective. In other public health legislation, such as food safety, occupational safety, and environmental pollution, the government does not rely on education but commands specific measures to ensure public health. Similar regulations are required to prevent unsafe indoor air. Such a regulatory system need not be radical or expensive. Moderate, cost-effective requirements on new construction and indoor products would go far to improve indoor air quality.

Litigation for private recoveries from indoor air pollution also requires some reform of common law rules. Current law often denies any remedy to those who suffer cancer from indoor air contamination. Permitting recovery for a risk of cancer, and medical surveillance for development of such cancer, can more equitably compensate deserving victims of indoor air pollution. Administrative reforms can facilitate plaintiffs' recoveries, while protecting defendants from unfairly large punitive damages awards. Recovery of costs for abating indoor air pollution must also be controlled, to enable recovery only when the pollution presents a genuine threat to public health.

11

DIRECTIONS FOR THE FUTURE LEGAL RESPONSE TO INDOOR AIR POLLUTION

The present legal response to indoor air pollution is woefully deficient. The health harms of indoor air contamination are enormous, both in absolute terms and relative to other environmental threats to health. Despite these risks, government has devoted few resources and little regulatory attention to indoor air quality issues. One can truthfully say that the government fiddles while tens of thousands of Americans contract fatal cancer and while millions of others suffer disease. We have known of the major sources of indoor air pollution risk for more than a decade, and little has been done.

The above critique is probably too harsh, however. Our democratic structures are not well poised for response to such insidious, nonintuitive threats as indoor air pollution. One author thus explained the government's progress on outdoor pollution sources:

> While many are critical of the glacial speed at which the government responds to toxic pollution, the author believes that the speed of eliminating toxic waste pollution is determined by human nature, namely the ability of many to recognize new factors and implement them in his life. This process involves several learning steps, starting with the collection of data that must slowly grow to an understanding of what the knowledge means. From there starts the painfully slow process of implementing knowledge. Viewed on a historic scale, our progress might not be as slow as it might seem. After all, even the most rapid social

changes, such as the Industrial Revolution, took longer than the twenty years during which [the National Environmental Protection Act] has been in effect.[1]

Given the costs attendant to government regulation and administrative realities, the prudence of gradualism has logic.

Notwithstanding the above concerns, it remains critical to press for rapid action against particularly hazardous conditions. Technological and social change occurs quickly in modern society, and government must adapt to keep pace. Progress in controlling environmental hazards is not in the hands of some uncontrollable machine but can be forced and directed by knowledgeable and concerned individuals. This chapter presents a series of future directions to better control the threat of indoor air pollution and to better compensate those who have suffered from breathing contaminated indoor air.

Raise the Priority of Indoor Air Quality

Perhaps the most significant shortcoming of the present government response to indoor air pollution is the extremely low priority assigned to indoor air problems. Given the reality of limited resources (money, staff, and public attention), the prioritization of those resources becomes critical to overall public health protection. A review of the resources devoted to indoor air issues vis-à-vis other environmental and public health concerns plainly reveals the low priority placed on indoor air quality. This low priority is disturbing and unjustifiable, because indoor air presents risks far exceeding those from environmental conditions afforded a much higher priority. Righting the government's prioritization in the battle to protect public health should be our foremost objective.

The Environmental Protection Agency's poor prioritization of attention on indoor air pollution is essentially confessed by the agency itself. A 1987 EPA self-study concluded that indoor air pollution was the greatest environmental public health threat extant. This study was followed by in-depth analyses by the agency's regional offices, which considered the regional threats from sources such as indoor air pollution, outdoor air pollution, water pollution, acid rain, hazardous wastes, pesticides, and other sources. After a two-year study, three administrative regions reported their conclusion that the most severe environmental risk was indoor air pollution from radon and the second most severe risk was nonradon indoor air pollution. There can be little doubt but that indoor air pollution should be the top priority of EPA. Yet EPA's regional study concluded that "[e]ach of the three highest health risk areas — radon, [indoor air pollution], and pesticide residues — are the subject of minimal regional program efforts. . . . By contrast, two of the low-risk problem areas — active and abandoned hazardous waste sites . . . are the subject of major regional programs."[2]

Indoor air pollution is also near the bottom of EPA's priorities in total spending. In 1989 EPA's indoor air quality budget tripled from $400,000 to $1.4 million. This substantial percentage increase, however, left indoor air quality with less than 0.01 percent of the budget for environmental hazards. Even passage of the controversial Mitchell-Kennedy indoor air quality bill would add funding of less than $50 million per year, still much less than 1 percent of EPA's budget. And this bill is unlikely to pass this year because Congress has given a higher priority to outdoor air pollution, pesticides, and other issues. President Bush's 1990 proposed budget for fiscal year 1991 perpetuates this misallocation of resources. Exhibit 11.1 shows the funding proposed for EPA programs in this budget and the increase over the previous fiscal year. This exhibit reveals not only the low priority accorded to the number one environmental health problem of radon but also that radon control is falling further behind less pressing threats to public health.

Exhibit 11.1
Proposed EPA Budget for FY 1991

Area	Amount	Increase
Total Budget	$5.58 billion	12%
Air programs	$252 million	35%
Superfund	$1.74 billion	14%
Hazardous waste	$317 million	15%
Water quality program	$379 million	9%
Safe drinking water	$132 million	8%
Radon control	$24.5 million	7%

EPA undertook the self-study of relative risks in order to reconsider its priorities and claims to be raising the priority of indoor air quality issues. Prospects for significantly increasing the resources allocated to correcting indoor air contamination remain slim, however. Structural features conspire to minimize regulatory attention for indoor air pollution.

The first structural problem is regulatory inertia. Change tends to come incrementally, if at all. Dramatic change is difficult and controversial, while continuity is politically secure. EPA has conceded that its priorities tend to be driven by past perceptions of environmental problems rather than current understanding of risks. Although it is difficult to overcome such inertia, it is possible to reorder priorities, given sufficient commitment. For example, abandoned hazardous waste sites were a low priority until Congress passed Superfund and helped focus public attention on the problem. Subsequently, attention and resources in this area bloomed to the point where it is the largest single element of EPA's budget. The irony is that abandoned hazardous waste sites present very little relative risk to the public. Yet Superfund demonstrates the ability of the political regulatory system to reorder priorities drastically.

A second difficulty in elevating the priority given indoor air pollution is public perception. For a variety of reasons, the public tends to place little importance on indoor air contamination. While EPA is an unelected bureaucracy, the agency indirectly responds to public opinion. Ultimately, EPA actions are beholden to the president and Congress, who tend to respond to public pressures. Some such responsiveness is both unavoidable and desirable in a democracy. However, "EPA's experience in the 1970s makes clear that being 'too responsive' can waste opportunities and fail to protect the public."[3] Public perceptions of risk, particularly risk from carcinogens, are "wildly inaccurate."[4] EPA reliance on public perceptions as a guide to regulation have produced a "carcinogen of the month" process, which misallocates money to small, exaggerated risks that happen to be publicized by the mass media, while ignoring much greater but less prominent risks. Public misperception of risks will remain a problem for EPA prioritization, but it need not remain an insurmountable one. The people rely on EPA's scientific expertise to lead the public, rather than to follow public opinion. When EPA places an issue at the front of its agenda, popular perceptions often follow and reinforce the agency's decision. While EPA runs some risk by rushing ahead of public perceptions, such action is one of the agency's primary tasks, which will inure to its benefit and credit over the long run.

Unfortunately, yet another barrier stands in the way of increasing the regulatory priority given to indoor air pollution. EPA is most likely to get ahead of public opinion when driven by concerned interest groups, but these groups have been guilty of underemphasizing indoor threats to health. Leading environmental organizations such as the Natural Resources Defense Council, which carry undeniable clout with EPA and with the public, have been slow to stress indoor air quality. This hesitancy is partially due to inertia within these organizations, which historically have focused upon outdoor pollution. In addition, these groups have feared a trade-off between indoor and outdoor air pollution, such that increased attention to indoor air problems would undermine their effort to control outdoor emissions. Such a trade-off is not necessarily ineluctable, though some degree of resource trade-off is probably a political reality. Yet it is ironic that these "public interest" groups have sought to address the less hazardous prong of the trade-off, at the expense of the much greater threat to public health posed by indoor air pollution. Choice, according to a great philosopher, is tragic, and the tragedy of the choice to emphasize outdoor pollution can be measured in thousands of lives. These environmental groups have compelling cause to reexamine their attention to indoor pollution sources, and some groups, such as the Environmental Defense Fund, have increasingly responded to indoor threats to health. While awaiting such a reexamination of priorities, EPA retains the responsibility not to be hostage to such interest groups but to take the lead and focus on indoor air quality. This action likely will precipitate a private reordering of priorities as well.

There remains one psychological obstacle to increasing the priority of indoor air quality, which probably explains something of the above barriers. EPA, the public, and interest groups tend to think of pollution problems in terms of an innocent and divine nature being selfishly ruined by the villainous actions of big business. For radon, the most significant indoor air pollution problem, the "pollution" is produced by nature itself. Interested organizations find it more difficult to mobilize government action in the absence of a compelling villain to bear responsibility for risking the health and welfare of individuals. A group of authors explained the difficulty of alerting Americans to the risks of radon in homes:

There is usually no villain to blame. Perceptions that individuals' rights to a safe, clean environment have been violated often complicate reactions to other environmental hazards. Affected individuals tend to focus on determining who caused the problem and, therefore, who should be responsible for its solution.[5]

Americans are accustomed to blaming industry, technology, and chemicals for health fears. The idea that nature could be responsible for greater cancer risks is unsettling. The idea that one's home, perceived as a refuge, could produce greater cancer risks is equally unsettling. These perceptions are pervasive and difficult to overcome. A certain environmental maturity is required to accept counterintuitive evidence. Development of this environmental maturity is increasingly essential and not merely for indoor air pollution. Many environmental problems are less attributable to the large smokestack industries than to small business, family farms, and other "less villainous" sources. EPA and the rest of the federal government must assume some responsibility for promoting this enhanced understanding of environmental problems.

Such a better understanding will not only permit indoor air pollution problems to achieve their deserved priority but also will enable better prioritization within indoor air programs. Indoor air pollution control resources are as misallocated as are overall environmental protection resources. By far the most money has been spent on prevention of indoor exposures to asbestos, with formaldehyde contamination probably the second highest indoor air priority in regulation. While both these sources warrant some government attention to potential risk, other pollutants such as radon and volatile organic compounds produce a much greater risk. Society will spend over $100 billion to abate and remove asbestos in buildings during the next decade.[6] This enormous expenditure will have little health benefit and may sometimes increase risk. Reallocation of these resources to address other indoor contaminants could produce much greater benefit.

While the above discussion has dealt with EPA, improved prioritization for indoor air pollution is required in other federal and state agencies. The Consumer Product Safety Commission is a logical locus for regulation of many product sources of volatile organic compounds, combustion byproducts, microbiological contaminants, and other pollutants. For a brief time, CPSC declared that indoor air quality was its top priority. But CPSC has a very limited budget and enough difficulty justifying its own significance in the federal government to take the primary responsibility for addressing the contamination of indoor air. Ultimately, the scope of a federal indoor air pollution control program will rest with EPA.

If EPA reprioritizes its resources to focus substantially upon indoor air pollution, this alone would represent tremendous progress. The skilled officers of that agency are capable of creating programs to control indoor exposure levels. Perhaps more importantly, assumption of a top priority at EPA will go far to raise the visibility of indoor air pollution issues with the public at large, who may then be motivated to take more private action to protect public health.

Adopt Comprehensive Statutory Authority

At the current time, authority to address indoor air pollution is both ambiguous and scattered throughout the federal government. There is relatively little authority that clearly includes indoor air quality. Jurisdictional disputes inevitably arise when enabling authority is so unclear. Most commentators cite the lack of overarching, unambiguous authority as a major reason for the federal government's lack of attention to indoor air pollution.

The power to act on indoor air pollution is not entirely lacking under current authority. Exhibit 11.2 sets forth EPA's determination of the authority provided by various statutes to respond to indoor air contamination. This exhibit shows that aggressive administrators, committed to improving indoor air quality, have sufficient statutory tools to make progress. New authority is necessary, however, in the absence of such an aggressive response from the present personnel of regulatory agencies.

The importance of clear authority is as much psychological as it is legal. Agencies are far more comfortable taking actions when it is clear that Congress desires such actions. Experience in indoor air pollution controls to date confirms the need for a clear congressional mandate. EPA has taken its most vigorous indoor air quality actions in response to asbestos in schools, after Congress passed a law commanding such measures. The second most vigorous regulatory response to indoor air quality has probably come in the field of pesticides, where EPA has a clear statutory authority for regulation. In fields where authority is less clear, EPA has done less.

Exhibit 11.2
EPA Interpretation of Federal Statutory Authorities

Statute	Agency	Regulations	Standards	Guidelines	Enforcement	Research	Coordination
Clean Air Act	EPA	B	B/A	B	B	B	B
Superfund	EPA	B	B	A	C	B/A	B/A
Radon Gas and Indoor Air Quality Act	EPA					A	A
FIFRA	EPA	B		B	B	B	
TSCA	EPA	B		B	B	B	B
AHERA	EPA	A		A	A		
Housing and Urban Development Act	HUD		B	B		B	
Energy Conservation and Production Act	DOE		B	A		A	A

A = Statutes that grant the agency explicit authority to conduct indoor air quality related activities.

B = Statutes that grant the agency authority which, by implication, include indoor air.

C = Statutes that give the agency authority which could be interpreted to include indoor air.

The new statutory power to protect public health from indoor air pollution should have at least two components. First, it should provide the full panoply of regulatory powers found in other statutes. The statute should authorize research, standard-setting, regulations, banning of products or processes, subsidies, incentives, and enforcement with sufficient penalties. While the terms of such a statute must be somewhat vague, the radon problem warrants specific authority, and the statute should differentiate between private residential problems and those in a commercial setting.

Second, the statutory authority should create EPA as a lead agency to respond to indoor air contamination. CPSC and other agencies could retain the power to ban or control harmful products, but EPA should be granted all necessary power to coordinate federal actions and override any activities that compromise indoor air quality. Such coordination is necessary to avoid the situation where different agencies act inconsistently or at cross-purposes. For example, EPA should have authority to prevent the Department of Energy from establishing energy conservation standards that have the effect of increasing indoor concentrations of radon and other hazardous substances. Increased government action in air pollution in offices will inevitably produce overlap and potential conflict between EPA and OSHA. Failures of government response to indoor air pollution is now partly attributable to the fact that "no one Federal agency has responsibility or authority for indoor air quality in the nonworkplace."[7]

Creation of clear statutory authority for response to indoor air pollution would produce great benefit. Such authority could be used to overcome existing jurisdictional conflicts and to reassure government agencies that indoor air pollution is a proper subject for action. In addition, passage of such a statute would help push indoor air problems to the forefront of the public health agenda, much as passage of Superfund focused public attention on the problem of hazardous waste sites.

Shift from Education to Regulation

The efforts taken to date against most indoor air pollution problems, particularly radon contamination, have been almost entirely informational. Government has researched the problem and disseminated information to potentially affected localities and individuals, who presumably will respond as necessary. In practice, this educational approach has largely failed to redress the problem and a more vigorous regulatory approach is required for effective indoor pollution control.

This position is not to demean the necessity for research and education. Research, of course, is essential to inform policymaking judgment, and the public should be fully informed of the risks they confront. But mere provision of information and even warning may fail to correct indoor air pollution risks and leave millions at substantial health risk. The success of informational campaigns is not yet demonstrated — reportedly, "the popularity of such information programs among public agencies rests more on philosophical and ideological grounds than on solid empirical evidence supporting their ability to alter consumer behavior."[8] Psychological studies have identified a number of reasons why warnings are insufficient to motivate action, or even to change perceptions of risk. One leading reason is the denial tendency, which may cause smokers to discount the true risks of smoking. This denial may be particularly problematic for informing of indoor air pollution risks, such as radon. One study suggested:

> I suggest that radon risk perception is a special case of ego-related risk, i.e., it is a risk that is closely related to self conceptions. This hypothesis is derived from evidence that people tend to perceive their homes as parts of their selves, especially if they have lived in them for a long time. And there is a tendency to deny that something as closely related to oneself as one's home (or body) could be threatening.
>
> Data indicate that people with a longer history of living in a house are more likely to deny radon risk.[9]

The existence of such denial behavior undermines any program that relies primarily upon raising public awareness.

A study of an educational campaign in Maine addressing the risks of indoor radon contamination illustrates the shortcomings of a purely educational approach.[10] The University of Maine produced an information pamphlet to inform homeowners about radon risks. While the homeowners considered the information materials to be understandable, their appreciation of radon risks remained limited. A majority of households significantly understated their risk levels. Relatively few households undertook significant radon mitigation, and longtime residents of a home were particularly unlikely to take mitigating actions.

The Maine study is not alone, as studies in Maryland, New Jersey, and other states have found at best a weak link between educational campaigns and remedial action for radon. Other studies have had some success in influencing individuals' perceptions of radon risk. This success is uneven, however, and there is no clear evidence that information produces effective remediation of high indoor radon concentrations. Nor is the educational approach likely to promise much success for other indoor pollutants. A report for EPA recently generalized:

> Don't expect too much. People *can* understand risk tradeoffs, risk comparisons, and risk probabilities when they are carefully explained. But usually people don't really want to understand.... Over the long haul, risk communication has more to do with fear, anger, powerlessness, optimism and overconfidence than with finding ways to simplify complex information.[11]

However attractive an educational approach may be to politicians and economists, the evidence indicates that information alone can do little to ensure indoor air quality.

Some would argue that the ineffectiveness of the educational approach is irrelevant, under the theory that homeowners have voluntarily assumed the risk of any indoor air pollution that they fail to abate. It is not government's responsibility, the argument goes, to protect these people from their own choices. As a commentator recently elaborated:

> The rationale for government regulation of outdoor air pollution is based in part on a definition of outdoor air as a "public good" and on the realization that those who suffer the effects of such pollution are neither compensated by nor powerful in influencing polluters. The situation is quite different for some indoor environments, especially private residences, for both the costs and benefits of pollution control are internalized within households.[12]

This argument ignores the realities of modern living. Subscribing to this argument would also invalidate all consumer protection legislation, occupational safety and health legislation, and other widely accepted government actions. While there is of course benefit to free choice, people have neither the time, inclination, nor ability to analyze every risk of modern living and adjust their lives accordingly. Rather, it can be more efficient to leave such relatively technical issues to government experts to design a structure beyond education, which directly protects public health from contaminated indoor air.

The alternative to an educational approach would involve some form of compulsory government regulation of indoor air quality. Government presently seems quite fearful of such regulation, and even strong proponents of indoor air quality legislation urgently stress that they propose no regulatory authority. Yet such regulation offers the best response to indoor air pollution, and a regulatory regime could be structured in a manner that avoids imposing great costs on building owners and real estate businesses.

Standard, traditional regulatory approaches cannot be used for much indoor air pollution. The national ambient air quality standards establish maximum permissible concentrations of certain pollutants in outdoor air. The national emission standards for hazardous air pollutants require specific control technology to prevent emission of certain pollutants into outdoor air. Neither approach could succeed for indoor air pollution in residential homes. First, homeowners would almost certainly rebel at any attempt by the government to set standards for the air in their homes. Second, such an approach would be "impractical because of the prohibitive monitoring costs and the difficulty of enforcement within approximately 62 million residences in the United States."[13]

Some regulation can succeed, however. Applying standards to new construction, for example, offers benefits at low cost. Builders could be required to test for radon and other pollutants prior to sale. In high-radon areas, builders might be required to install specific remediative technologies. Minimum ventilation standards prescribed by the federal government could be required in state and local building codes. Standards for new construction take a long time to protect a substantial portion of the population. The stock of residential housing turns over at a rate of only 2 percent per year. Extending the standards to any significant remodeling of buildings (such as that requiring a building permit) would significantly speed the implementation of the standards. This would be especially true in commercial buildings, where "about 30 percent of the average building's interior space is rebuilt each year."[14] Disclosure of indoor contamination levels to the purchaser could also be required as a condition of real estate sales.

Such standards for new construction could be accompanied by subsidies and other incentives to encourage voluntary abatement action for indoor air pollution.

Other indoor air pollution problems could be more simply addressed. Significant indoor air pollutants such as formaldehyde, volatile organic compounds, and combustion byproducts are caused by construction materials or other products. EPA, CPSC, or other agencies could set stricter standards for manufacture and use of such products. The current, relatively weak formaldehyde standards for certain wood products could be strengthened and expanded and used as a model for control of emissions from other products.

One remaining concern with the regulatory approach involves cost. Real estate interests are politically powerful and fearful that a new regulatory regime for indoor air pollution could spiral out of control and substantially raise the costs of new construction. New legislation should permit cost considerations and only mandate controls found to be cost-effective. In addition, regulation could have some positive economic effects:

> While comprehensive federal regulation is often seen as unwarranted interference, three peripheral effects of statutory regulation would actually enhance the real estate market. First, it would establish a certainty which is lacking in the haphazard way environmental law is applied in this area, allowing property owners to avoid litigation by adhering to definite standards. Secondly, regulation would force manufacturers, builders, architects, and designers to create and design products and buildings that mitigate or eliminate sources of indoor air pollution. Finally, contractual allocation of liability between the parties can be better accomplished where liabilities are defined by standards promulgated and mandated by a governmental authority.[15]

Additional efficiency benefits would result from federal action. States currently are passing legislation to protect indoor air quality, but these rules are at best haphazard. Different states have laws covering different pollutants, with different coverage, and imposing different requirements. Some states offer little protection. Overall national standards could bring some consistency to this process:

States claim that absent Federal standards, the Nation would be subjected to a patchwork of diverse State and local requirements which could be as counterproductive and confusing to meaningful control efforts as an absence of national air and water pollution control standards would be.[16]

A uniform national approach to indoor air pollution would make it far simpler for builders to identify the applicable regulatory requirements and more efficient for builders to develop procedures for compliance with such requirements.

A national regulatory approach to indoor air pollution is still considered a radical step, but it need not be so. Any national approach could be integrated with local building codes and enforced by local authorities. While regulation always involves compliance costs, there is no other potential area of regulation with so positive a benefit/cost ratio as indoor air pollution. The Clean Air Act has imposed far greater costs to achieve much less public health benefit. Even a regulatory regime for indoor air pollution that is structured to contain costs would offer considerable benefit. Development of such a regime should assume a prominent place on the public policy agenda.

Reform Compensation for Indoor Air Pollution

Whatever progress is made in reforming government regulation of indoor air pollution to protect public health, some significant number of adverse health effects will continue to be caused by indoor contamination. For these remaining health effects, we require an effective, efficient system to compensate the victims for their injuries. The present compensation structure offers no such system but rather produces haphazard results, where deserving plaintiffs are denied recovery even as less deserving plaintiffs receive windfall damages. Certain structural changes can ameliorate these problems.

Some change is needed to overcome the most serious obstacles to even a deserving plaintiff's recovery of certain health harms — the statute of limitations and the virtual impossibility of demonstrating causation for serious diseases such as cancer. Cancer, especially from radon and volatile organic compounds, is the most serious and one of the most frequent adverse health consequences of indoor air contamination. Yet it is particularly difficult to recover for indoor-pollution-caused cancers, and much easier to recover for far milder health effects. A major reason for the difficulty of recovery for cancer is that disease's long latency period before it is diagnosed and the multiple causes of most types of cancer. When cancer is found in a homeowner, he or she has a very difficult task tracing the past exposure that likely caused the cancer and the company responsible for that exposure. Even when the path of causation can be tracked, statutes of limitations may still preclude a person's ability to recover for suffering cancer.

The first key change in common law would be to recognize an opportunity for individuals to recover damages for incurring a risk of future cancer. Once recovery for a risk is accepted, a plaintiff need not await the decades of cancer latency but could sue responsible parties immediately following exposure to a carcinogen. Evidence would be more readily available and statutes of limitations would not bar actions.

Under a regime of recovery for a risk, a plaintiff still would be required to prove that the defendant violated some standard of liability (such as negligence, strict liability, etc.) and would also be compelled to demonstrate the magnitude of his or her exposure to a carcinogen. The plaintiff would then quantify the extent of risk, using accepted principles of quantitative risk assessment for carcinogens. If a plaintiff successfully demonstrated the above, and there were no successful affirmative defenses, the plaintiff would receive the present value of this future risk, discounted by its probability. Such damage assessment is practical:

> While damage measurement and valuation of future cancer risk under this proposal might appear complex, it need not be so. Actuaries have considerable expertise in assessing the present value of future risks, and these assessments form the basis of the insurance industry. A meaningful valuation of future cancer risk can be readily obtained.[17]

Assuming a reasonably functioning private market in insurance for future risks, a system of recovery for risk will enable plaintiffs to insure themselves against the potential consequences of carcinogenic exposures.

The above proposal does not imply that individuals should be able to recover for every exposure to carcinogenic risk, however. Every American has suffered some increased cancer risk from indoor exposures, not to mention other environmental sources of carcinogens.

In most cases, the relative risk of exposure is too small to justify the costs of litigation. For some exposures, however, particularly those involving high indoor radon levels, the risk may be so substantial that recovery is justified.

The benefits of the above-described recovery for a risk would be further enhanced by creating new administrative compensation structures. Even relatively large risks of future cancer (such as a 1 percent risk) may not provide recoveries sufficient to warrant litigation expenses. Yet these individuals are deserving of some compensation for a not insignificant danger of incurring future cancer. A kind of administrative cancer small claims court could be created. This court would use the quantitative risk assessments already produced by the federal government for most carcinogens, which estimate specific future risk levels for each defined exposure level. The court would also employ tables of present value for specified future cancer risks. Use of the above data sources would greatly simplify the trial process. A plaintiff would be called upon to show that a defendant violated some standard of liability, that this violation caused an exposure to a carcinogen, and what that exposure level was. Then, the court would simply calculate the proper damages based on existing data sources. In exchange for this simplified process, plaintiffs might give up their opportunity to recover other damages.

In regular trials, however, plaintiffs should be able to recover certain other damages from exposure to carcinogens. For example, after cancer risk passes a certain threshold, plaintiffs presumptively should be able to recover any costs of future medical surveillance. Plaintiffs should be able to recover for fear of future cancer, when the severity of risk makes such fear reasonable. Courts should be more hesitant, however, to grant punitive damages in indoor air pollution cases. Few indoor air pollution defendants are sufficiently culpable to warrant punitive damages, and courts are ill equipped to decide that punishment is warranted. Punitive damages have too often been made emotionally, without regard for all the facts of the case. As government regulation of indoor air pollution increases in effectiveness, the need for punitive damages also will be lowered correspondingly.

The above changes would help rationalize the recovery of health harms from indoor air pollution and other sources. The system already works reasonably well for irritant effects of indoor pollution. The suggested changes are far from a panacea, and many plaintiffs will still face a difficult task in accumulating the evidence necessary to justify a recovery. Permitting recovery for a risk, particularly with the new administrative structure suggested above, will at least facilitate plaintiffs' tasks and offers the best improvement of present structures, without imposing unreasonable costs on innocent defendants.

One additional common law change is also indicated, for economic recoveries for abatement of indoor air pollution harms. The courts have wisely disregarded much of the economic loss doctrine, permitting recovery in tort for even property damages. The courts have failed to scrutinize such claims strictly, however. The same courts that refuse to recognize health risks as high as 49 percent have authorized abatement actions in response to potential risks far below 1 percent. Some courts have not even required firm evidence of risk and have permitted recovery for abatement costs even when there may have been no human exposure. These holdings produce an enormous waste of economic resources. In addition, because abatement of asbestos can temporarily increase ambient levels, such actions might actually produce greater risk. When courts permit recovery of abatement costs in such circumstances, they create an incentive for unnecessary, harmful abatement actions. Before permitting such recoveries, courts should require plaintiffs to demonstrate the presence of a significant risk necessitating abatement and also that the abatement actions will be effective and reduce the significant risk caused by indoor air pollution.

The recognition of indoor air pollution risks and the response to such risks are still in a nascent state. The significant harms of polluted indoor air demand some improved government reaction. The above suggestions are meant to provide broad direction for such a government reaction. Putting such procedures into place will require certain trial-and-error and subsequent modification. Mere recognition of the magnitude of the indoor air pollution problem and establishment of action on such pollution as a top priority would go far toward protecting overall public health.

Notes

1. C. Meyer, *The Environmental Fate of Toxic Wastes, the Certainty of Harm, Toxic Torts, and Toxic Regulation*, 19 ENVT'L LAW 321, 387 (1988).

2. BNA ENVIRONMENT DAILY, January 2, 1990.

3. Daniel Byrd and Lester Lave, "Narrowing the Range: A Framework for Risk Regulators," *Issues in Science and Technology* (Summer 1987), 296.

4. Frank Cross, ENVIRONMENTALLY INDUCED CANCER AND THE LAW (1989), 34.

5. F. Reed Johnson, Ann Fisher, V. Kerry Smith & William H. Desvousges, *Informed Choice or Regulated Risk? Lessons from a Study in Radon Risk Communication*, 30 ENVIRONMENT (May 1988), 13–14.

6. Brooke Mossman & J. Bernard Gee, *Asbestos-Related Diseases*, 320 NEW ENGLAND JOURNAL OF MEDICINE (June 29, 1989), 1721.

7. Ken Sexton, *Indoor Air Quality: An Overview of Policy and Regulatory Issues*, 11 SCIENCE, TECHNOLOGY & HUMAN VALUES (Winter 1986), 59.

8. R. S. Adler and R. D. Pittle, *Cajolery or Command: Are Education Campaigns an Adequate Substitute for Regulation?* 1 YALE J. ON REGULATION 169, 161 (1984).

9. Lennart Sjoberg, RADON RISKS: ATTITUDES, PERCEPTIONS AND ACTIONS (March 1989), 3.

10. F. Reed Johnson & Ralph A. Luken, *Radon Risk Information and Voluntary Protection: Evidence from a Natural Experiment* 1 RISK ANALYSIS 97 (1987).

11. P. Sandman, *Explaining Environmental Risk. Some Notes on Environmental Risk Communication*, U.S.E.P.A. Office of Toxic Substances (1986), 23.

12. Sexton, 59.

13. Sexton, 60.

14. Diamond, *Liability in the Air: The Threat of Indoor Pollution*, ABA JOURNAL (November 1, 1987), 80.

15. Note, *Toxic Indoor Air: Commercial Real Estate Transactions May Be Hazardous to Your (Fiscal) Health*, 24 TULSA L.J. 449, 477–78 (1989).

16. Congressional Research Service, *Radon: Congressional and Federal Concerns* (March 2, 1987), CRS–11.

17. CROSS, 209.

SELECTED BIBLIOGRAPHY

Alter, H. W., and Oswald, R. A. "National Distribution of Indoor Radon Concentrations: A Preliminary Data Base." *Journal of Air Pollution Control Associations* 37 (1987): 227.

American Society of Heating, Refrigeration and Air-Conditioning Engineers, Inc. *Indoor Air Quality Position Paper.* Washington, D.C., 1987.

Annotation, *Measure of Damages for Landlord's Breach of Implied Warranty of Habitability* 1 A.L.R. 4th 1182 (1980).

Annotation, *Necessity of Real Estate Purchaser's Election between Remedy of Rescission and Remedy of Damages or Fraud* 40 A.L.R. 4th 627 (1985).

Annotation, *Products Liability: Construction Materials or Insulation Containing Formaldehyde* 45 A.L.R. 4th 751 (1986).

Annotation, *Recovery under Strict Liability for Injury or Damage Caused by Defects in Buildings or Land* 25 A.L.R. 4th 351 (1983).

Annotation, *Vender and Purchaser: Mutual Mistake as a Physical Condition of Realty as Ground for Rescission* 50 A.L.R. 3rd 1188 (1973).

Arness, John P., and Eliason, Randall D. "Insurance Coverage for 'Property Damage' in Asbestos and Other Toxic Tort Cases." *Virginia Law Review* 72 (1986): 943–80.

Blum, Andrew. "Structures Face Legal Scrutiny over Illnesses." *National Law Journal,* January 25, 1988, pp. 1+.

Brenza, Lindley J. "Asbestos in Schools and the Economic Loss Doctrine." *University of Chicago Law Review* 54 (1987): 277–311.

Brown, Ernest C. "What Lawyers Must Know about Asbestos." *ABA Journal,* November 1, 1987, pp. 74–76.

Brunao, R. C. "Sources of Indoor Radon in Houses: A Review." *Journal of Air Pollution Control Associations 33 (1983): 105.*

Bureau of National Affairs. "Radon: The Invisible Menace." Washington, D.C., 1987.

Bureau of National Affairs Special Report. *Indoor Air Pollution: The Complete Resource Guide, Volume I.* Washington, D.C. [1988].

Bureau of National Affairs Special Report. *Indoor Air Pollution: The Complete Resource Guide, Volume II.* Washington, D.C. [1988].

Burns, John P.; Cassidy, G. E.; Dodson, T. R.; Holladay, P. E.; Ney, P. C.; Parobek, D. T.; Payne, K.; Sanders, D. B.; Simmons, L. D.; Maguire, C. D.; and Blumenthal, L. "An Analysis of the Legal, Social, and Political Issues Raised by Asbestos Litigation." *Vanderbilt Law Review* 36 (1983): 573–847.

Christensen, Barbara M., and Larsceid, Kristine A. "Asbestos Abatement: The Second Wave of the Asbestos Litigation Industry." *Washburn Law Journal* 27 (1988): 455–94.

Cohen, B. L. "A National Survey of Radon-222 in U.S. Homes and Correlating Factors." *Health Physics* 51 (1986): 175.

Cohen, B. L., Kulwicki, D. R.; Warner, K. R., Jr.; and Grassi, C. L. "Radon Concentrations inside Public and Commercial Buildings in the Pittsburgh Area." *Health Physics* 47 (1984): 399.

Comstock, G. W.; Meyer, M. B.; Helsing, K. J.; and Tockman, M. S. "Respiratory Effects of Household Exposures to Tobacco Smoke and Gas Cooking." *American Review of Respiratory Diseases* 124 (1981): 143–48.

Conaway, Stephan F. "Grappling with Silent Invaders of the Home: Legal Remedies for Radon Gas Contamination." *Temple Environmental Law and Technical Journal* 5 (1986): 36–48.

Connaughton, James L. "Recovery for Risk Comes of Age: Asbestos in Schools and the Duty to Abate a Latent Environmental Hazard." *Northwestern Law Review* 83 (1&2) (1989): 512–45.

Cothern, C. R.; Lappenbusch, W. L.; and Michel, J. "Drinking Water Contribution to Natural Background Radiation." *Health Physics* 50 (1986): 33.

Coutant, R. W., and Scott, D. R. "Applicability of Passive Dosimeters for Ambient Air Monitoring of Toxic Organic Compounds." *Environment Science Technology* 16 (1982): 410–16.

Cross, Frank B. "Asbestos in Schools: A Remonstrance Against Panic." *Columbia Journal of Environmental Law* 11 (1986): 73–100.

"Danger Within." ABC News "20/20," broadcast February 4, 1982.

Diamond, Mark. "Liability in the Air: The Threat of Indoor Pollution." *American Bar Association,* November 1, 1987, pp. 78–85.

Dodge, R. "The Effects of Indoor Pollution on Arizona Children." *Archives of Environmental Health* 37 (3) (1982): 151–55.

Doll, R., and Peto, R. "The Causes of Cancer: Quantitative Estimates of Avoidable Risks of Cancer in the United States Today." *Journal of National Cancer Institutions* 66 (1981): 1191.

Eden, Barbara J. "Toxic Indoor Air: Commercial Real Estate Transactions May Be Hazardous to Your (Fiscal) Health." *Tulsa Law Journal* 24 (1989): 449–78.

Ekwo, E. E.; Weingerger, M. M.; Lachenbruch, P. A.; and Huntley, W. H. "Relationship of Parental Smoking and Gas Cooking to Respiratory Disease in Children." *Chest* 84 (6) (1983): 662–68.

Florey, C. du V.; Melia, R.J.W.; Chinn, S. "The Relation between Respiratory Illness in Primary School Children and the Use of Gas for Cooking. III. Nitrogen Dioxide, Respiratory Illness and Lung Infection." *International Journal of Epidemiology* 8(4) (1979): 347–53.

Gammage, Richard B., and Kaye, Stephan V. *Indoor Air and Human Health*. Chelsea, Mass.: Lewis Publishers, 1987.

Gesell, T. F. "Background Atmospheric Radon-222 Concentrations Outdoors and Indoors: A Review." *Health Physics* 45 (1983): 289.

Giampetro-Meyer, Andrea. "Rethinking Workplace Safety: An Integration and Evaluation of Sick Building Syndrome and Fetal Protection Cases." *Journal of Environmental Law* 8 (1988): 1–29.

Goldstein, B. D.; Melia, R.J.W.; Chinn, S., et al. "The Relation between Respiratory Illness in Primary School Children and the Use of Gas for Cooking. II. Factors Affecting Nitrogen Dioxide Levels in the Home." *International Journal of Epidemiology* 8 (4) (1979): 339–45.

Hasselblad, V.; Humble, C. G.; Graham, M. G.; and Anderson, H. S. "Indoor Environmental Determinants of Lung Function in Children." *American Review of Respiratory Disease* 123 (1981): 479–85.

Hess, C. T.; Weiffenbach, C. V.; and Norton, S. A. "Environmental Radon and Cancer Correlations in Maine." *Health Physics* 45 (1983): 339–48.

———. "Variations of Airborne and Waterborne Radon-222 in Houses in Maine." *Environment International* 8 (1982): 59.

Higham, Scott J., and Fleishman, Jeffrey G. "Radon Moves to Courts." *The Morning Call*, September 10, 1986, sec. A, p.1.

Ingersoll, J. G. "A Survey of Radionuclide Contents and Radon Emanation Rates in Building Materials Used in the U.S." *Health Physics* 45 (1983): 363–68.

International Commission on Radiological Protection. "Principles for Limiting Exposure of the Public to Natural Sources of Radiation." *ICRP Publication 39, Ann. ICRP* 14 (1) (1984).

Jacobi, W. "Possible Lung Cancer Risk from Indoor Exposure Radon Daughters." *Radiation Protection Dosimetry* 7 (1984): 395–401.

Jonassen, N. "Removal of Radon-Daughters by Filtration and Electric Fields." *Radiation Protection Dosimetry* 7 (1984): 407–11.

Keller, M. D.; Lanese, R. R.; Mitchell, R. I.; and Cote, R. W. "Respiratory Illness in Households Using Gas and Electricity for Cooking. I. Survey of Incidence." *Environmental Research.* 19 (1979): 495–503.

Kerr, R. A., "Indoor Radon: The Deadliest Pollutant." 240 *Science* 606 (1988).

Kirkland, Janis L. "What's Current in Asbestos Regulations." *University of Richmond Law Review* 23 (1989): 375–402.

Levin, L., and Purdom, P. W. "A Review of Health Effects of Energy Conserving Materials." *American Journal of Public Health* 73(6) (June 1983): 683–90.

Maloney, M.; Wray, B.; DuRant, R.; Smith, Larry; & Laura Smith. "Effect of an Electronic Air Cleaner and Negative Ionizer on the Population of Indoor Mold Spores." 59 *Annals of Allergy* 192 (1987).

Marcotte, Paul. "Toxic Blackarcre: Unprecedented Liability for Landowners." *ABA Journal*, November 1, 1987, pp. 67–70.

Mark, Gideon. "Issues in Asbestos Litigation." *The Hastings Law Journal* 34 (March 1983): 871–909.

Melia, R.J.W.; Florey, C. du V.; Altman, D. G.; and Swan, A. V. "Association between Gas Cooking and Respiratory Disease in Children." *British Medical Journal* 2 (1977): 149–52.

Melia, R.J.W.; Florey, C. du V.; and Chinn, S. "The Relation between Respiratory Illness in Primary School Children and the Use of Gas for Cooking. I. Results from a National Survey." *International Journal of Epidemiology* 8(4) (1979): 333–38.

Mossman, Brooke T., and Gee, J. Bernard L. "Asbestos-Related Diseases." *The New England Journal of Medicine*, June 29, 1989, pp. 1721–30.

National Research Council. *Formaldehyde and Other Aldehydes*. Washington, D.C.: National Academy Press, 1981.

———. *Indoor Pollutants*. Washington, D.C.: National Academy Press, 1981.

———. *Policies and Procedures for Control of Indoor Air Pollution*. Washington, D.C.; National Academy Press, 1987.

Nazaroff, W. W.; Boegal, M. L.; Hollowell, C. D.; and Rosemc, G. D. "The Use of Mechanical Ventilation with Heat Recovery for Controlling Radon and Radon-Daughter Concentrations in Houses." *Atmospheric Environment* 15 (1981): 263–70.

Nazaroff, W. W. Lewis, S. R.; Doyle, S. M.; Moed, B. A.; and Nero, A. V. "Experiments on Pollutant Transport from Soil into Residential Basements by Pressure-Driven Air Flow." *Environment Science Technology* 21 (1987): 459.

Nero, Anthony, V., Jr. "Airborne Radionuclides and Radiation in Buildings: A Review." *Health Physics* 45 (1983): 303.

———. "Controlling Indoor Air Pollution." *Scientific American*, May 1988, p. 42.

———. "Elements of a Strategy for Control of Indoor Radon." In *Radon and Its Decay Products in Indoor Air*, edited by William W. Nazaroff, pp. 459–85. New York: John Wiley & Sons, 1988.

———. "Indoor Radiation Exposures from Radon-222 and its Daughters: A View of the Issues." *Health Physics* 45 (1983): 277–88.

Nero, Anthony V., Jr.; Berk, A. V.; Boegal, M. L.; Hollowell, C. D.; Ingersoll, J. G.; and Nazaroff, W. W. "Radon Concentrations and Infiltration Rates Measured in Conventional and Energy-Efficient Houses." *Health Physics* 45 (1983): 401.

Nero, Anthony V., Jr., and Nazaroff, W. W. "Characterizing the Source of Radon Indoors." *Radiation Protection Dosimetry* 7 (1984): 23–39.

Nero, Anthony V., Jr., Schwehr, M. B.; Nazaroff, W. W.; and Revzan, K. L. "Distribution of Airborne Radon-222 Concentrations in U.S. Homes." *Science* 234 (1986): 992, 994.

New Jersey. *Asbestos Policy Committee Interim Report to the Governor*. September 1984.

"Personal Health." *New York Times*, December 22, 1988, p. 23.

Prichard, H. M., and Gesell, T. F. "An Estimate of Population Exposures Due to Radon in Public Water Supplies in the Area of Houston, Texas." *Health Physics* 41 (1981): 599

Preussmann, R. "Chemical Carcinogens in the Human Environment, Problems and Quantitative Aspects." *Oncology* 33 (1976): 51.

Samet, J. M.; Marbury, M. C.; Spengler, J. D. "Health Effects and Sources of Indoor Air Pollution. Part I." *American Review of Respiratory Disease* 136 (1987): 1486–1508.

Schenker, M. B.; Samet, J. M.; and Speizer, F. E. "Risk Factors for Childhood Respiratory Disease: The Effect of Host Factors and Home Environmental Exposures." *American Review of Respiratory Disease* 128 (1983): 1038–43.

Sexton, Ken. "Indoor Air Quality: An Overview of Policy and Regulatory Issues." *Science, Technology & Human Values* (Winter 1986): 53–67.

Sexton, K.; Letz, R.; and Spengler, J. D. "Estimating Human Exposure to Nitrogen Dioxide: An Indoor/Outdoor Modeling Approach." *Environmental Research* 32 (1983): 151–66.

Shuko, Carolyn Marie. "Radon Gas: Contractor Liability for an Indoor Health Hazard." *American Journal of Law and Medicine* 12 (2) (1986): 241–72.

Speizer, F. E.; Ferris, B. G., Jr.; Bishop, Y.M.M.; and Spengler, J. "Respiratory Disease Rates and Pulmonary Function in Children Associated with NO-2 Exposure." *American Review of Respiratory Diseases* 121 (1980): 3 –10.

Spengler, J. D.; Duffy, C. P.; Letz, R., et al. "Nitrogen Dioxide Inside and Outside 137 Homes and Implications for Ambient Air Quality Standards and Health Effects Research." *Environmental Science Technology* 17 (3) (1983): 164–68.

Spengler, J. D., and Sexton, K. "Indoor Air Pollution : A Public Health Perspective." *Science* 221 (1983): 9.

Stanevich, Rebecca S. "Indoor Air Pollution." *Office Systems* (December 1988): 21–26.

Steinhauser, F. "Possible Lung Cancer Risk from Indoor Exposure to Radon Daughters." *Radiation Protection Dosimetry.* 7 (1984): 389–94.

Steinhauser, F.; Hoffmann, W.; Pohl, E.; and Pohl-Ruling, J. "Radiation Exposure of the Respiratory Tract and Associated Carcinogenic Risk Due to Inhaled Radon Daughters." *Health Physics* 45 (1983): 331.

Stevens, William, K. "Despite Asbestos Risk, Experts See No Cause for 'Fiber Phobia' " *New York Times*, September 5, 1989, p. 19.

Strandon, E. "Radon in Dwellings and Lung Cancer – A Discussion." *Health Physics* 38 (March 1980): 301–6.

Strandon, E., and Berteig, L. "Radon in Dwellings and Influencing Factors." *Health Physics* 39 (1980): 275.

Strandon, E.; Kolstad, A. K.; and Lind, B. "The Influence of Moisture and Temperature on Radon Exhalation." *Radiation Protection Dosimetry* 7 (1984): 55.

Tancrede, M.; Wilson, R.; Zeise, L.; Crouch, E.A.C. "The Carcinogenic Risk of Some Organic Vapors Indoors: A Theoretical Survey." *Atmospheric Environment* 21 (1987): 2187–2205.

Turiel, Isaac. *Indoor Air Quality and Human Health.* Stanford, Calif.: Stanford University Press, 1985.

U.S. Congress. House. Committee on Environment and Public Works. *Hearings Before a Subcommittee on Toxic Substances and Environmental Oversight.* 99th Cong., 2d sess., 1986.

U.S. Congress. House. Representative Florio Speaking to Introduce the Asbestos Hazard Emergency Response Amendments. 101th Cong., 1st sess., April 25, 1989. *Congressional Record.* Vol. 135, no. 48.

U.S. Congress. House. Representative Luken Speaking for the Asbestos Act of 1988. H. Res. 5442, 100th Cong., 2d sess., October 4, 1988. *Congressional Record.* Vol. 134, no. 139.

U.S. Congress. House. Representative Luken Speaking to Amend the Asbestos Toxic Substances Control Act. H. Res. 3893, 100th Cong., 2d sess., June 27, 1988. *Congressional Record.* Vol. 134, no. 96.

U.S. Congress. House. Representative Malenee Introducing Legislation on Asbestos Cleanup. 101st Cong., 1st sess., April 27, 1989. *Congressional Record.* Vol. 135, no. 50.

U.S. Congress. Senate. Committee on Environmental and Public Works. *Health Effects of Indoor Air Pollution. Hearing Before a Subcommittee on Environmental Protection.* 100th Cong., 1st sess., 1987.

U.S. Congress. Senate. Committee on Environment and Public Works. *Hearings on the Asbestos School Health Hazard Act of 1984.* 99th Cong., 1st sess., 1985.

U.S. Congress. Senate. *Indoor Air Quality Act of 1988.* S. Rept. 100–442 to Accompany S. 1629. 100th Cong., 2d sess., 1988.

U.S. Congress. Senate. Senator Brud Speaking for the Submission of Asbestos Management Plan. H. Res. 3893. 100th Cong., 2d sess., June 29, 1988. *Congressional Record.* Vol. 134, no. 98.

U.S. Environmental Protection Agency. *EPA Study of Asbestos-Containing Materials in Public Buildings: A Report to Congress.* February 1988.

U.S. Environmental Protection Agency. *Report to Congress on Indoor Air Pollution and Radon Under Title IV, Superfund Amendments and Reauthorization Act of 1986.* April 1987.

U.S. Environmental Protection Agency. Office of Acid Deposition, Environmental Monitoring and Quality Assurance. *Project Summary: Indoor Air Quality in Public Buildings: Volumes 1 & 2.* September 1988.

U.S. Environmental Protection Agency. Office of Air and Radiation and Office of Research and Development. *EPA Indoor Air Quality Implementation Plan,* reproduced by U.S. Department of Commerce National Technical Information Service. Springfield, Va., June 1987.

U.S. Environmental Protection Agency. U.S. Consumer Product Safety Commission Co-operating. *The Inside Story: A Guide to Indoor Air Quality.* September 1988.

U.S. Library of Congress. "Radon: Congressional and Federal Concerns." Congressional Research Service, issue brief, updated March 2, 1987.

Wadden, R. A., and Schiff, P. A. *Indoor Air Pollution: Characterization, Prediction, and Control.* New York: Wiley, 1983.

Wallace, L. A.; Pellizzari, E.; Leaderer, B.; Zelon, H.; Sheldon, L. "Emissions of Volatile Organic Compounds from Building Materials and Consumer Products." *Atmospheric Environment* 21 (1987) 385–93.

Waltz, Donald A. "Radon Gas: Ramifications for Real Estate Transactions in Pennsylvania." *Dickinson Law Review* 91 (Summer 1987): 1113–55.

Ward, Catherine M. "Radon Litigation." Allan Kanner and Associates, Philadelphia, Pa. Typescript.

Ware, J. H.; Dockery, D. W.; Spiro, A., et al. "Passive Smoking, Gas Cooking." *American Review of Respiratory Disease* 124 (1981): 143–48.

Ware, J. H.; Dockery, D. W.; Spiro, A.; Speizer, F. E.; and Ferris, B. G. "Passive Smoking, Gas Cooking, and Respiratory Health of Children Living in Six Cities." *American Review of Respiratory Disease* 129 (1984): 366–74.

Winicour, Sheldon. "Clearing the Air on Radon Testing: The Duty of Real Estate Brokers to Protect Prospective Homebuyers." *Fordham Urban Law Journal* 15 (1987): 767–99.

INDEX

ABOUT THE AUTHOR

FRANK B. CROSS is an Associate Professor of Business Law at the University of Texas and Associate Director of the Center for Legal and Regulatory Studies. His articles have appeared in a variety of legal journals, and he is the author of four books, including *Environmentally Induced Cancer and the Law* (Quorum Books, 1989).